Oracle Blockchain Quick Start Guide

A practical approach to implementing blockchain in your enterprise

Vivek Acharya
Anand Eswararao Yerrapati
Nimesh Prakash

BIRMINGHAM - MUMBAI

Oracle Blockchain Quick Start Guide

Copyright © 2019 Packt Publishing

Commissioning Editor: Amey Varangaonkar
Acquisition Editor: Aditi Gour
Content Development Editor: Roshan Kumar
Senior Editor: Jack Cummings
Technical Editor: Manikandan Kurup
Copy Editor: Safis Editing
Project Coordinator: Kirti Pisat
Proofreader: Safis Editing
Indexer: Pratik Shirodkar
Production Designer: Shraddha Falebhai

First published: September 2019

Production reference: 1050919

Published by Packt Publishing Ltd.
Livery Place
35 Livery Street
Birmingham
B3 2PB, UK.

ISBN 978-1-78980-416-4

www.packt.com

You know how it is: you pick up a book, flip to the dedication, and find that, once again, the author has dedicated a book to someone else and not to you. Not this time. This one's for you. It is dedicated to all Enthusiast Evangelists and when you read it, you'll probably know why.

Along with you, I dedicate this book to my father, Ramesh Chandra, with love (actually, dad does not read technical books; he will never know about it unless someone tells him). A huge thanks to my wife, Richa, and son, Noah. Thanks for being patient with me while I was out at lakes and coffee shops writing, and could not spend weekends with you. Thank you for your sacrifice of weekends and vacations, and I'm sorry about that.

I would like to express my gratitude to Bill Swenton and Teresa Short for their support. I'm honored to have had Mark Rakhmilevich offer his guidance on the book.
I'm highly thankful to Nimesh Prakash and Anand Eswararao Yerrapati for joining me as coauthors of the book. You have enhanced the depth and value of the book multifold. I would like to express my deep gratitude for your generous support.

I'm deeply thankful to Navroop Sahdev, David Gadd, and Mary Hall for writing a foreword for the book. It certainly adds value to this edition. My deepest gratitude to you.
I would like to thank the talented team at Packt, including Aditi Gour and Roshan Kumar, who provided guidance, feedback, and added value to the book. I'm extremely thankful to the reviewer, Srihari Rayavarapu, who provided constructive and very useful feedback that helped us to tremendously improve the content of the book.

Foreword

Many of us who enjoy the benefits of internet technologies today don't possess a technical understanding of the software infrastructure layers of the internet. Indeed, understanding the architecture and technical layers of software has, until recently, been confined to software architects and engineers. This is partly due to the way the internet itself developed, in a patchy and almost "messy" manner. Ubiquitous interoperability was an afterthought. After all, there were no precedents to the internet and the technology hasn't *proven its worth*. Fast-forward to 2019 and we live in a very different era. Within the past 3 decades, the internet has transformed every conceivable industry in the world and human life, while accelerating the pace of growth and transformation of the global economy into something that would be unrecognizable – let alone imaginable – back in the 90s, when internet technologies were still in their infancy.

One more time, the new wave of emerging technologies, such as blockchain, artificial intelligence, big data, cloud computing, Internet of Things, 3D printing, augmented reality/virtual reality, and so on is going to transform human life and change the face of the global economy. Only this time, *the internet infrastructure already exists for the new technologies to piggyback on*. The future of technological growth and technology-led global economic transformation is abundant with opportunities. Five key pillars mark the characteristic features of the technologies of the future: decentralization, speed, scale, security, and usability. In this second inning, we have the opportunity to build a technology stack that is inherently interoperable from scratch. The timing couldn't be better as professionals from all fields are keen to understand and help build the infrastructure technologies of the future. The demand to understand the building blocks of technologies such as blockchain and the functional knowledge to work with them for future buildout is increasing at an accelerated rate. Vivek Acharya's *Oracle Blockchain Quick Start Guide* is a step forward in that direction, and is particularly focused on enterprise blockchain solutions. At the same time, the business models that emerged from the growth of the internet are also being replaced as emerging technologies transform business as we know it, bringing seamless interoperability, unprecedented speed, and breathtaking user experience to everyday life. However, **Platform-as-a-Service** continues to grow as the dominant business model, as businesses rush to deploy cutting edge technology to gain a first-mover advantage in their respective industries. This applies equally to large enterprises and start-ups. *Oracle Blockchain Quick Start Guide* marries this dominant business model with the most promising infrastructure technology of the future, blockchain, in the pages that follow.

What Vivek will show you in those pages will help you gain knowledge about blockchain technologies; key challenges and use cases; and Oracle blockchain platform's integrations into Hyperledger Fabric. In 2017, I had the opportunity to coauthor Hyperledger's Massive Open Online Course called *Blockchain for Business: An Introduction to Hyperledger Technologies*. 2 years on, Oracle's blockchain platform is an important step forward in making Hyperledger's open source technology infrastructure highly accessible to individuals and businesses.

Navroop Sahdev

CEO, Rethink Markets & Fellow, MIT Connection Science

Distributed ledger technologies (**DLTs**) such as Hyperledger are slowly taking over the world by offering solutions and applications that would otherwise not be possible with traditional enterprise IT systems. Hyperledger allows enterprises to reap the benefits of DLT in an unprecedented way that it is resulting in a different kind of marketplace. **Blockchain-as-a-Service** (**BaaS**) is slowly catalyzing the marketplace and this is evident with the existence of many big players in BaaS, such as Oracle, IBM, Microsoft, and so on. If you are a DLT, Hyperledger, and blockchain enthusiast who is exploring an effective BaaS option, then this book is for you.

David's involvement in the Blockchain ecosystem started in November 2017 when he was introduced to the technology and realized that its integration with existing systems and emerging technologies such as AI, IoT, and machine learning would change the way the general public, industries, and third parties do business going forward.

I was delighted when Vivek approached me. Vivek Acharya has experience in business process management, analytics, B2B, blockchain, and Hyperledger. In addition, he is the author of many technical and non-technical books. This allows him to effectively justify his Hyperledger prowess.

I am excited to write the foreword for this book on blockchain, which also covers Hyperledger and BaaS in depth. It will help readers design and build a solution on a BaaS platform. There are not many books on Hyperledger that emphasize its concepts, evolution, qualifiers, and approaches, and offer a sample, which users can build. Vivek Acharya and his contributor team have met that need, representing many disciplines that Hyperledger and BaaS have contributed to in the rapid adoption of enterprise solutions such as Hyperledger on a cloud platform.

The book is designed to start with accounting concepts, blockchain fundamentals, and its challenges and opportunities. It then navigates to adoption, use cases, and a detailed analysis of the Hyperledger platform with sample. It ends with approaches, qualifiers, and topologies. It offers an excellent kickstart for anyone to read though blockchain, Hyperledger, and BaaS, and then quickly practice it using Oracle Blockchain Platform. It serves as a one-stop shop to learn the various "nuts and bolts" of a DLT such as Hyperledger. This book will create a foundation for designers, developers, and architects to learn and build enterprise-grade solutions. The challenges in enterprises are both difficult and interesting. Enterprises are working on them with enthusiasm, tenacity, and dedication to design and develop new methods of analysis and provide new solutions to keep up with the ever-changing needs. In this new world, knowledge on the frontiers of DLT, blockchain, Hyperledger, and BaaS is paramount. This book is a good step in that direction and offers readers a chance to gain blockchain prowess.

All the best to Vivek Acharya and it is my hope and expectation that this book will provide an effective learning experience and reference resource for all Hyperledger and BaaS professionals.

David Gadd

Blockchain & Emerging Technologies Director, Consultancy Service & Talent Acquisition UK & Canada

Blockchain technology offers greater transparency and a single source of truth for participants doing business together and sharing selected data. With blockchain, a list of unalterable records (called blocks) are linked together to form a chain that is securely distributed among participants. This allows organizations that might not fully trust each other to agree on a single, distributed source of truth without any centralized authority. Blockchains can be public (open to all) or permissioned (only open to those parties granted access privileges).

Today's business transactions produce multiple data points, typically resulting in millions of daily transactions that need to be validated and confirmed. While all this "big data" presents opportunities, it can also be incredibly difficult to manage, especially if that data isn't properly validated by all parties. A lack of validation can expose organizations to risk, especially if they are trying to track supply chain goods, insurance claims, or financial transactions that are regulated by law. The promise of blockchain technology is the secure sharing of data that is tamper-evident, meaning if any party in the chain alters the data, the other parties in the chain will know who took that action and who the bad actor is.

The most popular enterprise blockchain is Hyperledger Fabric, a Linux Foundation-sponsored open source project. Hyperledger Fabric empowers organizations to build and manage permissioned, consortium-based blockchain business networks using a plug and play infrastructure. Because it is highly performant, secure and open sourced, Blockchain use cases built with Hyperledger Fabric are leading examples of the benefits of using Blockchain to accelerate the speed of business transactions.

Oracle Blockchain Platform is built with Hyperledger Fabric and offers users the ability to easily set up and manage a permissioned blockchain hosted in the cloud with preassembled components and enterprise-grade security and performance.

I've had the pleasure of being involved with blockchain technology for the past 3 years at both IBM and Oracle and have seen firsthand how this technology can transform the pace of a business, from verifying goods to ensure food safety freshness to preventing fraud, tracing complex supply chains and ensuring digital identity; the possibilities are literally endless.

If you're interested in blockchain technology, this book explains the technology, Hyperledger Fabric, and explores the benefits of BaaS (such as Oracle Blockchain Platform), with concrete use cases and samples for Hyperledger Fabric and Oracle Blockchain Platform. After establishing a theoretical foundation for blockchain and Hyperledger Fabric, readers are given a deep dive into various use cases, design strategies, and Hyperledger Fabric's architecture. This book can be used as a quick start guide, allowing you to delve into Oracle Blockchain Platform and experience the ease of building blockchain solutions with it.

Mary Hall

Blockchain Product Marketing, Oracle

Contributors

About the authors

Vivek Acharya is an IT professional and has been in the world of design, consulting, and architecture for approximately 12 years. He is a certified expert on blockchain, Hyperledger Fabric, **Software as a service (SaaS)**, and analytics. He loves all things associated with the cloud, **permissioned decentralized autonomous organization (pDAO)**, blockchain, predictive analytics, and social **business process management (BPM)**.

Anand Eswararao Yerrapati is an IT professional with about 12 years of experience in design, development, and the delivery of solutions for the various use cases of many customers. He works on **Platform-as-a-Service (PaaS)** primarily with mobile, chatbots, blockchain cloud service offerings, and their integrations. He loves to develop end-to-end solutions with the integration of multiple products and shares knowledge through blogs and sessions.

Nimesh Prakash is an IT solutions consultant with 13 years of experience. He has been part of multiple facets of enterprise IT solutions including development, design, solution consulting, and architecture. He works and evangelizes on PaaS cloud computing, involving blockchain, chatbots, cloud-native, and container technologies. He has been a regular at public technology events and likes to speak and to demonstrate his areas of interest.

About the reviewers

Srihari Rayavarapu (Sri) is a solution engineering manager at Oracle (Cloud Solution Engineering Hub), supporting customers across EMEA and JAPAC. He is currently leading a team of passionate solution engineers in modern application development. For the past 18 months, Srihari and his team have built expertise on Hyperledger Fabric and Oracle Blockchain Platform to deliver MVPs. He is passionate about emerging technologies (AI/ML, IoT, RPA, and AR/VR) and cloud-native/DevOps areas. He has over 18 years of industry experience in software development, presales, solution engineering, and technical leadership from various positions in IBM and Oracle. He holds a master's degree in software engineering from Dublin City University, Ireland.

Ankur Daharwal started his journey into blockchain with IBM Blockchain Garage in 2016. As a technology enthusiast and expert in both public and enterprise blockchains, he has been part of the decentralized world for around 3 years now. He has successfully developed and delivered numerous blockchain projects. He has devoted his career to devising real-life solutions for asset management and value exchange in a plethora of industry use cases worldwide. As an advisor to many blockchain start-ups, he focuses on providing expert guidance and solutions. Ankur strongly believes in fulfilling social responsibilities and supporting humanitarian causes with the use of his skills in technology.

Packt is searching for authors like you

If you're interested in becoming an author for Packt, please visit `authors.packtpub.com` and apply today. We have worked with thousands of developers and tech professionals, just like you, to help them share their insight with the global tech community. You can make a general application, apply for a specific hot topic that we are recruiting an author for, or submit your own idea.

Table of Contents

Preface

This book was created in the belief that, together, we will positively contribute to the evolution of blockchain technologies and continually inspire others to share their experiences and further influence others to do so. In this book, we will do the following:

- **Explore** distributed ledger technology; blockchain, its components, features, qualifiers, and architecture; and demystify the prominence of **Blockchain-as-a-Service (BaaS)**
- **Engage** in modeling a blockchain-based business network and gain exposure to developing business networks based on **Hyperledger Fabric (HLF)**, and appraise blockchain and HLF use cases and their potential effects and integration
- **Experiment** with **Oracle Blockchain Platform (OBP)** to utilize the practicality of translating network topology to OBP
- **Experience** the ease and richness of assimilating smartness in a business network by learning the full life cycle of chaincode, from development to updates; from installing, initiating, and testing to versioning; and finally, from integration to insight

Who this book is for

This book aims to address a diverse audience, from business stakeholders, to business leaders; from blockchain enthusiast evangelists to designers, architects, and developers; and to anyone and everyone who wants to benefit from the experience offered in this book. This book is intended to become a quick reference guide to learn blockchain, HLF, design strategies, and build chaincode on a blockchain platform. This book adopts a model that will allow readers to refer to this book as a reference for blockchain, its use cases, Hyperledger, design strategy, and quick development on the blockchain platform.

What this book covers

Chapter 1, *Exploring Blockchain and BaaS*, offers an in-depth exploration of blockchain and distributed ledger technology. It also takes you through blockchain-layered architecture, types of networks, actors, and structure. This chapter offers a prelude to blockchain, shows its relationship with distributed ledger technology, and demonstrates its pertinence to it. This chapter will demystify the prominence of the BaaS platform, its architecture, features, qualifiers, and the ease of use of prebuilt applications while exploring the eminence of OBP.

Chapter 2, *Construing Distributed Ledger Tech and Blockchain*, demonstrates the world of HLF design and implementation strategy, while diving into the comprehensive five-step design strategy—explore, engage, experiment, experience, and influence. In this chapter, we will build equations, coined by the author, to justify blockchain as the qualified solution for a given use case. We will look at various structures of permissioned business networks, such as joint venture, consortium, and founder initiated, and glance at a **permissioned distributed autonomous organization** (pDAO). We will also look at different types of use cases, ascertain the properties of blockchain, and witness them as the driving force behind various use cases and their adoption. The book includes a use case on FinTech; helping you to learn the art of modeling a blockchain business network (KonsensusChain) by defining its assets, participants, ledgers, consensus, transactions, events, permissions, and access controls. It also explores how to integrate a permissioned Hyperledger-based business network with BPM, SaaS, and other applications, while creating an infrastructure for the sample business network.

Chapter 3, *Delving into Hyperledger Fabric*, demonstrates Hyperledger's architecture and allows you to assemble a sample Hyperledger-based business network. You will look at a founder-based and a consortium-based business network. You will learn about business network components, adding peers to channels, working with chaincode, and smart contracts. It will guide you in enabling a dApp or application to transact with the business network. You will also take a deep dive into identity, security, privacy, membership services, and channels, as well as walking through ledger state and transaction flow via a PiggyBank example. These details will allow you to learn transaction flow and its steps, such as proposals, endorsement, packaging responses, verification, ordering, distribution, validation, committing, and notifications. Furthermore you'll see on-chain and off-chain architecture as an extension to a private data collection.

Chapter 4, *Engage in Business Case on Blockchain Platform*, allows you to engage with OBP. You'll learn how to design a solution inline with the constructs of OBP. You'll also see the sample business network topology, network artifacts, and solution and deployment architecture. Furthermore, you'll explore OBP in detail, its features, and components. You'll also delve into defining and creating an instance of a founder-based business network. In the chapter, you will see a rich history database working with channels.

Chapter 5, *Managing Solutions Using Oracle Blockchain Platform*, gets you into the practicality of translating network topology on OBP, creating network stakeholders, and configuring OBP instances. This ledger of knowledge illustrates a transaction infrastructure setup, joining participants to a business network, access control, adding smartness (chaincode) to a business network, and REST proxy configuration to expose chaincode to a dApp.

Chapter 6, *Developing Solutions on Oracle Blockchain Platform*, concludes the book with details on chaincode development, such as the programming languages required, development tools, and a development environment setup. This chapter teaches you about mapping asset models, operations, and developing chaincode functions and interfaces. It highlights the full life cycle of chaincode from development to updates; which includes installing, initiating, testing, and versioning. It demonstrates the full chaincode with a code base built on Go and Node.js. The chapter also illustrates endorsement policies, private data collections, and their functioning in concert with chaincode. It covers chaincode testing via shim and REST endpoints and integrating client apps with business networks using SDK, REST, and events. Finally, it concludes with insights into chaincode, transactions, and channels by experimenting with the monitoring of a business via chaincode logs and channel logs.

To get the most out of this book

The code samples were tested in a cloud environment as well as in a local environment, which can be created using a virtual machine in VirtualBox using an Oracle Linux ISO image. Download Oracle VirtualBox 6.x and install it on a machine (Windows/macOS/Linux) with 16 GB RAM and a minimum of 100 GB HDD. Visit Chapter 4, *Engage in Business Case on Blockchain Platform*, in the *Setting up OBP SDK* section, for more details on installation steps.

Download the example code files

You can download the example code files for this book from your account at www.packt.com. If you purchased this book elsewhere, you can visit www.packtpub.com/support and register to have the files emailed directly to you.

You can download the code files by following these steps:

1. Log in or register at www.packt.com.
2. Select the **Support** tab.
3. Click on **Code Downloads**.
4. Enter the name of the book in the **Search** box and follow the onscreen instructions.

Once the file is downloaded, please make sure that you unzip or extract the folder using the latest version of:

- WinRAR/7-Zip for Windows
- Zipeg/iZip/UnRarX for Mac
- 7-Zip/PeaZip for Linux

The code bundle for the book is also hosted on GitHub at `https://github.com/PacktPublishing/Oracle-Blockchain-Quick-Start-Guide`. In case there's an update to the code, it will be updated on the existing GitHub repository.

We also have other code bundles from our rich catalog of books and videos available at `https://github.com/PacktPublishing/`. Check them out!

Download the color images

We also provide a PDF file that has color images of the screenshots/diagrams used in this book. You can download it here: `https://static.packt-cdn.com/downloads/9781789804164_ColorImages.pdf`

Conventions used

There are a number of text conventions used throughout this book.

`CodeInText`: Indicates code words in text, database table names, folder names, filenames, file extensions, pathnames, dummy URLs, user input, and Twitter handles. Here is an example: "Then, from your local web browser, just enter `http://localhost:3000` and you should see the console's UI."

A block of code is set as follows:

```
#Create user Oracle
sudo useradd oracle
sudo passwd oracle
<newPassword>
```

Bold: Indicates a new term, an important word, or words that you see on screen. For example, words in menus or dialog boxes appear in the text like this. Here is an example: "Click **Sign In** in the top-right corner."

Warnings or important notes appear like this.

 Tips and tricks appear like this.

Get in touch

Feedback from our readers is always welcome.

General feedback: If you have questions about any aspect of this book, mention the book title in the subject of your message and email us at customercare@packtpub.com.

Errata: Although we have taken every care to ensure the accuracy of our content, mistakes do happen. If you have found a mistake in this book, we would be grateful if you would report this to us. Please visit www.packt.com/submit-errata, selecting your book, clicking on the Errata Submission Form link, and entering the details.

Piracy: If you come across any illegal copies of our works in any form on the internet, we would be grateful if you would provide us with the location address or website name. Please contact us at copyright@packt.com with a link to the material.

If you are interested in becoming an author: If there is a topic that you have expertise in, and you are interested in either writing or contributing to a book, please visit authors.packtpub.com.

Reviews

Please leave a review. Once you have read and used this book, why not leave a review on the site that you purchased it from? Potential readers can then see and use your unbiased opinion to make purchase decisions, we at Packt can understand what you think about our products, and our authors can see your feedback on their book. Thank you!

For more information about Packt, please visit packt.com.

1
Exploring Blockchain and BaaS

Blockchain is perceived to be a disruptive game-changing technology that will have an impact as huge as the internet in the next two decades. This programmable economy has use cases and applications in almost every industry. Blockchain has grown from being a buzzword to something of great interest to enthusiasts and real implementers. Evangelists are not confined to **proof of concepts** (**PoCs**), but have started real implementations and have started demonstrating concrete achievements. Although the adoption is slow, Gartner projects (at `https://www.gartner.com/` on June 3, 2019) that adoption will be $3.1 trillion by 2030.

Blockchain is a world where users are in full control of transactions and the information around them. The information flowing around is true, trusted, accurate, consistent, accepted, complete, timely available, widely available, transparent, and immutable. Blockchain, a type of **distributed ledger technology** (**DLT**), removes the risk of a central point of failure, while the underlying cryptography and algorithms will ensure the security in this immutable world. As the *trust* is in the blockchain network itself, there is no need for a trusted central third party. Welcome to the blockchain world, a world of distributed double-entry systems.

This chapter starts with accounting systems, centralized and decentralized ledgers, and coins the term *distributed double-entry system*. This chapter gradually moves toward the definition and analogy of blockchain and demonstrates the power of equity offered by **peer-to-peer** (**P2P**) networks. Here, you will also walk through various types of blockchain networks, such as permissioned and permissionless or public and private. This chapter then graduates toward the layered structure of the blockchain architecture and structure of transaction, as well as the blocks and the transaction flow. Finally, it covers how you can approach a blockchain solution and defines the cloud approach to ease blockchain adoption—from PoC to production using a **Blockchain-as-a-Service** (**BaaS**) platform such as the **Oracle Blockchain Platform** (**OBP**).

Accounting system – single and double–entry

Before we jump into blockchain and delve into Hyperledger Fabric and the Oracle Cloud solution, we need to start with two core principles—ledger and accounting. In an accounting system, business transactions are recorded in journals and ledgers. Fine-grained details of every transaction are entered into various journals. Summarized information from the journals is then transferred (also known as posted) to a ledger. It is the information from the ledger that becomes the source for trail balances and various financial statements. Every transaction is recorded in journals and then posted to a ledger that records this information in various accounts, such as asset accounts, liability accounts, equity accounts, revenue accounts, and expense accounts.

For any organization's accounting system, the ledger is the backbone. Anything that has financial value is posted to the organization's ledger. However, these ledgers are centralized ledgers and the organization has full control over them. We will talk about centralized and decentralized ledgers later in this chapter.

Accounting system – single–entry

Accounting systems address the purpose of producing an operating document to display ownership of assets, to protect assets, and various other tasks. Essentially, an accounting system is a powerful means to check the loss of assets due to malicious human activity, software, and so on, and to keep track of activities and transactions around those assets. Historically, as activities around assets were minimum, single-entry accounting was good enough to prove the ownership of assets. It is a form of accounting system where each transaction is a single-entry in the journal.

A single-entry account system resembles the check register that individuals use to track their checks, deposits, and balances. The information recorded is minimal and is owned by that individual. It's an efficient system for very small businesses that work on a cash basis of accounting, which have fairly low transactions each day. There are no credit-based transactions and the assets that are owned are very few and far between. Most importantly, there is no need to publish income, financial, and balance statements. Historically, it would have worked very well and, even today, it might work fine for very small firms that meet the aforementioned attributes.

There are various challenges with single-entry accounting systems—there are no scientific or systematic rules to record, post, and report on the transactions. It appears as an incomplete system as it does not have both the aspects of the accounts being recorded; hence, it fails to reflect the truth about the profit or loss and will miss reflecting the true financial position of the organization. With all of these shortcomings, a single-entry is vulnerable to frauds and various errors in the ledger. Hence, to check on vulnerability, you need to trust a centralized authority; therefore, historically, there was the need for a king to check for vulnerabilities and maintain trust around the ledger. However, since trade has expanded its boundaries, you need a mechanism to allow one ledger owner to trade with another ledger owner. This immediately led to a double-entry accounting system.

Accounting system – double–entry

The double-entry system offers error checks that are not inherently available in a single-entry system. Each account has two columns and each transaction is reflected in two accounts. Two entries are pushed for each transaction; however, every transaction has a debit entry in one account and an equivalent credit entry to another account. An example of a double-entry account system would be if an organization wants to purchase a new laptop for $2,000. In this case, the organization will enter a debit of $2,000 to an expense account and a credit of $2,000 to a cash account to show a decrease from the balance sheet.

Double-entry accounting is a way to show both of the effects of a transaction. For example, if an organization purchases a laptop, the accounting entry does not clarify whether the laptop was purchased for cash, in exchange for another laptop, or on credit. Information like this can only be available if both of the effects on a transaction are accounted for. In the accounting system, these two effects are known as debit and credit. A double-entry accounting system follows the principle of duality, which means that, for every debit entry, there is a mandatory equivalent credit entry. Debit entries demonstrate effects such as an increase in assets and expenses and a decrease in equity, income, and liability. Similarly, credit entries demonstrate effects such as a decrease in assets and expenses and an increase in equity, income, and liability. The double-entry system ensures that the accounting equation remains in equilibrium:

$$Assets = Liabilities + Equities$$

At the end of the reporting period, the total debits equalize the total credit. A balance sheet follows the equation, where the total assets are the sum of liabilities and equities. Any deviation from this equation will highlight an error.

Interestingly, a single-entry account system accounts for only revenue and expenses and does not monitor equities, liabilities, and assets. However, a double-entry system accounts for revenue, expenses, equity, liabilities, and assets, which makes it easy and precise to derive and calculate profits and loss, helps to detect fraud, reduces errors, and allows the generation of various financial statements. As both aspects of a transaction are recorded, it is easier to keep the account complete. Maintaining the double-entry system involves time, money, skill, and labor. There are chances of errors and mistakes. During an accounting year, transactions are posted and adjusted in final accounts; there are difficulties in adjusting transactions if tracking transactions is a challenge.

In the double-entry system, the first entry demonstrates what you have, while the second entry clarifies how you received it. If these entries are not in equilibrium, it is a clear indication that counterparty exposure might not be effectively accounted for which leads to audits and corrections. In the double-entry account system, it is mandatory to account for every single movement of the value of the counterparty. It has been a simple, proven, and effective accounting system for many years.

However, think about when there is no exposure to the counterparty. A what-if system does not know who owns it and is liable for the assets and the value recorded in the journal, which are posted in the ledger. To send or receive an asset of value, there must be a counterparty to receive and send it. Such fundamentals were far from question until today. A transaction is recorded in an organization's ledger, and the same transaction is recorded in the counterparty's ledger; for example, a supplier's ledger or bank's ledger. It reflects the counterparty's perspective for the same transaction. Various documents and statements such as contracts, invoices, notes, bank statements, and receipts support these transactions. This is prone to errors, such as reconciliation errors and missing cash, which then leads to disputes. This needs dispute resolution, and to check all of these, organizations invest in recording, analyzing, and auditing.

The double-entry account system worked well for hundreds of years. In this section, we will not emphasize the need for a triple-entry accounting system; however, we will delve into distributed ledgers. Double-entry mandates the need for each organization and its counterparty to maintain its own ledger, which in turn reflects the *truth*. However, there are multiple copies of the truth. In addition, the organization and the counterparty invest time, resources, and money to perform truth-reconciliation to actually derive and agree on a single truth.

Centralized versus distributed ledgers

This section highlights centralized and decentralized ledgers and distributed ledgers, and outlines the differences between them.

The following diagram shows different types of systems:

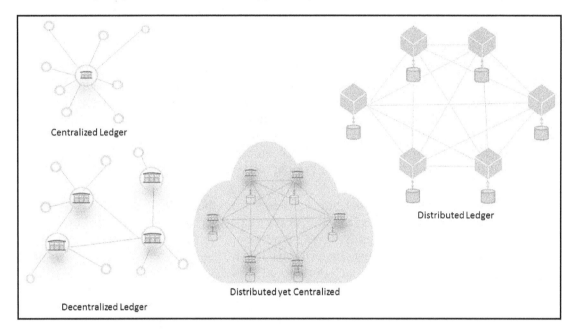

Types of systems and ledgers

Throughout this section, we will refer to the preceding diagram to understand the layout of various types of ledgers. Before we drill into the differences between centralized and distributed ledgers, let's understand the different types of system.

From the perspective of *control*, there are two types of systems—centralization and decentralization systems:

- **Centralized system**: One entity controls the entire system, where an entity can be a person or an enterprise.
- **Decentralized system**: In a decentralized system, there could be multiple entities controlling the system. There is no single point of control, and the control is shared between various independent entities.

From the perspective of *location*, there are two types of systems—centralized and distributed systems:

- **Centralized system**: All the constituting parts of the system, such as servers, ledgers, and so on, are co-located and exist at the same location
- **Distributed system**: All the constituting parts of the system, such as servers, ledgers, and so on, are NOT co-located and exist at different locations

These categories of the system lead to the following variants of the system:

- **Distributed yet centralized system**: Distributed yet centralized system is the category of system wherein the system is distributed, from the location's perspective, yet the system is controlled by a central authority or central entity. For example, cloud service providers offer various services such as compute, storage, SaaS, PaaS, IaaS, and so on. These services are offered via servers and databases that are distributed. However, the entire system is controlled by the cloud service provider. Such a system can be termed a distributed yet centralized system.
- **Distributed system**: Distributed systems, from the control's perspective, are decentralized, whereas from the location's perspective, they are distributed. This means that no single entity is the owner or authority of the system and the system doesn't have just one location—it is widely distributed. DLT and its type, such as blockchain, are such distributed systems, where control is not with one entity. Hence, no single entity can alter or modify the system (decentralized). Also, DLT and blockchain are based on the P2P network, where nodes (peers or participants) are independent and globally spread (distributed).

 A distributed system is a superset of a decentralized system, and is based on a P2P network.

Centralized ledgers

The double-entry accounting system we've discussed so far highlights an accounting system that has a centralized ledger. Anything with a financial value is recorded in journals and posted to ledgers. These ledgers are just like the central repository of the posted transactions, and they are the backbone of any organization.

However, centralized ledger systems have various drawbacks as well. For example, banks control the transactions that are posted into the bank's ledgers and they maintain total control over bank statements. In this case, they can penalize you at any given time and can transact money from your account at any given time. If such a centralized institute has malicious intent, then the consequences could be manifold; they could close down their business without prior notification, which prohibits any further transactions. These examples are used mostly by the blockchain evangelists who lean more toward complete decentralization of trust authorities.

Let's look at a more viable challenge, pertaining to banks. Double-entry mandates the need for each bank to maintain its own ledger to reflect their perspective of truth, and as more banks are transacting with each other, they need to reconcile their version of the truth to derive a single version of the truth. Banks today spend time, money, and resources to ensure a consensus over the single truth.

Obviously, they have their ledger and hence their own system, which allows the financial industry to avoid any chance of a single point of control and single point of failure. In addition, it becomes more interesting as a customer opens an account with a bank and puts his/her money with a level of trust in that banking institute. Now, the onus is on the banking institution to safeguard your money and information. On the other hand, the bank will invest a lot of time, money, resources, and effort into building and maintaining a system and then spend even more time, money, resources, and effort on integrating and checking with other banking institutes to ensure that their mastered system is in consensus with the other banking institutes' system to reach a common truth.

If you analyze this closely, you will see that each bank's ledger is actually replicating the functionality of the other banking institutions. Now, what if one of the banking institute's systems fail? Is this going to lead to a situation where reconciliation is not possible? Doesn't this sound more like a single point of failure? The answers lie in the distributed ledger discussed in the following section and throughout the book.

Distributed ledgers

Across the world, in the economical, legal, political, and institutional systems, the key elements are transactions, contracts, and documents. They dictate the relationship between countries, enterprises, organizations, communities, and individuals and, most importantly, they are perceived to offer trust. Interestingly, these have not joined the digital transformation to a greater extent and for the greater cause. So, what is the solution? Distributed ledgers and DLT, along with blockchain, offer the solution to such critical challenges. In this section, we will explore more about distributed ledgers and DLTs.

In a distributed ledger, there is no central authority or a central administrator. It is an asset database that is shared over the network, where each party on the network has an identical copy of the ledger. These assets can be financial, legal, and electronic assets. Changes to the value of these assets are reflected throughout the network, and each copy of the ledger is appended.

Many organizations, governments, and institutes use a central database of the ledger, which we discussed in the *Centralized ledgers* section. A centralized ledger needs a central authority to be trusted by transacting parties; however, in a distributed ledger, the need for a third party is omitted, which is one of the gravitational forces behind the attraction to DLT. Here, I have quietly used the term DLT because a distributed ledger can be pronounced as a shared ledger or a DLT, and they are one and the same.

What's disruptive about a DLT is that the ledger database is distributed, spread on all of the nodes or computing devices across the network, and each node has an identical copy of the ledger, where nodes update themselves independently. All of the participating nodes reach an agreement to establish a single truth (true copy) for the ledger through a process called **consensus**. Once a consensus is reached, the distributed ledger is updated automatically and the latest truth (true agreed copy) of the ledger is appended on each node separately. While reading this paragraph, you might think about the reconciliation process of banks to establish trust and an agreement on the ledger. With DLT, trust (reconciliation) and consensus (agreement) happen seamlessly and automatically.

What we just found out is that there is no central authority in the previous story to maintain the distributed ledger. DLT empowers systems to reduce the dependencies on various central authorities such as banks, lawyers, governments, regulatory offices, and third-party authorities. Distributed ledgers omit the need for a central authority to validate, authenticate, and process transactions. Transitions on DLT are timestamped and have a cryptographic unique identity, where all records in question are available for the participants to view, and this ensures that the verifiable and auditable history of the transaction is stored immutably.

In the decentralized distributed ledger, the transaction is replicated to the distributed ledger, which means all the participating nodes' copies of the ledger are appended; however, there is no central single database. It is the network that is decentralized. Such a system needs a decentralized consensus as there is no single point of contract, or single authority or party. Hence, to ensure trustlessness, consensus is a must. In a traditional database system, a single party acts on behalf of the transacting clients to modify the state of the system. However, in a distributed ledger, any party can record, and the protocols and algorithms govern the posting of transactions on the network's ledger.

The following table lists some of the differences between a centralized ledger and a distributed ledger:

Centralized ledger	Distributed ledger
Reconciliation is required (both internal and external).	Reconciliation is not required; however, a consensus is required to reach an agreement.
There's no restriction on DB operations.	It's append-only.
There's a single point of failure.	It's distributed; hence, there's no single point of failure.
There's a single point of contact.	It's decentralized; hence, there's no single authority.
There are third parties, middlemen, and gatekeepers.	It's P2P. There's no central party, and appending to the ledger is governed by the consensus.
Backup and disaster recovery are required.	Resilience and availability increases as more and more participating nodes get to the network.
Actions can be performed on behalf of someone.	There's cryptographic authentication and authorization.
NA	It's immutable as the data added to the ledger stays immutable.
NA	There's direct interaction of the nodes, allowing initiation of direct transactions of assets such as currency, real assets such as land titles or documents, and so on.

Equipped with the knowledge of ledgers, let's now dive into DLT and blockchain and understand the difference between them.

DLT and blockchain

Blockchain is a P2P network, where the ledger is distributed and transactions are posted to the ledger only upon consensus. Such a P2P network, along with various components such as smart contracts, cryptography, and algorithms, help to build a blockchain network that delivers trust. Blockchain allows participating parties (nodes) to establish consensus without an intermediary, which leads to a single distributed truth (ledger). There's no reconciliation, no delays, and no intermediary, and transactions are recorded in real time over an immutable ledger forever.

We have not covered the details about blockchain and, in this section too, we will just touch on the definition and jump into the difference between blockchain and DLT. So far, we know about distributed ledgers. Blockchain technology concentrates on securely and efficiently building an immutable record of transactions, also known as activities of high importance. Blockchain (one form of DLT) is the most accepted DLT; however, DLT by itself has a lot of potential for the future. There are various types of DLTs, as displayed in the following diagram:

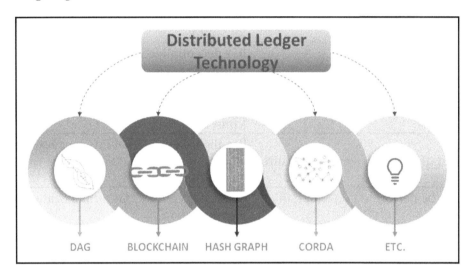

DLT

Blockchain groups data into blocks, chains them together, and firmly secures them through cryptography. Blockchain is an always growing append-only chain of blocks, where agreed upon transactions are appended only to the blocks. They can never be altered or deleted and this immutability has various use cases. Now, by virtue of the fact that blockchain is a form of DLT, it's the ledger that is distributed on the blockchain network. Each node has a copy of the ledger and transactions are only added securely when they reach a consensus by the participating nodes.

DLT is a broader term to highlight those technologies that allow the distribution of information among participants (public or private). Blockchain is one of the types of DLT that got wider acceptance and is very popular and, as a result, it turned out to be the synonym of DLT. DLT focus on a technology that does not have central authority, and interestingly, blockchain is a chain of blocks, while DLT neither mandates any requirement for chains nor for blocks. For the vision of blockchain, DLT resonated well; hence, every blockchain is a DLT. However, it is not mandatory for a DLT to be a blockchain. Here's an analogy of DLT and blockchain with the term vehicle and car, respectively. Hence, our equation is—every car is a vehicle; however, not every vehicle need be a car.

The following table summarizes the differences between DLT and blockchain:

DLT	Blockchain
It's a ledger that is distributed over the network.	It's a P2P distributed ledger.
The ledger remains immutable.	Transactions are grouped into blocks, and blocks are immutable.
DLT includes a consensus algorithm that ensures an agreement.	Blocks are added to the chain when a consensus is reached and each block has transactions.
There's no central authority or centralized data storage.	There's no central authority or centralized data storage.

A few other DLTs that have received popularity and acceptance are as follows:

- Chain Core
- Corda
- **Directed acyclic graph (DAG)**
- Hash graph
- peaq
- Quorum

In conclusion, DLT has broadly– and blockchain has specifically– created a system where the world can have a P2P distributed ledger that is trusted, immutable, secure, and consensus-based. There are various types of DLT, such as blockchain and DAG, and while blockchain has received wider acceptance, DAG is gaining momentum slowly but steadily. For the sake of this book, we will be concentrating on DLTs such as Hyperledger Fabric and blockchain. However, whichever DLT it is, the core benefits of DLTs are transparency, immutability, efficiency, and the absence of a third party.

DLTs that are blockchain:

Blockchain is a form of DLT where data is stored in the form of blocks. These blocks are linked and encrypted. Hence, it can also be termed an encrypted linked-list of blocks, where you can trace the provenance of the block (this means you can reach back to the genesis block). This linked-list of blocks (also known as a chain of blocks) is ever-growing. Such a massive growth leads to slow transactional speed and needs large storage capacity on a P2P network.

Blockchain technology as a platform:

Let's start by talking about the first application of blockchain technology—cryptocurrency. However, cryptocurrencies are not discussed further in this book. For cryptocurrency transactions, a ledger is distributed over the P2P network. Any user (node) can join the network without permission and can start transacting. As long as the user (node) adheres to transaction protocol, transactions can be executed. If they are valid, they will be added to the blockchain network. Similarly, any node can participate in the consensus process and start validating transactions.

Such blockchain networks are public and offer read access to everyone via explorer applications. Such transaction information does not contain user details. They just have the transaction details. Such public blockchain networks do not incur costs to system administrators as the mining is performed by participating nodes and the miners are paid incentives for their efforts to validate the transaction. In turn, the miner can afford the infrastructure themselves by taking care of the server, machines, and electricity costs. You can think of such an infrastructure as crowd-funded, crowd-maintained, and crowd-validated. The cost is shared among the participating nodes. With this approach, the upfront and maintenance cost for the infrastructure is greatly reduced in comparison to centralized systems. Some of the popular currencies are Litecoin, Ripple, EOS, Bitcoin, Ethereum (Ether), and so on.

Other than cryptocurrency, a blockchain platform fuels growth for permissionless networks or permissioned networks. It can be used as a platform for various types of transactions and consensus that represent an asset (a thing of value). Permissionless networks include Ethereum, while permissioned networks include Hyperledger Fabric and R3 Corda.

DLTs that are not blockchain:

There are various DLTs that are *not* blockchain, such as DAG, Hashgraph, and **Digital Asset Holdings** (**DAH**). They are also based on distributed ledger concepts; however, they are not based on a chain of blocks (also known as blockchain). They are mostly effective and their transaction volume is extremely high. DAH is mostly relevant to use cases such as financial services and banks. Hashgraphs are permissioned DLTs based on voting algorithms. DAG (table) is another DLT that is not based on blockchain. It is currently used for IOTA and micropayments.

Comparing blockchain and DAG:

Both blockchain and DAG are DLTs. However, let's look at the differences between these two for a better perspective on their technologies.

The following table compares DLT - Blockchain and DAG:

Properties	Blockchain	Directed Acyclic Graph
Structure	It is a linked-list of blocks where transactions are grouped into blocks.	It is a network of linked transactions. There are *no* blocks of transactions.
Data structure	It's a linked list (list of blocks).	It's a tree (tree of transactions).
Consensus	Transactions are validated block by block to meet the consensus.	Transactions are validated by one another.
Features	It offers transparency and immutability.	It offers high scalability and a negligible fee.
Use case	It's suitable for use cases with low volume and high worth of transactions.	It's suitable for high volume, of transactions.
Pitfalls	There's a high transaction cost, storage and bandwidth requirements, and computing power (for permissionless scenarios).	Low transaction volume can lead to attacks. For private versions of DAG, it uses coordinators, which do not allow DAG to be fully decentralized.
Approach	It's a linear, utilitarian DLT that offers near real-time updates for transactions and offers disintermediation.	It has a non-linear approach that actually results in faster transactions as the network grows.

Accounting system – triple–entry or distributed double–entry

Let me pull you back to accounting systems again. We've already talked about single-entry and double-entry accounting systems. Focusing more on ledgers drove us to familiarize ourselves with centralized and distributed decentralized ledgers. In addition, even before we had the definition of blockchain cemented in this chapter, we tried to compare it with DLT. Now, we are back to square one, to answer another important question about blockchain in the accounting world.

There are various discussions around the triple-entry accounting system. Many advocates believe that a triple-entry accounting system is an advanced enhancement to the age-old and proven double-entry accounting system. Debit and credit remain the two prime entries, and the third vertex entry is an immutable link to all of the previous debits and credits, which means all of the ledger entries have an immutable cryptographic seal.

Let's say two organizations are performing a transaction; one will post a debit to their account for the amount received while the other organization will post a credit to their account for the amount spent. However, these postings are into different ledgers. We have seen this previously in the banking institute example. Now, these organizations have separate copies of ledgers and then they will **reconcile** it to ensure that they have a common 'true' understanding. DLT will ensure that there aren't two ledgers. There will be one ledger, which will remains distributed, and blockchain technologies will ensure that the transactions that are posted to the distributed ledger are immutable and securely sealed. Immutability will ensure that it is never tampered with, and cryptography will take care of the security aspects. As a result, enterprise and business do not need to reconcile ledgers as there are no separate silos ledgers.

Although there are various definitions of a triple-entry accounting system, it will be extremely difficult to replace the proven double-entry accounting system. Triple-entry accounting is a complex term; we do not deny the fact that there are enormous benefits of posting transactions to a distributed ledger in a blockchain network. Posting and recording transactions in a distributed, append-only, immutable ledger has many benefits, and we will touch on these in this book.

For example, as soon as a contract is signed, a block is created on the blockchain and a transaction is posted to the distributed ledger in the blockchain network. Someone can issue a purchase order against that contract, and this transaction is appended as a block to the blockchain too, which means it is posted to the distributed ledger as well. Bills can be issued against those purchase orders and payments can be associated with those bills in separate transactions and recorded to the distributed ledger. You have a chain of blocks, which displays transactions from contracts to payments, in a single distributed ledger. This means you have an excellent audit record and real-time visibility of transactions by all of the transacting parties. Permissioned DLTs, such as Hyperledger Fabric, can further enable you to provide restricted access to those transactions. Moreover, those posted transactions need no reconciliations and are immutable and omnipresent.

We just learned that, in a distributed ledger on a blockchain network, transactions are immutable and no one can falsify them. Transactions are timestamped, verified, agreed upon via a consensus, and trusted; this offers an easy way to retrieve, access, analyze, and audit in real time, anytime. A chain of transactions, in the blocks, are tied together and are distributed across the blockchain network, where each participating node has the same copy of the ledger (single truth over the network). In this equation, we have not witnessed a single authority/party as there is no central trusted party; the trust is in the blockchain network and the distributed ledger. Welcome to the blockchain world, a world of distributed double-entry systems.

In conclusion, I personally believe in the distributed double-entry accounting system. You can term it a triple-entry account system if you want to. However, the essence of such an accounting system remains the same—a double-entry accounting system that is distributed, secure, and immutable. In this equation, DLT offers the distribution of the ledger, and blockchain technology will ensure the cryptography, security, digital receipt, and immutability of the single distributed ledger. Therefore, throughout this book, we will use the term distributed double-entry accounting system, which you can still term as a triple-entry accounting system.

Blockchain definition and analogy

With all of these fact checks about ledgers, types of systems, and knowing about the difference between DLT and blockchain, let's get into the definition and analogy of blockchain. Blockchain is a P2P network, where the ledger is distributed and transactions are posted to the ledger, but only upon consensus. Such a P2P network, along with various components, such as smart contracts, cryptography, and algorithms, help build a blockchain network that delivers trust. Blockchain allows participating parties (nodes) to establish consensus, without an intermediary, which leads to a single distributed truth (ledger). There's no reconciliation, no delays, and no intermediary, and transactions are recorded in real time over an immutable ledger forever.

Let's use an analogy for blockchain. Let's refer to blockchain as a notebook. Each page represents a block on this blockchain. You can record data of any kind, such as medical records and financial transactions, on this page, which is also known as a block, where each page (block) is chained to the previous page (block). This chain is not just a link to the previous page; it also contains information about the page in such a way that, once the data on the page is defined and added to the notebook, it cannot be changed. If it is changed, information about the page is changed. Then, the chain it holds with the other page is changed and so on. This is noticeable since the chain link is broken. Hence, the lines on each chained page are immutable.

Blockchain technology also includes smart contracts, which are intelligent programmatic contracts, also known as rules; these are defined and executed when an event of a certain type occurs on the blockchain network. It is called blockchain because the chain of blocks are a linked list of the blocks, where each block has one or many transactions. These transactions are verified and validated by the blockchain network in a given time span. The blockchain protocol's consensus algorithm, adopted for that blockchain network, defines the rules and incentive of the participating nodes. We will cover this in detail in the consensus algorithm section.

Blockchain is a chain of blocks, where each block has transactions that are recorded on a ledger (blockchain), which is distributed over all of the participating nodes in the blockchain network. This distributed ledger is the distributed double-entry ledger (as discussed previously), which records transactions for any digital asset or an asset of value. For a blockchain network, transactions are recorded on the distributed ledger from when it (the ledger) started, and they remain there immutably, forever. Hence, financial statements can be generated, traced, and validated from the start of the network. Interestingly, as the ledger is distributed and a copy of it is on all of the participating nodes, any node can verify the transaction and announce the transaction verification to reach consensus.

Analogy

Let's look at another analogy. Let's journey to a technology-less time. There was a beautiful village with a few families where, instead of currency, they exchanged goods.

A vegetable farmer would trade vegetables for rice, and a rice farmer would trade rice for peanuts, and so on. It worked fine until they started making promises to each other. Promises (transactions) were the credits, where a farmer would buy vegetables without giving away the rice; instead, the rice farmer would promise the vegetable farmer they would return rice when it was harvested. Similarly, the fruit farmer would get rice, with the promise of delivering oranges at the time of harvest.

The vegetable farmer trusted the rice farmer; however, over time, there were several promises transacted between various farmers and it was difficult to track those promises, which resulted in a breach of trust. Finally, the villagers appointed a person to keep track of these promises. This person was given the title LedgerMan (centralized third party). Soon, the LedgerMan established trust; however, he was overwhelmed with promises and started demanding a fee (transaction cost). The villagers agreed to pay him a portion of the promise as a fee. This eventually turned the LedgerMan into a rich person. Later, the LedgerMan indulged in corruption, started accepting bribes to tamper with the ledger, bribed villagers to keep his position safe, and sometimes enhanced the fee.

Soon, the villagers realized the challenges of having a LedgerMan (a centralized system). Hence, they decided that, instead of a single LedgerMan keeping the promises, promises would now be kept by everyone (decentralized). There would not be a single person holding the promises; the villagers would meet at a designated place to make promises, and every promise would be recorded by each villager (P2P network).

Once a week, they would validate the promises by reading out their version of the promise. If the majority of the villagers reached an agreement (consensus) over a promise, that promise would be considered valid and would be considered as truth (ledger). In the event of an issue, the promise, which had most of the entries, would be considered a correct promise and would help to resolve any promise-based issues (longest chain). Over the course of time, they added security and various other bells and whistles.

We will revisit this story and extend it as well. For now, we understand that blockchain is a solution (protocol) that allows a leaderless (decentralized) group of peers (P2P) to reach an agreement (consensus) on a transaction, and the moment they occur (synchronized), they are recorded (post) on an omnipresent tamper-proof (immutable) distributed linked-list (ledger), where each peer holds a copy (distributed) of it. We just learned that blockchain is a P2P network; now, let's find out exactly what a P2P network is.

Blockchain components

Blockchain comprises various components that work in tandem in a blockchain network. We will cover some of these components in this chapter, as well as a few others, such as member services, will be discussed in detail in subsequent chapters. The following is a list of blockchain components:

- **Ledger**: A ledger is a distributed ledger where transactions are recorded/posted immutably. Being a type of DLT, blockchain ensures immutability of transaction history, right from the genesis block to the current block. We have covered single-entry and double-entry accounting in this chapter. A blockchain ledger is a secure implementation of a distributed double-entry accounting system.

- **Peer network and nodes**: A P2P network is a computer network where computers (peers/nodes) are distributed and share the network's workload to reach the end goal. Nodes perform transactions on the blockchain. There are two kinds of nodes—full node and light node. DLT types such as blockchain or Hyperledger can be public or private. In public blockchain, each node has equity; however, they can operate with distinct roles, such as miners, as full nodes, where the entire copy of the blockchain will be replicated on such nodes. They can also act as light nodes and can hold key or block header values only.

- **Smart contracts or chaincode**: For a blockchain such as Ethereum, and a DLT such as Hyperledger, smart contracts, or chaincode, are the code logic that is executed on a blockchain network. Participating nodes or blockchain clients can issue transactions against that business logic (smart contracts or chaincode). With the inclusion of a blockchain layer, the ledger will store not only the immutable transactions but also the immutable code.

- **Membership services**: For DLTs such as Hyperledger, membership services offer identity and security solutions, which ensure the participation of users on a blockchain network. Authentication and authorization are functions of membership services. They are mostly used in private and permissioned blockchains or DLTs.

- **Events**: It's the responsibility of the blockchain or DLTs to raise events when certain defined actions happen on the blockchain/DLT. Events are effective ways to allow other subscriber applications or systems to interact with the blockchain network.
- **Consensus**: The consensus algorithm (or protocol) is the core for the existence of blockchain platforms. Needless to say, a blockchain network cannot exist without consensus. The consensus layer is the most critical and crucial layer for any blockchain (Ethereum or Hyperledger, or any other). Consensus is responsible for validating the blocks, ordering the blocks, and ensuring that everyone agrees on it. Visit the *Consensus algorithm* subsection, in this chapter for details about consensus algorithms.

In the previous section, we discussed ledgers and distributed systems in detail. In this section, we will focus on the P2P network. This chapter, *Exploring Blockchain and BaaS*, and `Chapter 2`, *Construing Distributed Ledger Tech and Blockchain*, cover all the enlisted components in detail.

P2P network

Blockchain technology leverages the internet and runs on a P2P network of computers. These computers run the blockchain protocol, which allows these computers to keep a copy of the ledger. This ledger includes transactions that are packaged in blocks and chained together in a genesis block. The inclusion of blocks in the chain is agreed over consensus, without an intermediary.

A blockchain distributed ledger runs on a P2P network, where transactions are validated using cryptography by consensus algorithms. A blockchain network defines the consensus algorithm for it, which is essentially the rule to validate transactions on the blockchain P2P network. Upon reaching the consensus, blocks are added to the ledger. The node adding the block to the network is then offered incentive (depending on the type of blockchain). Hence, the highlights are that, in the P2P network of a distributed ledger, transactions are verified using cryptography and validated using consensus.

The following diagram shows types of networks:

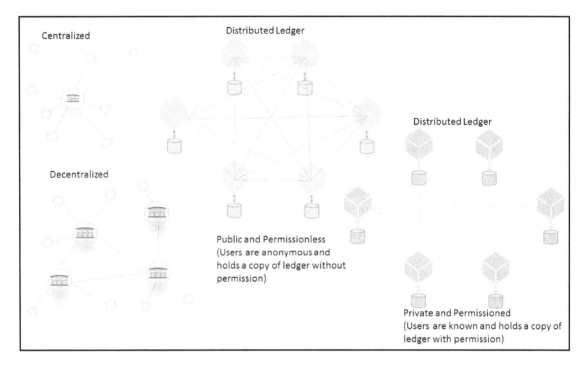

As shown in the previous diagram, a **Centralized** network has a central node, which defines and governs the validation and verification of the transactions. All other connecting nodes rely on the central authority. The central authority has full access and control of the data, information, and state of the transactions. Although it's a network that is highly regulated, it's also centrally controlled. On one hand, it's safe and secure as long as trust holds true between the central authority and participating nodes; however, human error, malicious intent, single point of failure, and power being in the hands of a single authority has its own challenges. It is suited for very small organizations, where decisions can be taken quickly and even the smallest decision is visible. **Decentralized** networks are almost the same as centralized ones; however, here, the central node itself is distributed. This means the centralization of authority is distributed. In a decentralized network, each node is not directly connected to node; however, in a P2P network, each node is connected to other nodes.

Network of equity or the peer-to-peer network

A P2P network leverages the network; however, the attachment and detachment of nodes is completely voluntary. The network is a network of *equity*, where each peer is the same as any other peer, and it is fair and impartial. One peer offers computing resources to other peers, without the need for a central authority to control, govern, or maintain the network. Even though it has equity, each node has a fair chance of adopting the role of the miner or can turn itself into a full node. Each node keeps a copy of the distributed ledger, and this protocol of the blockchain network ensures resilience and immutability of the blockchain network. A blockchain network can resurrect the entire system as long as there is a single node that holds the copy of the distributed ledger.

On a P2P network, information is recorded and replicated between all of the participating nodes; hence, the power, consistency, reliability, and trust in the P2P network grows more and more, as more and more nodes join the blockchain network. Also, as there is no single point of failure and no single authority, the system is not vulnerable to hacking, loss of data, inconsistency, human errors, or a single part controlling the network agenda, and so power and privacy remains with each node. Note that it's the consensus algorithms that ensure the synchronization of data on the blockchain. There are various consensus algorithms, such as **proof of work (PoW)** and **proof of stake (PoS)**. We will be talking about them in detail in this book.

Layered structure of the blockchain architecture

This section covers the layered architecture of blockchain. In this section, we will be diverging to Ethereum and Hyperledger Fabric as well. While discussing the Hyperledger Fabric infrastructure, we will drill into the OBP's infrastructure as well.

The following diagram displays the layered architecture of blockchain:

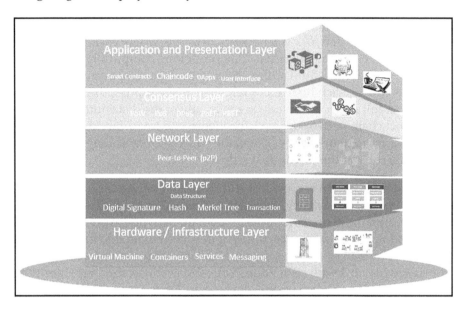

Blockchain layered architecture

Hardware and infrastructure layer

The content of the blockchain is hosted on a server that resides in a data center on this beautiful planet. While browsing the web or using any applications, clients request content or data from application servers, commonly referred to as client-server architecture. However, today, clients can connect with peer clients as well and share data among each other. Such a massive collection of computers sharing data with each other is termed a P2P network. Blockchain is a P2P network of computers that computes transactions, validates them, and stores them in an ordered form in a shared ledger. This results in a distributed database that records all the data, transactions, and other relevant information. Each computer in a P2P network is called a *node*. Nodes are responsible for validating transactions, organizing them into blocks, broadcasting them to the blockchain network, and so on. Upon reaching consensus, nodes commit the block to the blockchain network and update their local ledger copy. This layer comprises of virtualization (creation of virtual resources such as storage, network, servers etc.). Significantly, nodes are the core of this layer. When a device gets connected to a blockchain network, it is termed and considered as a node. On a blockchain network, these nodes are decentralized and distributed.

Ethereum - Infrastructure layer

Let's look at the nodes in Ethereum. Anyone and everyone can run an Ethereum node on their machine. This will enable their machine to participate on the Ethereum blockchain network. Nodes can run a client (compatible client), such as Geth, Parity, or Pantheon, to connect to Ethereum blockchain. Geth is written in Go, Parity is written in Rust, and Pantheon is written in Java. A node (node-running client), can be either a light node (client) or a full node (client). Light nodes store the cache, while full nodes (client) store the dataset, which grows linearly with time. Light nodes (clients) get high assurance from the Ethereum blockchain network about the state of the Ethereum, and they can participate to verify the execution of transactions. On the other hand, any node that participates in the full enforcement of consensus and downloads the entire blockchain to the node's local storage is known as a full node (client). Full nodes verify signatures, format the data of the transactions and blocks, check double spending, and so on. They essentially validate the transactions and use a gossip protocol to relay this information to other nodes, called peers.

These Ethereum nodes (clients) run the **Ethereum Virtual Machine (EVM)**. EVM is a Turing complete software; a stake-based virtual machine that enables untrusted code to be executed by a global P2P network of computers. EVM handles the internal state and computation. Ethereum blockchain is a Turing complete blockchain where developers can also develop programs (smart contracts) for the blockchain. EVMs are like JVMs, and they run on each node on the blockchain. EVMs are like transaction engines, which are responsible for changing the blockchain's world state. EVMs run as sandboxes and offer an execution environment for the smart contracts.

Hyperledger Fabric – Infrastructure Layer

This blockchain network, which is based on Hyperledger Framework, is comprised of peer nodes, and these nodes host ledgers and chaincode (also known as smart contracts). Essentially, peers host instances of the ledger and chaincode, which keeps an eye on single points of failure. As peer nodes are responsible for hosting the ledger and chaincode, applications and administrators need to interact with these peer nodes. A node in Hyperledger Fabric can host more than one ledger. In some cases, a peer node can only host a ledger, and not the chaincode (it is rare, but possible). Most nodes have at least one chaincode installed to update or query the node's ledger. A node can host multiple chaincode and multiple ledgers too, which are powered by channels. You will learn more about channels and the Hyperledger Fabric architecture in `Chapter 3`, *Delving into Hyperledger Fabric*.

To access the chaincode or ledger, applications and administrators (via admin applications) will always connect with peers via Fabric **software development kit** (**SDK**) APIs. These APIs allow applications to execute transactions on the blockchain network and receive events related to the confirmation of the process. There are two types of transaction—query and update transactions. For query transaction, consensus is not required, as the peer will return the result immediately from its local copy of the ledger. However, for update transactions, no individual peer can update the ledger because other peers need to agree before updating the ledger. This process of reaching an agreement to update the ledger is termed *consensus*. You can read more about the ledger-update transaction process in `Chapter 3`, *Delving into Hyperledger Fabric*.

A specific set of applications and peers can communicate via channels, since a channel is a partition – a pathway of communication – between the specific application and peer(s). Hyperledger Fabric is for enterprises and it caters to private-permissioned (consortium) and private-permissionless use cases. Various like-minded organizations form a consortium to build a blockchain business network. Hence, peers are owned by various organizations. These organizations offer resources for the setup, maintenance, and operations of the blockchain network. One of the resources is nodes (peers), and the business network can continue to exist as long as one organization with one peer remains alive on the blockchain business network.

The administrators of that organization assign nodes to the blockchain business network. Each organization has a certificate authority, which assigns a digital certificate to these nodes. This digital certificate (X.509) is the digital identity of these peers. This digital identity helps in identifying the owning organization of the peer when the peer tries to connect to a channel on the blockchain business network. A channel has policies, which determine the rights and privileges of the peer. This mapping of the peer's role in an organization and the peer's identity to an organization is provided the **Membership Service Provider** (**MSP**). Anything that interacts with the blockchain business network, such as peers, applications, admins, orderers, and so on, must have an identity and an associated MSP to enable their integration with it.

Orderers nodes ensure the consistency of the ledger across the blockchain business network. Let's take a quick glance at the transaction flow of a blockchain network based on Hyperledger Fabric. This entire process is mediated by orderers (orderers' nodes), where all the peers reach a consensus on the content of the transaction, and also the order of the transactions.

Transaction Flow: Transactions in a Hyperledger Fabric-based blockchain network happen in a multi-phase process. Please visit the *Transaction flow* section of `Chapter 3`, *Delving into Hyperledger Fabric*, for more details. Here is the glimpse of the transaction flow:

1. **First phase (endorsing phase)**: The application initiates a ledger-update transaction. This transaction request is handled by endorsing peers (nodes as endorsers). These nodes endorse the proposed ledger update and send the endorsement to the application. However, no commits are performed to the ledger.

2. **Second phase (ordering phase)**: Proposal response from endorsed transaction, from various applications are received by the orderers' nodes. These nodes order the transactions into blocks.

3. **Third phase (distribution phase)**: Finally, ordered blocks are distributed to all the peers in the blockchain business network. These peers will validate the transaction and, upon successful validation, commit the transaction to the local copy of the ledger.

Orderers' nodes are the mediators of the entire transaction process. This transaction process is known as a consensus, as all the peers in the blockchain business network have agreed about the transactions and the data of the transactions. The ordering service leverages a message-oriented architecture, Ordering service can be implemented in one of the following three ways:

- Solo
- Kafka
- Raft

The following table highlights the features of various order service implementations:

Features	**Solo**	**Kafka**	**Raft**
Number of nodes	Single ordering node	Multiple ordering nodes from one organization.	Multiple ordering nodes from different organizations.
Fault-tolerant	Not fault-tolerant	**Crash fault-tolerant** (**CFT**), which uses a ledger and follows node configuration. Uses ZooKeeper ensemble for management.	CFT based on Raft protocol.
Implementation	Development and testing (not for production)	Production grade, however has management overhead.	Production grade and easier to implement than Kafka.
Distributed order service		Kafka clusters are practically run by one organization (maybe a founder organization). Hence, all the ordering actually goes to one single organization. Hence it's partially decentralized.	Allows distributed ordering service as various organizations can contribute their nodes to form a distributed order service. Hence, it is fully decentralized.

From a physical presence perspective, nodes can reside in one of the following locations:

- Cloud tenanted or owned by one of the organizations
- Data center or on-premise owned by one of the organizations
- On a local machine

Essentially, identity of the peer associates its affiliation with an organization and determines that it is owned by that organization. These nodes are the basis and core of the blockchain network. They are of different types and perform various functions, such as endorsement, ordering, committing, and hosting chaincode, and ensure the consistency of the ledger. So far, we've discussed infrastructure from an Ethereum and Hyperledger Fabric perspective. If you want to check the infrastructure offerings for a specific vendor, you can visit the *Oracle's Baas – OBP* section of this chapter.

Data layer

Blockchain is a decentralized, massively replicated database (distributed ledger), where transactions are arranged in blocks, and placed in a P2P network. The current state of all accounts is stored in such a database. A network (public or private) is comprised of many nodes and without a common consensus, data cannot be altered. The data structure of a blockchain can be represented as a linked-list of blocks, where transactions are ordered. The blockchain's data structure includes two primary components—pointers and a linked list. The pointers are the variables, which refer to the location of another variable, and linked list is a list of chained blocks, where each block has data and pointers to the previous block. A **Merkle tree** is a binary tree of hashes. Each block contains a hash of the Merkle root with information such as the hash of the previous block, timestamp, nonce, the block version number, and the current difficulty target. A Merkle tree offers security, integrity, and irrefutability for the blockchain technology. Merkle trees, along with cryptography and consensus algorithms, are the basis of the blockchain technology. For example, Ethereum blockchain uses a Patricia tree database to store information. Patricia tree (Trie) is a Merkle tree, which is like a key-value store. Just like Merkle tree, a Patricia tree has a *root hash*. This root hash can be used to refer to the entire tree. Hence, you cannot modify the content of the tree without modifying the root hash. Each block contains a list of transactions that happened since the last block, and after applying those transactions, the root hash of the Patricia tree represents the new state (*state tree*).

The genesis block (the first block) does not contain the pointer, as it's the first in the chain. The following diagram shows the connected list of blocks in a blockchain:

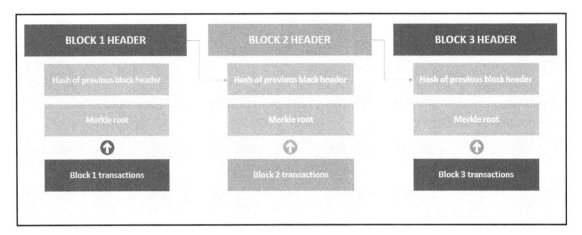

Blockchain structure

Depending on the type of blockchain, data is stored in blocks. For example, Hyperledger Fabric's blocks will include channel information, while a Bitcoin blockchain will have data about the sender, receiver, and the amount. We've used the term *hash* a few times already. A hash is a unique digest of the data. A cryptographic hash algorithm (such as the SHA 256 algorithm) can generate a fixed length hash value of the data. These hashes help in identifying blocks easily and also help to detect any changes that are made to the blocks. Each block has a hash of the previous block; hence, blockchain is essentially a chain of hashes. Any new node connected to the blockchain will receive a copy of the blockchain network. Only upon consensus are blocks added to the local blockchain.

Transactions are digitally signed on the blockchain to ensure the security and integrity of the data stored on it. They secure information about the block, transactions, transacting parties, and so via a digital signature, which uses asymmetric cryptography. Transactions are signed using a private key, and anyone in possession of the public key can verify the signer. The digital signature checks for tampering. Digital signatures guarantee integrity as the data that is encrypted is also signed. Hence, any tampering will invalidate the signature. As the data is already encrypted, it cannot be detected. Even if it is detected, it cannot be tampered with. A digital signature secures the sender's (owner) identity as well. Private keys are linked to owners (users); hence, signatures are legally associated with the owner and cannot be repudiated. In this section, we talked about transactions in detail. We will walk through the transaction flow for Ethereum-based blockchain platforms in the next section.

Network layer

The network layer, also known as the P2P layer, is the one that is responsible for internode communication. It takes care of discovery, transactions, and block propagation. This layer can also be termed as propagation layer. This P2P layer ensures that nodes can discover each other and can communicate, propagate and synchronize with each other to maintain valid current state of the blockchain network. Visit the following *Transaction flow* subsection, in this chapter to experience the P2P layer in terms of transaction broadcast, transaction proposals, transaction validation and transaction commit. This layer also takes care of the world state propagation. A P2P network is a computer network where computers (nodes) are distributed and share the network's workload to reach the end goal. Nodes perform transactions on the blockchain. There are two kinds of nodes—full node and light node. Full nodes ensure the verification and validation of transactions, mining, and the enforcement of consensus rules. They are responsible for maintaining trust in the network. Light nodes only keep the header of the blockchain (keys) and can send transactions.

Transaction flow

The transaction flow described here highlights the interaction between nodes in a P2P network layer. The following diagram displays the transaction flow for the Ethereum blockchain:

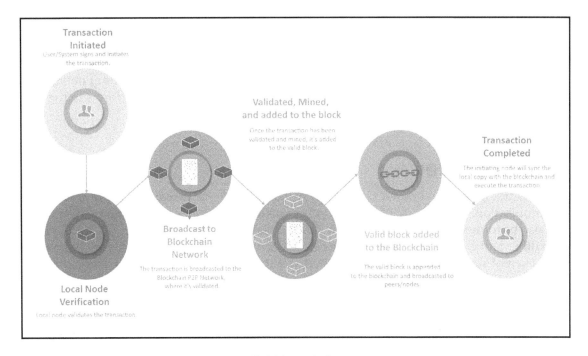

Blockchain transaction flow

The following bullet points highlight the transaction flow of Ethereum blockchain, as shown in the preceding diagram:

- **Transaction Initiated**: A light node or a full node that has an Ethereum client digitally signs and initiates the transaction
- **Local Node Verification**: Once the local Ethereum node receives the transaction, the local Ethereum node will perform the following checks:
    - Check the digital signature's consistency with the sender's address and transaction's content
    - Check if the sender has enough gas to fuel the transaction being processed
    - Check if the transaction will result in a smart contract's functions to fail

- **Broadcast to Blockchain Network**: Transactions are broadcasted to the blockchain P2P network, where the full nodes will perform the following checks:
  - Repeat the aforementioned validation checks
  - Full nodes communicate with each other
  - Miner nodes will put the transaction in a pending block and start the consensus (for example, PoW) so that it can try to solve the puzzle
- **Validated, mined, and added to the block**: Following steps ensure the block validation and addition to blockchain :
  - Once the transaction is validated and mined, it's added to the valid block
  - The miner will solve the puzzle and find the valid block, which will be added to the blockchain
- **Valid Block added to the Blockchain**: The valid block is appended to the blockchain and broadcasted to nodes:
  - The miner node will append the valid block to the blockchain.
  - The miner will broadcast the valid block to nodes.
  - Upon appending the block to the blockchain, the miner will broadcast this to blockchain peer nodes, and each node will again validate the block to ensure the consistency of the current (new) block with the previous block. Once validation is successful, the node will broadcast to its nodes and so on.
- **Transaction Completed**: The initiating node will sync the local copy with the blockchain and execute the transaction:
  - Finally, the block reaches the node that initiated the transaction
  - The local node will sync its local copy with the blockchain and will execute the transactions in the block
  - Transaction is marked as completed

Consensus layer

The consensus protocol is the core to the existence of blockchain platforms. As the saying goes, *behind every blockchain, there is a consensus algorithm*. The consensus layer is the most critical and crucial layer for any blockchain (Ethereum, Hyperledger, or any other). Consensus is responsible for validating the blocks, ordering the blocks, and ensuring everyone agrees on it. The following are the key points regarding the consensus layer:

- Consensus protocols (algorithms) create an irrefutable set of agreements between nodes across the distributed P2P network.
- Consensus keeps all the nodes synchronized. Consensus ensures that all the nodes agree to the *truth*.
- Consensus ensures that power remains distributed and decentralized. No single entity can control the entire blockchain network.
- Consensus guarantees that a single chain is followed and that it holds the *truth*.
- Consensus is the rules that nodes follow to ensure that transactions are validated within the boundaries of those rules and that blocks follow those rules.
- Consensus results in unanimous acceptance of *truth* among the participating nodes.
- For a blockchain with cryptocurrency (for example, Ethereum), consensus also rewards the nodes for validating the transactions and maintaining the blockchain network.
- By design, consensus protocols cannot be replicated as replication or imitating them is costly and time-consuming.
- Reliability in a P2P network is achieved by a consensus protocol.

Consensus methods vary for different types of blockchain. For example, consensus, when followed by a permissionless blockchain network such as Ethereum, Bitcoin, and so on, is known as a probabilistic consensus. Such a consensus guarantees consistency of the ledger, though there is a possibility that various participants have different views of the blocks. This means that they remain vulnerable to ledger forks (also known as divergent ledgers). Permissioned blockchains such as Hyperledger Fabric follow deterministic algorithms. Such blockchain networks have specific nodes called ordering nodes; blocks validated by these ordering nodes are considered as final and true. Hence, there is no probability of a fork.

The following table outlines a quick comparison of some of the consensus algorithms mentioned in this book:

Facts	PoW	PoS	PBFT
Type of Blockchain	Permissionless	Permissionless and Permissioned	Permissioned
Finality of Transaction	Probabilistic	Probabilistic	Deterministic
Needs Token	Yes	Yes	No
Example Usage	Bitcoin, Ethereum	Ethereum	Hyperledger Fabric

Visit the *Structure of the blockchain* section for a detailed analysis of the various types of consensus algorithms.

Application layer

The application layer is comprised of smart contracts, chaincode, and dApps. Application layer can be further divided into two sub-layers –application layer and execution layer. Application layer has the applications that are used by end users to interact with the blockchain network. It comprises of scripts, APIs, user interfaces, frameworks. For these applications, blockchain network is the back-end system and they often connect with blockchain network via APIs. Execution layer is the sublayer which constitutes of smart contracts, underlying rules and chaincode. This sublayer has the actual code that gets executed and rules that are executed. A transaction propagates from application layer to execution layer, however the transaction is validated and executed at the semantic layer (smart contracts and rules). Applications sends instructions to execution layer (chaincode; in case of Hyperledger fabric), which performs the execution of transactions and ensure the deterministic nature of the blockchain (such as permissioned blockchain like hyperledger fabric).

Smart contracts to be executed on the **Ethereum runtime engine** are written in Solidity. It needs a compiler to syntactically prove the code. Since it is compiled, the bytecode is smaller and runs faster on EVM. Code executed on EVM is fully isolated and does not have any interaction with the network or filesystem.

Smart contract: A code with business logic is identified by a unique address, and it resides on the EVM. A smart contract contains functions that are executed when a transaction is performed against those functions. Depending on the logic of the smart contract, a transaction can result in a change of state in the contract. Developers can use any language such as Solidity or Python, to write a smart contract, and can use a specific complier to compile the code into bytecode and then deploy those bytecodes to blockchain. Once deployed, a unique address is assigned to the smart contract. Any user on the blockchain can execute a transaction against that smart contract. Refer to the following transaction flow for the steps of a transaction on an Ethereum blockchain. Smart contracts are written in a high language such as Solidity and deployed to EVM for execution. However, there are codes that link the smart contract to the outside world; for example, inter-blockchain, logic execution, and so on. These are called oracles and dApps.

Oracles: Smart contracts operate on values and trigger contract state change, but only when the defined logic is met. An oracle is an agent whose task is to securely provide these values to a smart contract. Oracles are like data feeds from third-party services, which supply values to smart contracts.

Chaincode (**Hyperledger Fabric**): Smart contracts are the transaction logic that controls the life cycle of business objects, which are contained in the world state. Smart contracts are then packaged together into chaincode, which is then deployed to the blockchain business network. In Hyperledger, smart contracts govern the transactions, while chaincode governs the packaging and deployment of smart contracts. A chaincode can contain many smart contracts. For example, in an insurance chaincode, there can be smart contracts for claims, liability, processing, and so on. Chaincode defines the ledger's data schema, initiates it, performs updates to ledgers (consensus-based), and responds to queries for ledger data. Chaincode also emits events, which allows other applications to subscribe to chaincode events and perform subsequent downstream functions or processes.

In Hyperledger Fabric, there is no VM like EVM (Ethereum). Chaincode is deployed on network nodes, and smart contracts run on a peer node owned by an organization, mostly written in standard languages such as Java, Node.js, and Go. Chaincode runs on a secure Docker container that's available to each blockchain instance. These containers are independent of other nodes in the network; however, these chaincodes are orchestrated by the peer nodes and act as proxies, allowing access to client applications via REST APIs or SDK.

Chaincodes are initiated for channels. An administrator can define an endorsement policy for a chaincode for a given channel. This ensures that all the smart contracts, which are packaged in the chaincode, are available for that channel. Because of this, a chaincode might follow different endorsement policies on different channels based on the endorsement policy that's been configured for that channel. Smart contracts can communicate with other smart contracts on the same channel or other channels.

dApps: dApps is a distributed application that runs on top of a distributed technology like Blockchain, such as Ethereum, Bitcoin, or Hyperledger Fabric. It's a decentralized application that leverages smart contracts or chaincode. dApps can be considered a web application that interacts with the smart contract or chaincode; however, the dApps are not controlled by a single entity or an organization. Once deployed, they belong to the blockchain network. dApps are user-friendly applications, which business users can use to transact onto a blockchain network. Smart contracts allow you to connect to blockchains, whereas dApps allows you to connect to a smart contract or chaincode. For example, if you go to LinkedIn, the web page calls APIs, which gather data from a database. However, in dApps and the smart contract world, dApps are API-based web applications that connect with smart contracts, which in turn execute transactions on the ledger. A few examples of dApps are financial applications such as invoice factoring, KYC, and so on.

Structure of the blockchain

When a user performs a transaction on a traditional system, there is a trusted third party involved who takes care of transaction processing, transaction logging, maintaining the ledgers and balances, and, in return, charge a transaction fee. With a DLT such as blockchain (for example, Ethereum), every participating full node has a copy of the ledger (blockchain). The trust is on the system itself as there is no party involved. Users initiate transactions, which are validated and grouped (in a block) and, based on consensus, the block is added to the ledger (blockchain).

This section is dedicated to the structure of block headers, transactions, adding transactions to a block, and finally, adding blocks to the blockchain. We have discussed blockchain and, in particular, Ethereum, in this section. However, we will be delving into DLTs such as Hyperledger in detail in subsequent chapters. There, we will walk through the structure, transaction flow, participants, and algorithms that are specific to Hyperledger Fabric. Visit Chapter 3, *Delving into Hyperledger Fabric*, for details about Hyperledger Fabric.

Transaction state machine

The Ethereum blockchain is a transaction-based state machine that starts with a **genesis state**. A transaction will then lead to a change of state, where the recent state is termed the current state. Hence, a transaction is a representation of a *valid* sequence flow between two states; the blockchain should contain only valid state transactions that occur because of a valid transaction.

Transactions are grouped into blocks. A block is chained to a previous block with a cryptographic hash, representing a chain of blocks called a blockchain. Here, the cryptographic hash is used as a reference. Blocks themselves are the journals, and the blockchain is the ledger where blocks record one or more transactions. Incentives are offered to miners, and incentivization occurs at the state transition. A blockchain that offers incentives to miners needs to have a consensus to transmit value to the miner. For example, Ethereum considers Ether as the value in the Ethereum blockchain, and it's used to offer incentives to the miner. The smallest unit of value, Wei, is used for incentivization in Ethereum.

Mining is a process where various nodes solve a puzzle to validate a transaction so that more transactions can be added as a block within the blockchain. This process of validating transactions is known as mining. Many miners act at the same time to validate the transaction and, once done, they submit a proof of their work, which is mathematical proof. Miners not only have to solve the puzzle – they need to solve it way before other miners to be able to add their block to the blockchain. This is the process of miners solving a puzzle and submitting a PoW. The winning miner is rewarded with some form of value. If it's Ethereum, then a certain amount of Ether is offered as a reward to the miner.

As Ethereum is decentralized, every node has equity and can participate in creating new blocks. There could be malicious participants as well who might propose a new path. Hence, the system makes sure to reach a consensus that follows on from the genesis block to the current block. Ethereum uses the **GHOST** (which stands for **Greedy Heaviest Observed Subtree**) protocol to check the creation of multiple branches in the blockchain and to follow the best valid path.

Types of accounts

Mapping between account addresses (160-bit unique identifier) and the account state is termed the world state, which is maintained in the Merkle tree (Trie). The Trie is maintained in the state database. Since the root node is dependent cryptographically on all of the internal nodes' data, the root node's hash can be used as a global secure identity for the blockchain network.

Small objects constitute the shared global state of Ethereum. These objects interact via message-passing framework. These objects are termed as **accounts**. A state is associated with each account and each account has a 20-byte address, where accounts are identified by a 160-bit identifier. Ethereum has two kinds of accounts, where externally owned accounts have no codes associated and they can initiate new transactions. However, contract accounts have contract codes attached to them, along with a unique address, and they cannot initiate new transactions. Contract accounts can only perform contract-to-contract messaging. Remember, external accounts initiate transactions by signing them with their private keys and sending those transactions to another external account or to a contract account. If the transaction is sent to a contract account, this will result in the execution of the business logic of the contract account (smart contract's account).

Both of these accounts have an account state that is represented by four components: nonce, balance, storage root, and code hash. For an externally owned account, the nonce highlights the transactions initiated from account's address, while for a contract account, it represents the contracts that have been created by that contract account. Balance shows the base unit of the Ether (in the Ethereum blockchain). The storage root holds the hash of the root node of the Merkle tree, while the code hash contains the hash of the code on the contract account, which is deployed on EVM.

Delving into Block Structure

A block is comprised of a block header (BH), transaction set (BT), and the other block's headers for the current block's ommers (BU), as shown in the following code:

```
B = (BH, BT, BU)
```

Ommers are those miners whose blocks were orphaned and didn't make it to the blockchain. However, they were successful in mining the block, but their block was added in time. Ethereum offers a low incentive to those miners as well.

Ethereum block headers contain the following components:

- **Parent Hash**: Hash of the parent block's header
- **Ommers Hash**: Hash of the ommer's list portion of the current block
- **Beneficiary**: Miner's account address, who is entitled to the incentive
- **State Root**: Hash of the Trie's root node
- **Transactions Root**: Trie's root node's hash that has the transaction list portion of the block
- **Receipts Root**: Trie's root node's hash that has the receipts for each transaction that is listed in the block

- **Logs Bloom**: Log information such as logger address and log topics
- **Difficulty**: Value representing the difficulty level of the block
- **Number**: Number showcasing the value of ancestor blocks; for example, for the genesis block, this number is zero
- **Gas Limit**: Value that shows the gas limit per block
- **Gas Used**: Value showing the gas used for the transactions in the block
- **Timestamp**: Time at the block's inception; essentially, it's the system time
- **Extra Data**: Array containing the block data; it's just 32 bytes and should contain relevant data only
- **mixHash**: A hash value that, when mixed with the nonce, will prove the sufficiency of the computations performed on the block
- **Nonce**: A hash value that, when mixed with the mixHash, will prove the sufficiency of the computations performed on the block

The receipt of each transaction comprises cumulative gas prices of the block in which the transaction resides, the set of logs created for the transaction, the bloom filter from the transaction log, and the transaction's status code.

Transactions

A transaction is signed and created by external accounts. These transactions result in messages being sent between contract accounts and the creation of a contract account. Each transaction has the following fields:

- **Nonce**: Enlists the number of transactions initiated by the sender
- **Gas Price**: Value (price) paid in Wei for the cost of computation to execute the transaction
- **Gas Limit**: Maximum gas limit for the given transaction; the given transaction should not cost more than this limit
- **To**: Address of the recipient of the message or transaction
- **Value**: The transacted value to be transferred to the recipient
- **V, r, s**: Signature of the sender of the transaction
- **Init**: Usually associated with a contract creation transaction, which specifies the EVM code for the initialization of the account; it's executed once at the time of creation of the account and is discarded afterwards
- **Data**: Message call's input data

The following diagram shows the transaction, block, and inclusion of the block to the blockchain, which are discussed in detail in this section. Please refer to this diagram while reading about the transaction components, block header components, blockchain, and transaction flow. It also shows the inclusion of consensus in the entire process:

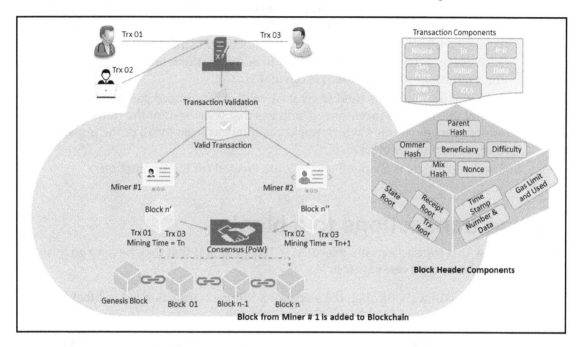

Transactions

Transactions are executed in the EVM. When a transaction is executed, it passes through initial validation:

1. The validity of the signature of the initiator
2. Validity of the transaction's nonce (must match the sender's current nonce)
3. Check the gas limit (it should be more than the intrinsic gas used by the transaction)
4. Well-formedness of the transaction
5. The sender's account should have sufficient funds for the upfront payment

Once the transaction has been validated successfully, the following steps are performed:

1. The cost of the transaction is deducted upfront from the sender's account balance.
2. The nonce value of the sender's account is incremented by one.
3. The transaction is executed, and during transaction execution, the logic of the transaction in the contract (smart contract) is executed.
4. While the transaction is executing, various sub-state information is collected, such as log series and refund balance. In addition, the remaining gas (total gas limit minus intrinsic gas used) is calculated.
5. Once the transaction is used to create a valid state, unused gas is refunded to the sender, the miner is incentivized, and gas that was used for the transaction is added to a gas counter, which tracks the total gas used by all of the transactions that are part of the block.
6. Finally, the state is changed and logs are created for the transaction.

Adding transactions to a block

Now, we know that transactions are executed in the EVM and that they have to go through various validation and processing steps.

In this section, we will walk through the steps for adding a transaction to the block, which are as follows:

1. **Validate ommer**: Within the blockchain header, each ommer block must be a valid header
2. **Validate transactions**: The gas that's used for the block should be equal to or less than the gas that's used for all of the transactions to be listed on the block
3. **Apply the rewards, also known as incentives**: Miners are awarded
4. **Verify the state and block nonce**: Apply state changes to each transaction and define the new block

Appending blocks to blockchain

Now, we understand how transactions are added to a block. In this section, we'll look at how a block is added to the blockchain. We already know that the block header contains mixHash and nonce, which prove the sufficiency of the computations performed on the block. This sufficiency of computation is defined as the *total difficulty* a miner had to go through to create a new block. The algorithm for *total difficulty* or the *block difficulty* is called the PoW algorithm (also known as Ethash in Ethereum). A block is only valid if it contains PoW of a given difficulty (maybe soon to be replaced with PoS).

A seed is calculated for each block by scanning the header of the block until that point in time. From the seed, a pseudo-random cache is computed and, from the cache, a dataset is generated. Full clients and miners need to store this dataset. Miners will randomly pick a few slices of the dataset and will hash them together into mixHash. Each miner will continue to repeat this set of generating mixHashes, until the mixHash matches the nonce. When the mixHash matches the nonce, the nonce is considered valid and hence the block is considered valid and can be added to the blockchain. Transactions that are part of this block are also considered to be confirmed.

Remember, there are many miners on the network, and they get to hear about the transaction at different times. Hence, each miner is mining different transactions (this could also be based on the transaction fee associated with each transaction), and so is generating its own block. Since each miner is building its own block with its own set of transactions in it, how does the block that gets mined and validated come to a common agreement? They reach a common agreement based on the consensus.

Consensus algorithm

It is evident that miners perform validation of the transaction and build their own block of transactions. Once they solve the puzzle and create a new valid block, they broadcast it to the blockchain network. This is where the consensus algorithm of the blockchain appears, which will ensure that the blockchain network reaches a consensus about the ordering of the transactions and about whose valid block needs to be added to the blockchain. Remember, the decision about *whose block to be considered* as the next block on the blockchain also determines the reward to the miner. This is taken care of by consensus algorithms such as PoW or PoS.

Ethereum uses PoW and will move to PoS soon. With PoS being the consensus algorithm for the blockchain network, any miner who solves the problem first and broadcasts the valid block will be considered the winner. With PoS, the creator of a new block is chosen in a deterministic way, depending on its wealth, which is also defined as its stake. Interestingly, there are no block rewards in PoS and so the miners will be offered transaction fees. This is the reason why miners are forgers in PoS and not miners. The following table lists the differences between PoW and PoS:

PoW	PoS
PoW is the original consensus algorithm in a blockchain network.	The next consensus algorithm for a blockchain, such as Ethereum.
Miners compete with each other to validate and propose a valid block to be added to the blockchain so that the miners get rewarded.	There are no miners and no mining rewards. Forgers (creators of new blocks) are chosen deterministically and are offered transaction fees.
The first miner of the valid block is rewarded.	The creator of a block is determined by their share, or stake, in a currency.
Solving difficulty by many miners is expensive and needs computation power and energy.	The PoS method is greener and cheaper.
The main benefits are the anti-DoS attack defenses and the low impact of stake on mining possibilities. Mining possibilities may result in cases, where the holders of a high stake, can turn out to be in charge of the blockchain network.	With PoS Casper, there will be a validator pool and network that will select the forger from this pool. Forgers need to submit a deposit to participate and be listed as a validator in the validator pool. If they violate or misbehave, they will be charged economically, their deposits will be taken away, and the forger will be delisted.
The main disadvantages are huge expenditures, *uselessness* of computations, and 51% attacks, where a 51% attack means a user or a group is in charge of the majority of the mining power of the network.	For a validator to perform a 51% attack, they need to own 51% of the overall supply of the value (currency). So, for someone to attack Ethereum, the dollar amount is in billions, and its occurrence is far from reality.

The following outlines some of the consensus methods in detail:

- **PoW**: This is the pioneer consensus algorithm. It is used in Bitcoin and other cryptocurrencies. Consensus is an algorithm that processes blocks of transactions and adds them to blockchain when an agreement is reached between the nodes. Hence, for a network that follows PoW consensus, that network is following the PoW rules to establish various processing blocks of transactions and add them to blockchain. The process of generating PoW and to allow a node to add a block to the blockchain is known as *mining*, and nodes that participate in mining are called *miners*. Before a miner adds a block to blockchain, PoW requires miners to solve a complex business problem (also known as a puzzle). In exchange for solving the business problem (puzzle), miners are rewarded. In a currency-based blockchain like Bitcoin or Ethereum, they are awarded with cryptocurrency. Essentially, miners compete with other miners to find a correct hash for each hash function. As soon as a miner reaches the solution and finds the correct hash, it propagates it to all the other nodes in the P2P network. Other nodes verify the hash before adding the block (set of transactions) to the blockchain. To maintain block time, the difficulty level of the problem (puzzle) is dynamically changed by the network. In the event of multiple miners solving the problem at the same time, then the longest chain is considered the winner, as the longest chain is the most trustworthy chain.
It solves the double spending problem, but is slow and costly from an energy and fee perspective, and not considered scalable.

- **PoS**: This is an alternative to PoW, suggested in 2011, and was first implemented by Peercoin (2012). In PoS, the miner's probability to mine depends on the stake (coins) the miners own in the system. For example, a miner with 15% of the stake (coins) has a 15% probability of mining the next block. It is expensive to attack a blockchain network based on PoS consensus, and it is energy efficient as well. Hence, in PoS, the probability of creating a block and being rewarded is determined by the stake in the network. Essentially, the probability of creating a block is directly proportional to the stake in the underlying cryptocurrency. But doesn't this mean the rich get richer? To prevent this, PoS follows randomization, that is, checking centralization, which may arise when a rich node gets richer and finally takes over the entire network. An attacker loses its stake for every attempt it makes to attach the blockchain network based on PoS. The problem with PoS is the *nothing at stake* problem, where a block generator can vote for multiple blockchain(s), also known as forks, and so, they can block the system from achieving consensus.

- **Proof of Elapsed Time** (**PoET**): Introduced by Intel in 2016, the PoET consensus algorithm suits permissioned blockchain networks such as Hyperledger sawtooth. The PoET algorithm is based on wait time, where the participating nodes (known as validators) wait for a randomly selected period. Essentially, validators generate a random wait time and sleep for that time. The first one that wakes up (also known as the one with the shortest wake time) will get the chance to commit a new block to the blockchain and propagate that information to all the nodes in the P2P network. With this random wait time, each node has a fair and similar probability to add blocks to the network. The PoET algorithm needs to take care of two tasks—firstly, it needs to ensure that participating nodes have really selected a random sleep time (not the shortest sleep time), and secondly, that the node has reached the sleep time and not woke up in the middle of the sleep time. PoET is cost-effective and offers equal opportunity to all participants. However, it is not suited for permissionless public blockchain networks.

  PoET results in a leader selection, where leadership is randomly distributed to the validators in the entire network. As the cost of the participation of the validators is low, it enlarges the population of validators, and therefore, enhances the robustness of the consensus algorithm.

- **Byzantine Fault Tolerance** (**BFT**): This is not from the family of *Proof* algorithms. Its name is derived from the classic Byzantine general's problem. An army, along with their Byzantine generals, surrounded a fort city. Generals are scattered around the fort city and, for an attack to succeed, they need to attack in unison. If all the generals do not attack in unison, they will lose the war. Now, they need to communicate with each other to reach a consensus so that they attack at the same time.

  In technical terms, it needs a system with several peer nodes to reach a consensus, even if there are few attackers and malicious nodes trying to influence the nodes. The Practical Byzantine Fault Tolerance algorithm can help solve the BFT.

- **Practical Byzantine Fault Tolerance** (**PBFT**): Hyperledger Fabric uses this consensus mechanism. PBFT offers a Byzantine state machine replication that is designed to tolerate malicious nodes (Byzantine faults). All the nodes are sequentially ordered, where one node is declared as the leader node (primary node) and other nodes are known as follower nodes (secondary/backup nodes). Any node will become a leader by transitioning from follower node to leader node, mostly via a round-robin algorithm. All nodes communicate and need to perform two tasks—firstly, they need to verify that the message came from a specific peer node, and secondly, they need to verify and ensure that the message was not modified during its communication. All nodes will reach a consensus, irrespective of the state of the network, using majority rule. The entire network is based on the assumption that no more than one-third of the network nodes are malicious. The more nodes, the more secure the network will be. It has the following phases:

1. A client sends a request to a leader node
2. Leader node propagates this message to all the follower (secondary) nodes
3. All the nodes (leader and follower) will perform a task, as requested by the client, and send a response back to the client
4. The client will verify the responses and ensure that the request (attack or retreat) is served successfully when it receives $n + 1$ replies with the same result, where n is the max number of malicious nodes

This is also based on the fact that the nodes are deterministic. The final result is attained when all honest nodes reach an agreement on the order and collectively accept or reject the order.

Types of blockchain networks

Broadly, there are two kinds of blockchain network—public and private. Both are P2P networks, where the ledger is distributed among those that can participate in the transaction. The ledger copy is replicated among participants, and those parties that can execute append-only transactions to the ledger will hold a copy of the ledger and will participate to reach a consensus to add a block to the blockchain. Along with being public or private, a blockchain can be both **permissionless** (such as Bitcoin or Ethereum) and **permissioned** (such as the Hyperledger blockchain framework).

A permissionless blockchain is also known as a public blockchain because anyone can join the network. Permissionless P2P systems do not require a set amount of peers to be online and are generally slower. Parties communicate on a permissionless blockchain without verifying the transacting parties' identities. Anyone can join a permissionless blockchain such as Ethereum and can perform read and write transactions. As the actors are not known, there are chances of malicious actors being in a network.

Permissioned networks are the blockchain networks where only pre-authorized users or organizations can perform write transactions. By virtue of the limited nodes, they are faster and inexpensive, can comply with regulations, and can easily be maintained. Pre-verification of the participating parties is mandatory for a permissioned blockchain and, hence, transacting parties are made. *Permissioned P2P networks have to guarantee uptime and require a high level of quality of service on communication links.* Permissioned blockchains such as Hyperledger Fabric ensure that only transacting parties are part of the transaction and that records of the transaction are displayed to only those participants and not to the whole network. Hence, capabilities such as data privacy, immutability, and security are the primary capabilities that Hyperledger offers to enterprises.

Although there are two kinds of blockchain network—public and private – on permissions, they can be classified as **PUBLIC AND PERMISSIONLESS**, **PUBLIC AND PERMISSIONED**, **PRIVATE AND PERMISSIONLESS**, and **PRIVATE AND PERMISSIONED**, as shown in the following diagram:

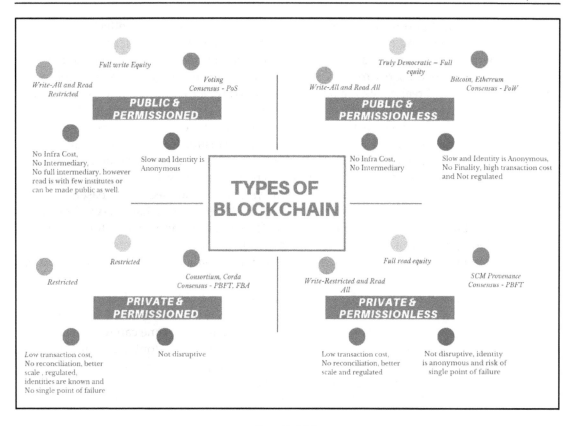

Types of blockchain

Blockchain networks based on permissions can be classified as follows:

- **Public and permissionless blockchain**: These are open and transparent and offer disintermediation and anonymity. They are trustless and offer immutability. This means they are *open* for anybody to join the blockchain network. The user (on a node) can enable his/her system with the required software and join the blockchain network. Public blockchain removes *intermediaries*, which reduces the cost, reduces the time it takes for reconciliation, and offers *transparency* in the network. Public blockchains are *trustless*, and trust is in the consensus. Transactions are replicated to each participating node, and consensus takes care of validation and synchronizes the transactions to be added to the blockchain. This allows *trustless* parties to execute transactions with confidence. The more nodes there are, the more impossible it becomes to undo a transaction; hence, public blockchain is immutable. Although transactions can be read by anyone, the identities of users are protected, hence offering *anonymity*.

- **Public and permissioned blockchain**: These are scalable, cost-effective, transparent, and offer disintermediation and anonymity. Public and permissioned blockchain allows anyone to read transactions, but only a few permissioned users can write transactions (for example, government employees' salaries and real-estate registries). Alternatively, it can allow a few to read transactions and everyone to write transactions (for example, voting). Public and permissioned blockchain is designated for such use cases where people or authorities (such as a designated employee or institution) sanction a transaction with data that's viewable by the public. If a public and permissioned blockchain is of the type where it allows anyone to read it and only a few permissioned participants to write on it, then such a system does not need to be based on expensive consensus algorithms such as PoW. Such blockchain networks can be scalable. Not everyone will participate for validation, and a validator is chosen. Hence, it is not slow and costly compared to a public and permissionless network. Although there are no intermediaries, only a few institutes can read or write.

- **Private and permissionless blockchain**: Only individual or selected members can run a full node to transact, validate, and read transactions. A few can execute write transactions and validate transactions, while everyone can read. It can be applied to use cases that include audits and are mostly adopted by enterprises that want to explore blockchain within the enterprise. All of the permissions are central to an enterprise; hence, they are not decentralized, and they can just be distributed. On the positive side, it allows the enterprise to be compliant and meet privacy needs to implement blockchain. Moreover, it allows cryptographic auditing. However, the whole idea of a decentralized network is lost.

- **Private and permissioned blockchain**: Public blockchain leads to scenarios where we run one full node, which means the node is performing computation for all of the applications for that network. This slows down the performance of the blockchain network. This can be a fit for some use cases; however, for enterprise requirements, public blockchain is not the answer. Enterprises are looking for a blockchain network where a node performs only those computations that are required for given applications. In addition, they need a blockchain network where parties are identifiable (not necessarily trusted) and permissions can be granted. In addition, the privacy of data can be guaranteed between a certain set of participants, even if all of the participants are on the same blockchain network. Furthermore, consensus is controlled by a predefined set of nodes, which leads to a faster and low-cost business network.

The answer to enterprise needs is a private and permissioned blockchain network. Private and permissioned blockchain can also be termed a consortium blockchain. A consortia (a consortium of members) controls them. Nodes are predefined and access rights are defined. Examples of such blockchain networks are R3 and Hyperledger Fabric.

Private and permissioned blockchain/consortia offer the following:

- **Better governance than public blockchain**: Public blockchain networks lack the governance to ensure an effective evolution of the blockchain network (for example, updates, changes to operational mechanisms, and consensus). As a result, it's slow to rectify defects and hinders innovation. On the other hand, consortiums can move fast as like-minded enterprises can quickly decide on innovations and evolve the business network to meet the dynamic needs of businesses.
- **Cost-effective**: The upfront cost for public blockchain is low; however, it gets expensive for nodes that are initiating transactions. Initial infrastructure costs might be low, but the operational cost increases over time, which is reflected in the increased cost of transactions. As public networks are trustless, trust lies in the consensus mechanism. Expensive consensus mechanisms such as PoW and PoS are not applicable. In a consortium, like-minded trusted parties are involved. Hence, costly consensus mechanisms are not required. In addition, a consortium does not include transaction fees. In many ways, a consortium is not only cost-effective, but also faster.
- **Privacy and security**: A consortium or private and permissioned blockchain network is highly secure. The access control layer is a first-class citizen for consortiums and ensures that a defined set of people get access to the network. Access is defined for reading, writing, and deploying code (smart contract/chaincode) and validating transactions. Public blockchain are secured by *miners*—also called **validators**. They solve complex problems (mining) to validate the transaction and, in return, receive incentives and rewards. In a private and permissioned network, security is ensured by the predictive distribution of control over the creation of blocks among identifiable nodes that are highly unlikely to collude. Malicious colluding and 51% attacks are not applicable as such malicious activities can be easily detected and the parties involved will be penalized based on consortium governing rules. Transactions are not visible to everyone. This offers enterprises and businesses the ability to transact with confidence, with trust in privacy offered by the business network.

The following table highlights the similarities and differences between different types of blockchain from the permissions perspective:

Public and Permissionless	Public and Permissioned	Private and Permissionless	Private and Permissioned
Open and transparent.	Open and restricted.	Restricted yet read transparent.	Restricted (hybrid approach).
Write all and read all.	Write all and read restricted.	Write restricted and read all.	Write restricted and read restricted.
Everyone can join, transact, read, and audit.	Everyone can join and transact, but only permissioned users can read and audit.	Everyone can join, nobody can transact, and everyone can read and audit.	Nobody can join, transact, read, and audit.
Anyone can download the protocol and participate with validate transactions.	Anyone who meets the predefined criteria can download the protocol and participate with validate transactions.	Anyone in the network can participate and validate transactions. However, this is only within the enterprise.	Only consortium members can validate the transaction.

The following table highlights the similarities and differences between different types of blockchain from a transaction and anonymity perspective:

Public and Permissionless	Public and Permissioned	Private and Permissionless	Private and Permissioned
Transactions are anonymous and transparent.	Transactions are anonymous and not read transparent.	Transactions are not anonymous and are read transparent.	Transactions are not anonymous and not transparent.

Write transactions can be authored or initiated by anyone; for example, I'm sending 10 Bitcoin to Bill. Everyone will know that 10 bitcoins were transacted.	Write transactions can be authored or initiated by anyone; for example, I'm casting my vote. However, whom I have cast my vote for can be counted by the authorized institution only. Another example is that a write can be performed by few and it can be read by all.	A write transaction is performed by few and it can be read by anyone. For example, an authorized party writes about the source of the inventory, and subsequent writes are performed by a few other intermediary parties or devices; however, it can be read by anyone.	A write transaction can be authored or initiated by authorized users; for example, I'm sending 10 USD to Bill. Authorized institutions will know that 10 USD was transacted.
Everyone will participate in transaction validation, and the validators are not the chosen ones.	Nobody can participate in transaction validation, and the validators are the chosen ones.	Nobody can participate in transaction validation, and the validators are the chosen ones.	Nobody can participate in transaction validation, and the validators are the chosen ones.
Truly democratic: full equity.	Full write equity.	Full read equity.	Restricted.
Transaction approval is long. It usually takes minutes.	Transaction approval is long. It usually takes minutes.	Transaction approval is short.	Transaction approval is short.

The following table shows the **consensus** and **use case** for different types of blockchain:

Public and Permissionless	Public and Permissioned	Private and Permissionless	Private and Permissioned
Open and decentralized.	Open and controlled.	Restricted.	Closed and restricted.
Anyone can run a full node to transact, validate, and read transactions.	Not just anyone can run a full node to transact, validate, and read transactions. Everyone can execute write transactions, while few can validate and read transactions.	Only individual or selected members can run a full node to transact, validate, and read transactions. A few can execute write transactions and validate transactions, while everyone can read.	Only members of the consortium can run a full node to transact, validate, and read transactions. In addition, only permissioned users can read.
For example, Bitcoin, Ethereum, and Litecoin.	For example, Ethereum.	For example, Hyperledger Fabric.	For example, Hyperledger Fabric, R3, and Corda.
Consensus - PoW.	PoS, PoA.	PBFT.	PBFT and FBA.
Use case—cryptocurrency, video games.	Use case—voting, poll records.	Use case—supply chain provenance, government record keeping, and assessor records.	Use case—tax returns, consortium, federations.

The advantages of **public and permissionless** blockchain are as follows:

- There's no infrastructure costs for creating and running **decentralized applications** (**dApps**)
- There's no need for a trusted party or intermediary; there is no intermediary
- The network is open and transparent and offers anonymity
- The network offers trustlessness and immutability

The advantages of **public and permissioned** blockchain are as follows:

- No infrastructure costs for creating and running dApps
- No need for a trusted party or intermediary; there is no intermediary
- Scalable, fast, and lower cost

The advantages of **private and permissionless** blockchain are as follows:

- Cost of transaction is reduced
- No need for reconciliations
- Simplified document handling
- Reduced data redundancy
- Scales better
- Better compliance with regulations
- Automated compliance functionalities
- Enables finality

The advantages of **private and permissioned** blockchain are as follows:

- There's better governance than public blockchain
- The cost of transactions is reduced. There is no need for reconciliations.
- Document handling is simplified and data redundancy is reduced
- As participants are preapproved and identities are known, there is better privacy and security
- Consortia is into decision-making and not using a single party
- There are no single points of failure
- It scales better and adheres to compliance with regulations
- It enables finality

The disadvantages of **public and permissionless** blockchain are as follows:

- **Scalability**: There is a limitation on the number of transactions that can be created, which can often reach to minutes at the peak period. Hence, such decentralized systems are not scalable.
- **Slowness and higher cost**: This includes the following:
  - Everyone will participate in validation, and a validator is not chosen. Consensus can be reached when every node executes the same task, such as executing the code (smart contract) or validating the transaction. This replication is slow, time-consuming, and costly from many perspectives, such as storage, electricity, and processing power.
  - As the number of transactions increases, so does the cost of executing those transactions, which leads to the clogging of miners to execute high-value transactions, and so, the system becomes slow and costly.

- **Identity is anonymous**: Anonymous participants could be malicious.
- **Immutability is a challenge**: Although immutability of transactions and blocks is the major feature of public blockchain, immutability of code (smart contract) is a challenge for the blockchain network. Blockchain considers smart contract deployment as a transaction and as they are transactions, they are immutable. Hence, any bug or issue or a code loop cannot be corrected. This means that, smart contracts need to be meticulously built and tested before being deployed and should have operations to **KILL** (also known as **shutdown**) the invocation to stop further damages.
- **Finality :** There's no finality and 51% attack (theory).
- **Can lead to centralization**: To realize the tokenized benefits of public blockchain, nodes operate as full nodes. A full node means the nodes carry a full copy of the blockchain. As the blockchain network grows in size, it becomes costly for smaller players and individual nodes to operate as full nodes. Only bigger players will then be able to operate as full nodes, and such scenarios can lead to centralization, which can influence the blockchain network.

The disadvantages of **public and permissioned** blockchain are as follows:

- Identity is anonymous—participants, being anonymous, can be malicious
- Immutability is a challenge
- There's no finality and 51% attack (theory)
- It can lead to centralization

The disadvantages of **private and permissionless** blockchain are as follows:

- It still has an intermediary and hence it is not decentralized.
- It is centralized and hence it is not decentralized. However, it can be distributed.
- As participants are not preapproved, identities are not known, although malicious users cannot perform write transactions and can only read information.

The disadvantages of **private and permissioned** blockchain are as follows:

- **Not fully distributed**: It still has an intermediary and hence it is not fully distributed.

- **Consortium formation is a challenge**: Formation of a consortium needs like-minded enterprises to collaborate over common business problems. Along with defining the structure and operation and governance model of the consortium, there are various questions that need to be answered for a formal setup of a consortium:
    - How to ensure that the consortia does not lead to concentration of power?
    - Who controls the consortium?
    - Do primary consortium members benefit more than late joiners?
    - Who benefits from the already existing infrastructure? Does this create confusion and infrastructure dependency or locking for new joiners or late joiners?
    - Who decides on new member inclusion or any member exclusion?
    - Who decides on the inclusion/exclusion of non-core members to the consortium?
    - How will the operational decisions be executed?
    - How will the consortium be financed?
    - How are disputes realized?
- **Dispute resolution and arbitrators**: This includes the following:
    - As a consortium includes various enterprises and discrete parties, it has its own business complexities. These complexities can lead to disputes. Hence, a consortium must have arbitrators to settle disputes. This means there is a need for an arbitration function for a consortium, which takes care of participation contracts (via a legal document) between members of the consortia.
    - A consortium can also need smart contract (chaincode) auditors to verify the smart contracts and verify the interface and integration of the smart contract with external applications and data sources. Such independent auditors will offer assurance to the consortium and help in surfacing vulnerabilities.

In this section, we compared different types of blockchain and learned about their advantages, disadvantages, and so on. In the next section, the emphasis will be on the layered structure of the blockchain architecture.

Blockchain platform

Until now, we have explored different types of blockchain network. In this section, we will quickly look at two major blockchain platforms—Ethereum and Hyperledger Fabric.

Following is the overview of these two platforms:

- **Ethereum**: It's an open source, public blockchain network. It is an extension of the core blockchain concept and now supports applications beyond currencies. Developers can build decentralized applications (via smart contracts) and can even build **decentralized autonomous organizations** (**DAOs**). It is a generic platform, and transactions are validated by PoW consensus. Ethereum is used as an idea for **business-to-consumer** (**B2C**) use cases and applications. It's a public blockchain; hence, all of the participants can access the ledger. It supports Solidity and has built-in currency (Ether).
- **Hyperledger Fabric**: It is a platform for enterprise applications. This platform is open source and modular and runs the BFT consensus algorithm. Hyperledger does not truly have a consensus mechanism. Due to its pluggable architecture, consensus can be plugged to it, based on the use case. Ledger is not public and it's mostly suited for **business-to-business** (**B2B**) use cases or applications. Chaincode (also known as smart contracts) can be written in standard languages such as Java, Go, and Node.js. It does not have a built-in currency.

Operations include the following:

- **Ethereum**: It is a public blockchain, where participants (nodes) can participate any time
- **Hyperledger Fabric**: It is a private blockchain, where participants (nodes) are given permission to participate

Consensus is as follows:

- **Ethereum**: Roles played by each participating node are similar. All of the nodes need to reach consensus for a transaction to commit. Every node needs to participate in consensus, even if that node is participating in a transaction. Ethereum consensus is based on PoW algorithms or a hybrid of PoW/PoS (called Casper).

- **Hyperledger Fabric**: Roles played by each participating node can be different. Some nodes are validating nodes, some are endorsing nodes, some are ordering nodes, and so on. Hence, during the process of establishing a consensus, different nodes will be performing different tasks. Nodes can opt for No consensus (No-op) or an agreement protocol such as PBFT. There is no third party that is forcing the choice of consensus mechanism. In addition to consensus, Hyperledger Fabric also offers identity verification during the life cycle of the transaction. It also supports channels and private data collection for a more private transaction between parties. Transactions are ordered and then added to blocks, which are then distributed across the channel. Channels further control the visibility of transactions to the business network participants.

Choice: Depending on the use case and application, you can opt for Ethereum versus Hyperledger. The following are a few points to note:

- **Ethereum**: Ethereum is public and permissionless and offers transparency. Its various advantages listed in the previous section. However, privacy and scalability are low in Ethereum.
- **Hyperledger Fabric**: It solves privacy and scalability issues and offers access control, high transaction speed, and resilience. On top of that, it is modular and pluggable, which can suit various B2B enterprise use cases.

Code execution is as follows:

- **Ethereum**: Code, also known as smart contracts, is executed on the EVM. Ethereum networks offer services to execute smart contracts and allow them to reach consensus. They also offer services to invoke external *oracles*. The scope of a smart contract is until the lifetime of the business network concludes. Hence, it's good development practice to write smart contracts with KILL methods.
- **Hyperledger Fabric**: Code, also known as chaincode, can be written in a standard programming language such as Java, Node.js, and Go. Chaincode is executed on the business network and validated and endorsed by business network nodes. Unlike Ethereum, Hyperledger Fabric supports chaincode versioning and upgrading. Following are some highlights of Hyperledger fabric from chaincode perspective -
  - Chaincode can be upgraded to a new version, as long as you maintain the same name of the chaincode; otherwise, it will be considered a different chaincode. Update is a transaction on the blockchain network and results in the binding of the new version of the chaincode to the channel. Before you update the chaincode, install a new version of the chaincode on the endorsers.

- What happens to the old version? All the other channels that are binding to the previous (old) version of the chaincode can continue to execute the older version. You submit the chaincode *upgrade* transaction to a channel. Hence, only one channel is affected, to which you have executed the upgrade transaction. All other channels, on which the upgrade transaction is not executed, will continue to run the older version.

- Chaincode can even be stopped. However, the start and stop life cycle transactions are *not* implemented in v1.4. These are future enhancements. Stop transactions will be a logical way to stop chaincode transactions before upgrading it.

- Optionally, you can STOP a chaincode by removing the chaincode container from the endorsers. Practically, you can delete the chaincode's container from each host (VM) on which the endorsing peers are running.

 Hyperledger Fabric supports Ethereum. With Hyperledger Fabric version 1.3 onward, smart contracts written in Solidity and Vyper can now be executed on Hyperledger Fabric as it supports the EVM. It's a new smart contract runtime and supports web3.js for enhancing the development of dApps (decentralized applications). This further boosts the development of dApps on permissioned blockchain. Visit `https://www.hyperledger.org/` for more details on this feature.

Blockchain actors

An entity that can participate in an action or in a blockchain network is known as an **actor**, which is an abbreviation of *blockchain actor*. In this section, we will cover various actors involved in blockchain. However, before we get into the details, let's briefly revisit the private blockchain. The previous section covered various types of blockchain networks. However, in this section, we will focus on defining actors primarily for private blockchain networks.

The following table lists some of the main properties of private blockchain networks that are essential to understanding blockchain actors:

Characteristics	Private and Permissionless	Private and Permissioned (consortium)
Owner	Single owner	Consortia or a founder organization
Consensus	Managed by single owner	Managed by a consortium (set of designated participants)
Read transaction	Any node	Only permissioned nodes
Network	Distributed	Decentralized

Private blockchain is meant to solve enterprise business cases, and this evolution is gaining momentum. Private and permissioned is a consortium blockchain that works across various organizations; however, it has a controlled user group. Participants, although not fully trusted, are identifiable (have identities). Like-minded enterprises or enterprises trying to chase similar goals can form a consortium to address business needs, improve trust, transparency, and accountability, and enhance existing business processes and workflows.

Private and permissionless blockchains, are not truly distributed. They are decentralized and are fully controlled by a single owner. As it is owned and operated by a single authority, consensus that's established in such a network cannot be trusted as the power lies with the central authority to choose users and influence consensus. A consortium blockchain (private and permissioned blockchain) is owned by a founder organization, but managed by a consortia (set of participants from different organizations). Consensus can be trusted as various organizations participate in it and they have a collective interest in the outcomes.

A consortium offers many benefits, such as the following:

- Not every enterprise or organization needs to build solutions to leverage blockchain. They can share the business network and build it together, which is cost-effective and less time-consuming.
- Smaller organizations can join the league and join the network on a pay-per-use basis and yet fully scale their business on blockchain.
- Member organizations of the consortia need to identify the use cases that reflect their common problems. They can then define a governing body and build solutions together to meet business needs.
- The identities of the participants are known, which enhances the level of trust.

- Consensus cannot be influenced as consortium members manage the blockchain network.
- The blockchain network access control and features of the blockchain network can ensure the privacy of data and enhanced security.
- Licenses to participate are issued by regulatory authorities of the blockchain network.
- Access to transaction data and knowledge about transactions is limited to permissioned participants for particular transactions.
- Consortia are resilient and offer high security, performance, scalability, and transactional throughput.

So far, we've discussed various private blockchain networks and the benefits of a consortium. Now, let's get back to the main topic of this section—actors. The following figure shows various actors for private blockchain network:

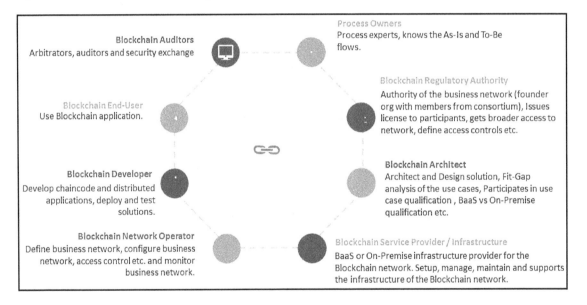

Blockchain actors

Each actor has a defined and key role to play in the development, operation, and maintenance of the blockchain network. However, the most challenging work lies with the architect.

The architecture of designing, building, maintaining, and using blockchain applications involve various actors, which are discussed as follows:

- **Process owner**: Process owners are subject matter experts on business processes. They are key to identifying business challenges and helping define common problems, which become the base to form a consortium. Process owners are key participants for defining use cases. They are subject matter experts on as-is processes, define the to-be processes from a functional standpoint, and lay the foundation for the blockchain business network.

- **Blockchain regulatory authority**: They are the primary authority of the business network (founder organization with members from the consortium). They issue licenses (certificates) to participants and usually have broader access to the network. They define access controls, issue certificates, and so on. They have functional knowledge about the processes and they ensure the correct participants get access to the relevant parts of blockchain network. They are key in defining the consortium, as private and permissioned blockchain networks are based on identifiable participants with defined access controls. Along with architects, they are responsible for identifying and defining the following:

  - Funding for the establishment, development, and operations of the consortium and blockchain network
  - Choosing the infrastructure for the blockchain network
  - Access control and participation of the actors and end users in the blockchain network
  - Defining and establishing trust authorities
  - Defining governance for the programs that will lead to the development of the blockchain network
  - Establish ROI for the consortium and its members
  - Define tracking, tracking of the program, and so on

- **Blockchain architect**: They should have a background in business analysis and should have an understanding of technology. A blockchain architect should have knowledge about their peers, consensus, security, chaincode, integration, ledgers, and applications. They, along with the authority, define and decide on the usage of consensus algorithms, standards, best practices, and so on for the consortium and its solutions. A blockchain architect is responsible for the following activities:

  - Delves into identifying use cases
  - Analyzes and chooses a specific blockchain solution for the given use case(s)
  - Defines which blockchain/DLT solution fits the gaps

- Offers estimates, plans risk, and defines milestones
- Architecting and designing the solution
- Works in tandem with infrastructure, blockchain operator, and development teams for the correct realization of the blockchain solution
- Defines reuse, auditability, and monitoring of the blockchain network
- Analyzes and quantifies the performance, resilience, security, scalability, and transactional throughput of the blockchain network
- Defines the versioning strategy, governance model, and production readiness of the blockchain network

- **Blockchain solution providers**: A consortium can opt for a BaaS (cloud) offering as blockchain business network's infrastructure. They can also set up an on-premise solution. Blockchain architects, along with the blockchain authority, can decide on the infrastructure. Once decided, the blockchain solution provider (either cloud or on-premise) can take care of the setup, management, maintenance, and support for the infrastructure of the blockchain network. The blockchain solution providers are the team from the blockchain cloud service providers who are responsible for creating and maintaining the blockchain network, offering security solutions, and providing ease of deploying and maintaining smart contracts or chain codes.

- **Blockchain network operators**: They define the business network, configure the business network, access control, and monitor the business network. They focus on the operational part of the blockchain business network. They mostly care about peers, consensus, and security of the blockchain network and are not concerned about smart contract and user interface codes.

- **Blockchain developer**: Blockchain developers focus on code (chaincode, UI, and analytics). They also take care of integration of blockchain network's chaincode with other applications, data sources, events, and ledgers. They are transparent to the working of blockchain network, consensus, security, peers, and orderers. However, they should understand the fundamentals of blockchain. Anyone with an acumen to code in any high-level programming language and who has a basic understating of blockchain/DLT technology can execute the following responsibilities as a blockchain developer:
  - Develop smart contracts or chaincode
  - Deploy and test smart contracts or chaincode
  - Use APIs in code to interact with blockchain networks
  - Develop, deploy, and maintain dApps and user interfaces as web applications for smart contracts

- **Blockchain end user**: With access to dApps web applications, end users are capable of consuming blockchain smart contracts via a UI or web application. This allows the end users to execute transactions against smart contracts, and yet the underlying blockchain technology remains transparent to them.
- **Blockchain auditors**: As the consortium includes various enterprises and discrete parties, it has its own business complexities. These complexities can lead to disputes. Hence, a consortium must have arbitrators to settle disputes. This means there is a need for an arbitration function for a consortium, which takes care of the participation contract (via a legal document) between members of the consortia. For now, the CPA authorities will handle these legal documents, until the time they turn into smart contracts (chaincode) and act as smart arbitrators. A consortium can engage smart contract (chaincode) auditors to verify the smart contracts and verify the interface and integration of smart contracts with external applications and data sources. Such independent auditors will offer assurance to the consortium and help surface vulnerabilities. Also, it allows regulatory bodies such as SEC to have a read-only pull on data so that they can identify transaction details among *the universe of available information*.

BaaS

Blockchain is a disruptive technology and is the future. However, due to technical complexities, lack of expertise and skills, and operational overhead, the adoption of blockchain is slow. These challenges were gradually addressed by cloud service providers who entered into blockchain solutions with the BaaS offering, which offered clarity on *where* we should host the solution.

So far, we've discussed DLT, blockchain, centralized and decentralized systems, and ledgers. We also looked at the blockchain structure, blocks, and so on. Now, I want to conclude this chapter by laying the foundation for *what's next* in the subsequent chapters. This section talks about the **center of gravity** (**CG**) of this book. Subsequent chapters will revolve around use cases and the implementation of a use case using Oracle's Blockchain Cloud Platform (BaaS). At this stage, you might be curious about how we will implement this. Consider this section as a glimpse into a blockchain solution provider and where it should reside. There are various steps before implementing blockchain. They start with identifying the use case and choosing the solution providers. Some of the questions you will need to answer are as follows:

- Why do you need blockchain and what's the rationale behind it?
- Is there a strategic choice or a tactical push?
- What are you building and how are you building it?

- Who is involved, how are they involved, who will decide, and so on?
- Where will the solution reside-on-premises or on the cloud?
- Who will be managing it?
- Who will take care of resilience?

Many of the answers lie with BaaS.

BaaS qualifiers

BaaS is a blockchain platform that hosts a consumer's blockchain applications and solutions. The blockchain platform (BaaS) provider, for a fee, handles the setup, maintenance, and support of the blockchain infrastructure. It is a boost to businesses and entrepreneurs as it offloads a lot from customers and allows them to focus on identifying use cases and developing blockchain applications and solutions. Things such as network availability, scalability, performance, and so on stay with the service provider. Blockchain touches on a wide range of audiences, which includes architects, designers, developers, enthusiastic evangelists, business and process owners, IT strategists, and economists. In addition, BaaS, being a full-stake cloud-based solution, empowers entrepreneurs, enthusiastic evangelists, enterprises, and so on to grasp the potential of DLT and blockchain in a timely and efficient manner. BaaS is turning into a true catalyst to expand the adoption of DLT and blockchain.

The following are some of the qualifying factors to look at when choosing a BaaS provider:

- **Standard**: These include the following:
    - Is it an established cloud provider?
    - Is it based on industry standards?
    - Is it compatible and interoperable? Is it interoperable with other ledgers too?
- **Quick setup**: Does it allow for the quick provisioning of a blockchain network?
- **Integration and other service offerings**: These include the following:
    - Does it support REST proxies for integrating OBP with SaaS, PaaS, and other on-premises applications?
    - Does it offer services such as data security, integration services, and object/document storage?
    - Does it offer cloud services such as containers and compute and storage services?

- **Security and privacy**: These include the following:
    - Does it offer integrated identity management and security?
    - Does it take care of privacy, data partitioning, and private channels?
- **Is it resilient**: These include the following:
    - Does it offer high availability?
    - Does it offer backup and disaster recovery?
    - Does it offer enhanced performance (both blockchain network and consensus)?
- **Smart contract/chaincode—deployment, versioning, standards, auditing, and testing**: These include the following:
    - Does it offer the deployment of chaincode in standard languages such as Java and Node.js?
    - Does it allow rollback to the previous version of chaincode?
    - Does it offer/support tools to test chaincode?
    - Does it have a credible development community?
- **Eat your own pill**: Does it offer applications on the marketplace and build on its own BaaS?
- **Monitoring**: Does it offer transaction monitoring and dashboards?

The following diagram highlights the key qualifiers for a BaaS platform:

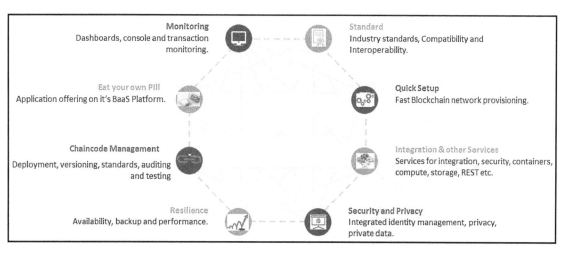

BaaS qualifiers

BaaS use cases

To keep it simple, BaaS solves cost, efficiency, and transparency challenges. It allows the business to explore, experiment, experience, and then engage in blockchain. It takes away the intricacies of implementation and allows the business to focus on the core. It's analogous to an aged whiskey. You can trust its manufacturer and pay for it to enjoy it. You do not need to get into the details of where it was manufactured, under what conditions, how it was treated, and so on. Blockchain enables product provenance.

There is an explosion of ideas around use cases, which can be advantageous for DLT, and blockchain and BaaS will drive the wave in the adoption of DLT and blockchain, thereby realizing and fulfilling these ideas for enterprises, customers, and entrepreneurs. There are various use cases that can be addressed by leveraging BaaS:

- **Prowess (education and profession)**: A *ledger of prowess* can act as a single source of truth for certificates, assessments, skills, and so on. It offers prowess ownership, full authority on the asset (certificate, transcripts, skills, evidence, and so on), and offers a solution to fully track and trace an individual's certificates, skills, and knowledge. There are various use cases beyond certificates. For example, while hiring someone, organizations need authentic and trustworthy information about the credentials of an applicant. *A ledger of prowess* will offer the ledger that holds the applicant's certificates, skills, experience, expertise, and other relevant reports, immutably. In addition, as these records are immutable, even the applicants cannot fabricate it to meet specific job requirements. We easily calculate the risk involved in hiring an applicant who has fabricated his/her skills.
- **Supply chain**: A *ledger of supply* can act as a single source of truth for asset management, procurement, product life cycle management, logistics, provenance, fraud detection, and so on. It can go beyond the provenance (tracking of products) to a full life cycle of SCM on blockchain.
- **Government**: Government agencies hold citizen data and various other kinds of sensitive information. The sensitivity quotient poses security and privacy risks. Blockchain's public repository, along with hashing, cryptography, and other proven technologies, can take care of hacking, data modifications, loss of information, and so on. A *ledger of trust* can take care of citizen rights, votes, donations, and so on. A voting platform with *ledger of trust* can ensure fraud-free voting and fraud-free counting, and check vote rigging. Results are quick and the entire exercise of executing elections can be made cost-effective, timely, and trustworthy. A *ledger of* **unique identity** (**UID**) can digitize secure identity management.

- **Real estate**: A *ledger of ownership* can act as a truth for the ownership of properties, ease the listing of properties, allow the transferral of ownership in minutes, reduce the cost of listing properties, and so on.
- **Healthcare**: A *ledger of wellness* can evolve as a truth to track patient and doctor information. This will take care of drug counterfeits, secured and controlled exchange of information such as prescriptions and medical history, and so on. The current system stores medical information in silos with massive restrictions on sharing and its usage. A *ledger of wellness* will lead to storing information on an immutable and secure ledger, where discrete stakeholders have access to it based on their privileges. Blockchain and its chaincode can automatically keep audit and track an individual's health and history, and can even allow patients to monetize their medical records for research, which is a huge gain for humanity.
- **Insurance**: A *ledger of assurance* can be a source of truth from policy sales to settlement, which includes sale of a policy, maintenance of a policy (renewals, terminations, adjustments, and so on), claims, evaluation and evidence, and settlements. This will eliminate cumbersome processes, reduce third-party involvement, allow for faster settlements, and so on.
- **Intellectual properties**: A *ledger of IP* can be a proven source for patents and trademarking of IP; it reduces IP abuse, ensures IP owners receive credits and monetary benefits for their IP, and so on.
- **Fintech**: A *ledger of affluence* can be the base for cross-broader payments and faster B2B transactions. It eliminates reconciliations, infuses trust among traders, and so on. It can also be used for clearing and settlements, trade finance, KYC, and AML.
- **Other industries**: These can use BaaS as well, and they are as follows:
    - **Travel**: It can be used for passenger processing, travel trace and tracking, single source of truth for passenger identity, and so on. With critical documents being on the ledger, passport forging, pass-through, illegal immigration, and so on can be checked.
    - **Humanitarianism**: It can be used for charity, donations, and so on.
    - **Transportation**: The use cases include track, trace, and so on.
    - **Oil and gas**: It can be used for freight management, payments, shipments, and so on.

- **Analytics**: I'm pushing analytics as a horizontal industry here, as I believe in the quote: *Where there is data, there is analytics* (Vivek Acharya). Referring to the aforementioned example on *Healthcare*—patients trying to monetize their medical records also serves humanity a lot. If that happens, it needs an efficient analytics platform to make sense of the blockchain data. Other than that, transactional data on ledgers can lead to greater insights. Blockchain, along with AI, can lead to better forecasting, effective predications, and answers to business and end-users questions in real time.

Key advantages of BaaS

BaaS is a platform with a magnitude of features on the top of a platform such as Hyperledger Fabric. Using BaaS offerings, customers can create networks and channels and build and deploy chaincode and dApps. Cloud service providers take care of the mundane necessary activities such as infrastructure agility, scalability, and operational efficiency, while customers can focus on building applications and chaincode. BaaS is a major boost to the adoption of blockchain, which is a BaaS offering in most of the major cloud solution providers.

With a cloud platform such as Oracle's Blockchain Cloud Service, you don't need to bring your own security, identity management, container management, admin console management, infrastructure, HA, and recovery. It is all with the cloud service provider. The following are a few of the key advantages of BaaS:

- Fast provisioning
- Ease to configure
- Quick on-boarding of members
- Embedded identity management
- Enhanced security and confidentiality
- Efficient development and testing
- Enhanced integration with processes and applications
- Better performance and scalability
- High availability and operational resilience
- Excellent scalability
- Decouples infrastructure from the customer's primary task of developing smart contracts and applications
- Allows customers to explore the magnitude of possibilities with their legacy applications and business processes.

Oracle's BaaS – OBP

BaaS offers a lot on top of its base (also known as its core). Hyperledger Fabric (base) is not preassembled. Hence, the enterprise needs to build chaincode and benefit from Hyperledger Fabric; they need to set up the Hyperledger Fabric infrastructure, handle its prerequisites, and configure and maintain it. The enterprise needs to ensure the integration of the installed Hyperledger Fabric environment with a security stake and manage the life cycle of all of the containers. The enterprise needs to handle the patching and upgrades and needs to ensure the system's huge availability, performance, business network management, and so on. Oracle's blockchain platform is based on Hyperledger Fabric. With OBP, the enterprise's responsibilities to set up, manage, and maintain the blockchain platform will shift toward Oracle (BaaS provider), and the enterprise can continue to focus on building work class blockchain applications and solutions.

Linux foundation's Hyperledger Fabric is the foundational base (core) for OBP. With Hyperledger Fabric being the base, any vendor (including Oracle) offering solutions on top of it must automatically adhere to industry standards. Blockchain platforms, such as Oracle's Blockchain platform, ease the creation of a network where participants from different organizations can participate and work together. Interoperability challenges such as governance, naming convention standards, and unified data models need to meet common consensus. For example, a consortium where participants mutually agree on standards, rules of participation, sharing of cost and profits, governance mechanism, and collective risk mitigation, along with the inclusion of analytics, auditing, and validation to ensure smooth blockchain network operations.

OBP offers a console to manage networks, channels, and users. It offers a REST proxy and various other infrastructure services to set up, build, and maintain a blockchain network. It's built on top of Hyperledger Fabric and adds a lot of rich features to allow for the ease of operations, enhanced security, and high accessibility. Oracle OBP is a BaaS offering from Oracle, which has the potential to address enterprise DLT/blockchain use cases. The Oracle offering includes infrastructure services and various embedded resources such as compute, containers, storage, event streaming, and identity management. Oracle has the following features:

- **Standard-based**: Oracle BaaS's core is Hyperledger Fabric; hence, it automatically adheres to industry standards. As a result, applications built on OBP are interoperable and compatible. This feature matches the BaaS qualifier *standard* listed in the previous section.

- **Preassembled**: Oracle's blockchain platform includes a preassembled identity solution (Oracle's identity management), object store (embedded archiving), and RESTful APIs. The Oracle offering includes an operational console to configure and manage the entire blockchain business network. Onboarding of B2B partners to the blockchain network is simplified and partners can be verified with a built-in identity solution. This feature resembles the BaaS qualifiers: *quick setup, security, privacy, and chaincode management and monitoring.*

- **Pluggable**: It offers integration services with **Oracle Integration Cloud Service (OICS)**, which allows for quick integration with SaaS and PaaS applications. This feature fits into the BaaS qualifier integration and other services, which are as follows:

  - The enterprise can leverage OICS tools in order to process cloud services to build and extend BPM (workflow) applications. The enterprise can extend its SaaS applications using SDKs or RESTful APIs.

  - Applications built on the Oracle development platform (for example, VBCS) can invoke operations on chaincode using various standards (Java, Node.js, and Go) and APIs.

  - Enterprises can build applications on application container cloud services, Java cloud services, mobile cloud services, or application builder cloud services and can initiate blockchain transactions using SOA cloud services, process cloud services, and APIs.

- **Enterprise-grade solution**: It is a managed service with high availability, enhanced security, and continuous backup of ledgers. This feature resonates with the BaaS qualifier—*resilience.*

- **Automated**: Oracle's autonomous database anchors OBP. Hence, it leverages the benefits of Oracle's autonomous database, such as self-provisioning, auto upgrades, enhanced security, and monitoring. It auto-applies security patches without a downtime, enhancing security multifold and storing data in an encrypted state. It offers self-repairing features, which ensures the highest availability and reduces planned and unplanned downtime to less than two and a half minutes. This feature fits into the *resilience* and *monitoring* BaaS qualifiers.

- **Privacy**: Hyperledger Fabric offers channels and private data collection (refer to Chapter 3, *Delving into Hyperledger Fabric* for more details) to allow the enterprise to conduct confidential transactions. The Oracle offering allows only approved peers to join channels. This feature fits with the *security* and *privacy* BaaS qualifiers.

While analyzing the blockchain solution, identifying the use cases, and choosing the most relevant blockchain platform, it's strategically important to look at the core systems, business processes, and benefits the enterprise will reap from the inclusion of blockchain in your ecosystem. We are in an era of *cloudifying (cloud)* infrastructure, applications, and processes. Blockchain cloud platform is an excellent addition to your cloud strategy. Cloud and blockchain strategies go hand in hand with a vision toward the future of autonomous organizations. This book contains details and practices around Hyperledger Fabric and its realization though Oracle's blockchain cloud platform. We will be going though this in detail in subsequent chapters.

Pre–built blockchain applications

The previous section listed OBP and its features. It also tried to match them with BaaS qualifiers. Almost all of the OBP features matched the BaaS qualifiers, except one (*Eat your own pill*). In this section, we will expand on the OBP features and match them with the *Eat your own pill* qualifier. This qualifier essentially displays the capability and maturity of BaaS offerings from a vendor. In this context, Oracle offers many applications that are built on OBP.

Oracle is the pioneer in creating SaaS-based blockchain applications that allow business applications to leverage blockchain technology for traceability, enhanced security, and streamlined consensus. These SaaS-based blockchain applications are built using OBP and run on Oracle's cloud platform. They are seamlessly integrated with other SaaS applications, such as **supply chain management (SCM)**, **enterprise resource planning (ERP)**, and other cloud-based applications. They are also integrated with machine learning applications and IoT and AI applications.

These applications solve common challenges faced by enterprises such as tracking, tracing, visibility, and root cause analysis. Blockchain is a technology that remembers. It is a technology that removes the hurdle in the tracking, tracing, and visibility of products. Oracle Blockchain Applications allow the tracking, tracing, and analytics for products through their supply chain cycle. These applications also allow root cause analysis and offer recommendations in challenging situations such as damaged products, delayed transportation, delayed delivery, and low quality.

These blockchain applications offer the following advantages:

- They offer pre-built solutions to common business challenges
- These applications are configurable, allowing for the faster interconnection of applications with blockchain technology to meet business needs
- It's a one-stop shop to add B2B partners to blockchain business networks
- It allows quick solutions to business challenges and saves time for business
- It leads to business agility for SaaS and on-premise applications, allowing them to quickly leverage the benefits of blockchain technology
- It seamlessly integrates IoT and AI-based applications
- It offers a pre-built analytics dashboard to enhance transparency, trust, and visibility among businesses, its partners, and suppliers

These applications offer solutions to business problems such as recalls, disputes, frauds, compliance issues, and counterfeits. They offer analysis and end-to-end traceability across the supply chain. They offer a pre-built dashboard, which surfaces IoT, AI, and blockchain transactions. This allows real-time insights for businesses. The following are the applications offered by Oracle (at the time of writing this book):

- **Oracle Intelligent Track and Trace**: It offers end-to-end asset tracking and tracing. It allows a digital footprint for each step and event in the process of the supply chain. It offers real-time insight into these events and steps in the process of the supply chain, from manufacturing to transportation, to sales and delivery.
- **Oracle Product Lineage and Provenance**: It allows users to verify the provenance of the product.
- **Oracle Intelligent Cold Chain**: It tracks the product's state from manufacturing to sales and offers a full audit trail of it. It emits alterations for excursions and offers preventive recommendations.
- **Oracle Warranty and Usage Tracking**: It tracks high-value assets and offers a complete audit trail of an asset's usage. These audit trails are verifiable logs and can be used for product warranty and liability claims.

Enterprises can transform their existing business processes and attain immediate benefits from these business-friendly applications. These applications allow enterprises to develop a blockchain network that allows secure, transparent, and efficient transactions with their suppliers and partners. Moreover, it solves common business problems with tracking, tracing, visibility, and root cause analysis. This is indeed the future for applications. Such applications work seamlessly with existing on-premise and cloud applications. Businesses can use out-of-the-box blockchain applications, set up their blockchain business network with blockchain network templates, and expand and integrate with applications using pre-built integration. We are going to learn more about this in subsequent chapters.

Summary

In this chapter, we delved into ledgers, blockchain definitions, blockchain structure, and layers. We also glanced at blockchain structure, blocks, transactions, and how blocks are added to the blockchain. We have familiarized ourselves with actors, components, and algorithms in blockchain. We also tried to coin the term distributed double-entry (also known as triple-entry). Chapter 2, *Construing Distributed Ledger Tech and Blockchain*, will enlist use cases on blockchain and Hyperledger and help us identify a possible approach for them. Enterprises are exploring the immense opportunities of DLT and blockchain, and they acknowledge the strategic and long-term benefits of this distributed technology; however, there are various challenges tagged with DLT and blockchain that need to be mitigated before it is adopted by enterprises. Although there are challenges, there is a wide array of opportunities available. As the trust and benefits of DLT and blockchain grows, businesses will explore and engage more in adopting DLT/blockchain. Let's delve into Chapter 2, *Construing Distributed Ledger Tech and Blockchain*, and explore the plethora of opportunities DLT-like blockchain offers by addressing various use cases.

2
Construing Distributed Ledger Tech and Blockchain

A blockchain is a time-sequenced chain of transactions that are agreed upon consensus and grouped into blocks. This guarantees that information of the ledger (chain) is reliable and can be trusted, since each entry (block) is validated by the network and is agreed by the network. For a ledger of records, **distributed ledger technology** (**DLT**) and its variant (blockchain) are revolutions. By virtue of its nature, such as being an immutable trustworthy ledger of records, no single point of failure, no centralized third party, and decentralized trust, DLT and blockchain have created a hype (catalyzed by imagination) that allows us to envision various use cases of DLT and blockchain.

One such application of blockchain that grabbed everyone's attention is Bitcoin, which is a globally distributed immutable ledger of records. Since its discovery (I'm not referring to it as an invention), enterprises, organizations, businesses, entrepreneurs, and lately, individuals, have learned the significance of this disruptive technology. For some time, the massive journey of Bitcoin overshadowed its underlying technology. However, when the world witnessed the massive volatility of cryptocurrency, everyone showed interest in the headlines that were created by the underlying disruptive technology. Today, there are many consensus protocols, various DLTs, and blockchains, and the world is trying to identify different use cases that can be addressed by DLT and blockchain.

Since its discovery, DLT and blockchain have outgrown themselves. Billions of dollars are pumped into blockchain initiatives, and the trend is only growing year after year. Explorers are exploring and proving various use cases, from the prevention of human trafficking to digital identities, from education to healthcare, and so on.

The previous chapter focused on ledgers, an introduction to blockchain, DLT technologies, and their structure. This chapter will delve into DLT, its challenges and opportunities, and will drill into various use cases. We will also focus on design strategy and how it allows us to explore and engage with business scenarios.

Challenges and opportunities of DLT

Enterprises are exploring the immense opportunities of DLT and blockchain, and they acknowledge the strategic and long-term benefits of this disruptive technology. However, there are various challenges associated with DLT and blockchain that need to be mitigated before they are adopted by enterprises. This section summarizes the challenges faced by DLT and the opportunities it offers.

Challenges associated with DLT

This section covers the main challenges of the adoption of DLT.

Perception

The perceived immaturity of the underlying technology: The perceived immaturity of the technology catalyzes the belief that solutions built with it might face challenges. Lately, it is also evident that DLT struggles with handling a higher number of transactions for concurrent users. Under-performing DLT and blockchain applications, from the transaction and performance perspectives, reduce the appeal and competitiveness of DLT and blockchain.

The perceived challenges related to the security of data: Enterprises need secure data access and permissioned implementation of DLT and blockchain. DLT and blockchain, by their very nature of being decentralized distributed ledgers, are perceived to be more secure than centralized ledgers, yet this needs data to back the facts. Most of the analysis is centered on the impact of DLT and blockchain; however, the attention needs to shift toward the usage of the technology and the regulations around it. To me, the more established a regulatory framework is, the more widely a technology will be adopted, and this holds true for DLT and blockchain.

Consensus

Consensus on the terminologies and clarity: The obscurity of DLT versus blockchain, consensus, regulations, and security, along with their relationships, add to the confusion around this disruptive technology. Business stakeholders, decision-makers, consumers, and businesses are still analyzing the use cases of DLT and blockchain. The better the clarity, the higher the adoption, since businesses will be clearer about the use cases.

Regulation uncertainty: Considering the fact that enterprises have invested considerably to remain compliant with standards and regulations, it is critical to establish regulations around DLT and blockchain. Otherwise, without regulations, the adoption of DLT and blockchain will remain in question.

Facts

Missing structured governance around the technology: Governance around DLT and blockchain is challenging, especially when the ledgers are distributed. Since DLT and blockchain are P2P, users use their keys to transact; this is why the governance around key management, as well as the clarity and legality around the loss of keys, still needs to evolve.

It is not urgent: Another important factor for the adoption of any technology revolves around the need for it. If there is a need and urgency for it, the technology will witness a monumental shift toward the adoption of it, both from regulators and businesses. Since enterprises are already invested in the current IT infrastructure, which is also compliant with regulations, they don't have the urgency to shift to DLT and blockchain; it is a huge architecture change and a giant leap. It also involves cost, and enterprises need to gauge the **return on investment** (**ROI**). These factors reduce the urgency of DLT and blockchain, as well as its adoption.

The unknowns

Unknown risks for an early adopter: Today, every enterprise has well-defined processes, IT systems, and analytics solutions that serve their current requirements and comply with regulations and standards. The adoption of yet-to-be standardized solutions around DLT and blockchain requires considerable redesign of their existing solutions, and the risks are unknown. There's also this issue of their clarity. Even with some level of calculated strategic benefits of DLT and blockchain, enterprises are reluctant to adopt DLT and blockchain due to the cost of resources—both software and talent. A shift toward DLT and blockchain will only happen when the benefits to business outweigh the cost and risk.

Lack of clarity on the replacement of real contracts with smart contracts: There is lack of clarity when it comes to smart contracts and chaincodes as well. They are assumed to replace real legal contracts with simple auto-executable conditions. This, lack of clarity, will eventually die out with the evolution of smart contracts and smart contracts will shine when enterprises share the influencing stories of smart contracts as a replacement for complex real contracts.

Lack of data to highlight the advantages businesses can gain: Since DLT and blockchain aren't widely adopted yet, data on their performance is yet to be shared and widely known. A precise assessment of their performance and their impact on the traditional centralized ledger approach versus the decentralized ledger approach are not clearly known. Clarity on the benefits of businesses adopting DLT and blockchain still need to be cemented.

Being a DLT and blockchain enthusiast and evangelist, I firmly believe that the challenges around DLT and blockchain will not hinder the acceptance and adoption of such a disruptive technology. As we discussed previously, the more trust grows, the more likely the technology is going to be adopted. The more businesses see the value and benefits of them, the more regulations will be legislated and standards will be defined. Interestingly, there is a difference between maturity and adoption, which is fully based on the benefits enterprises find in the usage of DLT and blockchain. The more benefits there are (even if the maturity of DLT and blockchain are low), the more likely they are to be adopted. DLT and blockchain might take a little more time to mature than they will to be adopted.

Opportunities offered by DLT and blockchain

This is an era of disintermediation, where Uber owns no vehicles, Facebook allows billions to connect, Airbnb owns no real estate, and Amazon sells almost everything without holding much inventory. Various industries, such as insurance, healthcare, finance, transportation, logistics, retail, and real estate include intermediaries. All of those cases where intermediaries are involved are potential use cases for blockchain. This allows the removal of intermediaries between consumer and producer while injecting trust, reliability, robustness, immutability, and confidentiality. Financial and non-financial industries have quickly understood the potential of DLT and blockchain technology and its disruptive applications. DLT and blockchain can be applied to several industries, from the financial sector to music, from intellectual property rights to education and healthcare. The continuous application of DLT and blockchain to address various use cases is so huge that the World Economic Forum predicted that, by 2027, 10% of global GDP would be stored on blockchain.

Now, it's time to check out the opportunities that DLT and blockchain offer.

Gain in efficiency and novel revenue streams

Gain in efficiency: Various enterprise processes that involve third parties and processes that are human-centric can be automated and re-engineered to gain efficiency. For example, with DLT and blockchain, there is no need for data synchronization and control by a third party, which makes the need for a third party obsolete, thus improving the efficiency of transactions. Previously, we discussed cases where reconciliation is required by transacting parties where assets and their values are included. With DLT and blockchain, everyone has the same trusted copy of the ledger, and so reconciliation isn't required. This is a significant cost saving and a driver for wide adoption.

Novel revenue streams: Efficient, improvised, and integrated processes will attract novel revenue streams for enterprises because they will be able to scale quickly, integrate with other organizations more quickly, address new challenges quickly by inducing agility.

Business models and enhanced resilience

Wide array of business models: The absence of a third party opens up a wide array of possibilities around applications and business models. Businesses can adopt **peer-to-peer (P2P)** transactions so that they can fuel the growth of a crowd economy, a shared economy, or a system where the underprivileged population can be brought to the mainstream.

Enhanced resilience: DLT and blockchain, by virtue of their distributed nature, allow participating nodes to have a copy of the ledger. Even if the network fails, each node holds a copy of the ledger and the transactions on it. No single entity owns it; everyone owns it, and this enhances the network's resilience.

Inheritance of trust

As there is no single point of failure and no single or third party acts as the central authority, everyone owns the network, but at the same time doesn't. Transactions are added as blocks, but only when a consensus is reached; once appended to the block and the block is added to the chain, it remains omnipresent and immutable. Without a third party being involved and no reliance on a centralized database, DLT and blockchain offer opportunities in terms of identity verification, security, and authentication of trust on an immutable, trusted, distributed platform.

Immutability and a smarter world

Advantages of recording and reporting on immutability: Since transactions are immutable in DLT and blockchain, consistency and clarity reporting is provided. Since they are immutable, the chance of errors occurring is extremely low and the network itself checks against fraud.

Smarter world: In DLT and blockchain, agreements between businesses, businesses and consumers, individuals and machines, machines and machines, and so on are implemented using smart contracts. These smart contracts are self-executing, and so the administrative and execution costs of agreements are reduced drastically. Risk, in terms of contract or agreement interpretation, is reduced significantly, which further reduces any legal costs that arise in the case of conflicts in traditional contracts and agreements.

Plethora of use cases: DLT and blockchain find opportunities in abundant use cases, from government to finance and **supply chain management** (**SCM**) to human empowerment. This chapter will cover a few of those use cases.

Challenges of traditional technologies and solutions

The evolution of a human being to being able to understand exchanging value has its roots in the level of uncertainty. The greater the uncertainty, the less the trust in the exchange of value. The higher the certainty, the greater the exchange of value. There are various traditional challenges that blockchain tries to solve, such as trust, intermediaries, confidentiality, robustness, resilience, and availability. Let's go over them now:

- **Trustless**: When you deal with a centralized system, you place trust on the system and the underlying set of people and machines that are responsible for taking care of the system and its security. Your inherent trust is in the organization you are dealing with. For example, we are using an email service for many years and sometimes send important personal emails as well. We have inherent trust in the organization that is offering those email services, with trust and certainty that our emails will neither be tampered nor lost. However, can it be modified, and can the data that you are trying to access from a bank or an institution such as a government be tampered with? The answer is yes. On the other hand, blockchain offers a trustless ecosystem, where information cannot be tampered and is delivered with certainty. A human's quest to look for a trustless ecosystem is addressed by blockchain.

- **No intermediary**: While talking about trust, we can sense that it is the foundation for the exchange of value between a business and a business or a business and its consumers. In addition, trust becomes more complicated, costly, inefficient, error-prone, and slow when it crosses borders, boundaries, and regulations. This equation is complicated when an intermediary gets involved. Blockchain is proven as a powerful alternative to a dis-intermediary, trust-free economy, where the trust is between businesses directly, between humans directly, or between business and humans directly, without an institutionalized intermediary or a third party as a centralized trust authority. With no intermediary and trust residing in the system/ecosystem itself, collaborations, partnerships, and opportunities are limitless. Moreover, blockchain allows organizations to transact with organizations, consumers, machines, or each other without any intermediary. To me, this is an evolution of trust, where the trust is in an ecosystem and technology that now allows parties to transact without a trusted intermediary. When it comes to transactions, it is paramount to understand confidentiality.

- **Confidentiality**: This is a person's, organization's, or party's right to keep their data private, where their actions are neither recorded nor monitored. They can obtain privacy by being either anonymous by not letting others know anything about them, or by not posting any sensitive information or documentation in the transaction itself or transacting encrypted information. Confidentiality is all about a secure and controlled exchange of sensitive information to a person, an organization, or parties based on an agreement. It can also be termed as permissioned access, where permissions are granted to allow parties to access information. It's in this technologically advanced era that technology has invaded privacy. Individuals', organizations', and institutions' data and information is out in the public domain, which is hosted outside their firewalls or used by others to monitor and derive patterns and gauge activities.

An example of this is facial recognition, which isn't just a technology; it's a biometric identification that (interestingly) doesn't need your consensus. Fingerprints and retinal scans need your consensus; however, with facial recognition, someone can use your identity without your approval. Information can be derived and your patterns can be recognized with facial technology. Paying with a smile or linking an individual to photos or dynamic pricing are some examples of facial recognition applications prevailing today. With sophisticated pattern matching, technology can even relate data to an individual or an organization.

With blockchain technology, users are the owners and can decide the depth and level of information that can be shared and with whom. For example, a user can choose to share their facial recognition biometric identity for their government's security initiatives and not for the commercial use of pattern identification of the user's buying behavior.

Blockchain offers confidentiality and privacy through encryption and access control. Persisted data is encrypted and stored, while in-transit data is secured by enabling two-way **Transport Layer Security (TLS)**. Also, it encrypts transactions that are executed against the smart contract or chaincode. Role-based access control or attribute-based access control defines who can execute transactions based on users' role profiles or users' attributes. On top of that, you should only share data and information with those parties that should have access to it (for example, Hyperledger Fabric's private channels). This way, an organization assumes that information is only shared with those parties that should have access to it. Confidentiality can be enhanced to the next level if you use distributed ledgers, which aren't public, but are specific to channels on which only agreed parties are transacting.

- **Robustness**: We discussed trust in the previous section, and we learned that trust is about executing transactions correctly. However, trust extends to managing exceptions too. The ability of the system to manage trustworthy exceptions is called robustness. Robustness is paramount in blockchain as its consensus-based ecosystem that establishes trust without an intermediary. Blockchain can meet exceptions when, let's say, two miners reach a solution to a puzzle at the same time. Blockchain offers the solution of following the longest chain, and consolidating a single chain within a cycle will help solve such a double mining issue. Similarly, the exception of double spending can be resolved by allowing the first transaction that is referring the digital asset to be accepted, and rejecting the second transaction that references the same asset. There are challenges with this, but the underlying robustness of the system enhances the trust. After all, in blockchain, trust is on the system itself, and it's the robustness of the blockchain system that will attract businesses and individuals to it.

- **Resilience:** Resilience means the ability of an individual to recover from a state of shock, for example, a large mobile bill or if you just dropped your phone in water. How soon and positively you recover from these shocks defines your resilience. Similarly, in blockchain, resilience is the ability of the blockchain network to recover from a fault. Interestingly, due to the nature of blockchain technology, it is inherently resilient. With DLT, transactions are backed up and available on the participating nodes. As more and more nodes are added to the blockchain network, its availability increases. Since the data is available in each node, resilience is not an issue. It's distributed, and so there's no single point of failure, and it's also decentralized, which means there's no single authority. This leads to excellent disaster recovery in a system where nodes can attach or detach from the blockchain network at any time.
- **Availability:** Since a blockchain network doesn't need a centralized authority to trust and maintain it, and it's also resilient and nodes can attach and detach anytime, the availability of the system is enhanced. As more and more nodes get attached to the network, the network becomes more available. It's even classed as available when a single node is alive in the blockchain network. With no missed transactions and no human errors, and a system where all transactions meet the consensus, blockchain offers a resilient, robust system. Transactions are immutable and can be validated, and the results of such validations are always consistent. Imagine a system with so many benefits over traditional technology; it entices businesses and enterprises to believe that blockchain is a revolution.

Design strategy

This section will cover the details around designing a blockchain solution to build a business network. Many enterprises, entrepreneurs, and organizations are analyzing blockchain. They are adopting blockchain to gain transactional speed for business-to-business transactions, store information in an immutable way, and share it securely. For businesses, blockchain is a platform where peers exchange values via transactions, without the interference of a central arbitrator. All of this is good; however, where should we start? This section covers defining a design strategy for blockchain.

I have used the following terms from my book, *We Wake With Noah,* and found it interesting that the self-improvement concepts I explored in that book can be applied to technology as well :

Explore	Engage	Experiment	Experience	Influence
Use case identification	*As-is* flow	Acquire skills	Analyze outcome	Share
Justifying the use case	*To-be flow*	Be agile	Measure outcome	Influence
Structure of the blockchain network	Holistic solution design	Develop, test	Analyze lessons	
Business network goals	Choosing MVP	Elevate, test		
Governance	Draw long term vision	Deploy		
Dispute and arbitrator	Future enhancements			
	Define scope			
	Define storyboard			

The preceding table lists the design strategy for a blockchain solution. This section will discuss it in more detail.

It is always conducive to run workshops and sessions with enterprise key stakeholders when you're making various decisions, such as use case identifying and justifying the use case though blockchain technology. It also helps to determine the type of blockchain, define, governance and arbitrators, and so on. The following principles can be followed during workshops:

- Define the workshop as a business workshop and list technical questions that can be answered in subsequent technology workshops.
- Put an emphasis on identifying the use case and justifying them by answering and rating various factors.
- Continually gauge the audience's reactions, questions, and inclination toward factors, which maybe align toward or away from blockchain. Feed that to the justifying question (as listed in the following section) for further enhancement of the question's outcome.
- Understand the *as-is* and *to-be* processes as they help align the solution with the business needs.
- Include blockchain experts, technology experts, and security experts in the workshops, as they help to answer specific technology questions, and also help them gravitate toward the real business needs.

- Identify key stakeholders and build a consortium of stakeholders (business consortium and technology consortium) so that you can run subsequent workshops more effectively.
- Run parallel design sessions with the technology consortium. An early design session brings two very important things to the equation: simplicity and clarity.
- Use the business consortium's feedback at the start and end of the design session and, similarly, technology consortium feedback at the end of the business sessions. This will help you establish equilibrium and keep things on track.

Explore

This section covers the identification and justification of use cases as candidates for blockchain technology. We will also cover identifying a blockchain's type, governance, and arbitrators.

Identifying and justifying use cases

Kick-start workshops will identify the use case, draft it at a high level, and analyze blockchain as a candidate to address the use case at hand. This exploration is critical as it ensures that all the parties reach a consensus to employ blockchain in order to address use case. It helps to quantify the need for a blockchain-based solution.

The following is a list of factors that will be used in the equation to quantify the need for blockchain as a solution for the use case. For the chosen use case, quantify the need for blockchain based on the following factors:

- **Truth**:
    - Is there a need for reconciliation between parties?
    - Is there a silo of information among the enterprise, its partners and suppliers, and so on?
- **Intermediaries**:
    - Are there existing intermediaries?
    - Are these intermediaries only ensuring trust?
    - Is there a need to include participants with similar common problems?

- **Multi-party**:
    - Does this use case result in sharing information with others?
    - Do multiple parties need to update reports?
    - Do you need information from other sources or stakeholders?
    - Is it a similar problem that other parties encounter?

- **Transaction**:
    - Does this use case need the enterprise to report the accuracy of transactions?
    - Does this use case need transactions to be transparent?
    - Does this use case need transaction privacy?
    - Does it require high transaction throughput?

- **Authority**:
    - Do you need regulatory authority among participants?
    - Do you foresee the inclusion of other parties?

- **Standards and other solutions**:
    - Does this use case easily highlight assets (or can you easily identify assets?), transactions, and events?
    - Does this use case lead to ease in digitalizing the asset in your business value chain?
    - Can you address it better with a traditional technology?

What is the algorithm to quantify the need for blockchain?

For the aforementioned factors, ensure that you draft two separate factors for each question—a criticality factor question and a satisfaction factor question. The answers to these questions should be given by the participants. For example, the first factor on **truth** can be expanded with the following questions:

- **Criticality factor**: Is reconciliation between parties critical?
- **Satisfaction factor**: Is the current reconciliation between parties satisfactory?

Formulate all other factors and expand them to gauge the criticality factor and satisfaction factor. This becomes key to the equation that will help justify the need for blockchain. Here, I'm attempting to formulate an equation to justify the need for blockchain: let me call it the **blockchain justifying equation (BJE)**.

Let's use this BJE to quantify the need for blockchain. Assign a number to the use case factor and check whether the employment of blockchain is justified or not for the given use case. In other words, we can say that use case factors are paramount in highlighting the usability of blockchain. In this section, I will try to draft an equation to justify the need for blockchain. The need for blockchain is as follows:

- **Justified**: When the use case is critical to the enterprise, but it is not well served currently. This means that they are not satisfied with the current solution.
- **Not Justified**: When the use case is not critical to the enterprise, but it is currently well served. This means that they are satisfied with the current solution.

Conclusively, we will consider the need for blockchain when the **outcome** is justified; otherwise, there is no need for blockchain.

Building the equation

Work through the workshops and sessions to make the participants rate the aforementioned questions based on two factors: **criticality factor** (**CF**) and **satisfaction factor** (**SF**). These factors need to be independently answered on a scale of zero to five, where five is extremely critical and zero is not critical; similarly, five is extremely satisfied and zero is not satisfied.

Let me formulate the equation:

$$BN = CF + (CF - SF)$$

Here, *BN* is the blockchain need, *CF* is the criticality factor, and *SF* is the satisfaction factor.

This means: *blockchain need = criticality factor + (criticality factor – satisfaction factor)*. Here, the *criticality factor* is the percentage of people who rated the factors as extremely critical, and the *satisfaction factor* is the percentage of people who rated the factor as extremely satisfactory. In this equation, *criticality* is the percentage of people rating the outcome very or extremely important and *satisfaction* is the percentage of people rating the outcome very or extremely satisfying.

If 80% of respondents rate the factors as extremely critical and only 20% of respondents rate it as extremely satisfactory, then the need for blockchain is justified. However, if only 20% of respondents rate the factors as extremely critical and 80% of respondents' rate it as extremely satisfactory, then the need for blockchain is not justified.

I will be developing this equation and plots around it in more detail in my next book, *Blockchain for Solution Designers*. For now, we will explore the equation and see how it can quickly help to quantify (justify) the need for blockchain for given a use case based on the various factors at hand.

Types of blockchain

Once you have justified the need for blockchain, you can analyze various factors to determine which blockchain solution fits the use case. The following diagram is self-explanatory in terms of identifying which type of blockchain suffices your requirement. However, if you want to get into the details for each type of blockchain, you can refer to the *Types of blockchain networks* section in `Chapter 1`, *Exploring Blockchain and BaaS*, where we provide details about the different types of blockchain.

The following diagram illustrates the qualifiers to identify the need for a specific type of blockchain:

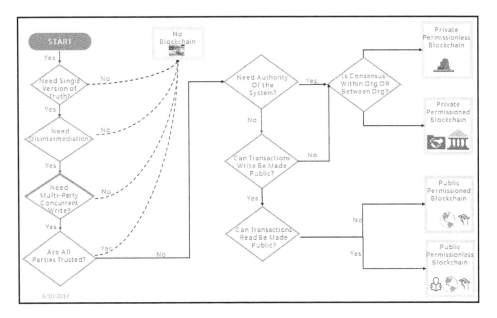

Types of blockchain

The preceding diagram clearly highlights the qualifiers that can help you identify the type of blockchain network needed for the use case.

Structure of the business network

Up until now, as part of the design strategy, we have identified the use case and the qualifiers/factors to justify the need for blockchain. We have also analyzed the use case and reached a consensus on the type of blockchain network needed. From this chapter onward, we will focus on permissioned blockchain since this book is about Hyperledger Fabric and permissioned blockchain. In this section, we will focus on defining a structure for the blockchain-based business network, particularly for permissioned blockchain networks. Permissioned blockchain business networks consist of more than one enterprise. They solve a common business problem and they want to reap the benefits of blockchain technology. Hence, the first question that arises is how to define the scope and structure of the permissioned blockchain network.

Defining a structure is paramount as it has impacts on tax, laws, jurisdiction, and governance. A permissioned blockchain network can be structured as follows:

- **Consortium-based business networks**: They can be a joint venture, where all the members are just like the founder:
    - **Joint ventures** (**JVs**): These are usually a massive centralized structure. JVs are rigid and usually put the founders in the driving seat. However, if the pitfalls of JVs are neglected, then it is an effective choice to form a consortium. Each member (with financial participation) can be added as a founder, and a JV legal entity can be formed between founders. They can democratically decide on the setup, maintenance, and operation of the consortium.
- **Founder-driven business networks**: Founder-driven business networks are set up and maintained by the founder. In such case, founders are able to handle business networks and can decide on future direction in technology. They can be of the following types:
    - **Software license-driven**: This is when a technology company or a solution/platform provider takes care of the founder-driven business network; for example, IBM or Oracle build a solution from the ground up that takes care of the consortium. It might be possible that such configurations may lead to technological centralization.
    - **Open source driven**: Such networks are run by an open source giant; the Hyperledger project by the Linux foundation and Ethereum are examples. Open source still lacks the capability for enterprise support, governance of the project, finance of the project, and so on.

- **Community-based business network**: These are blockchain networks that are driven by communities, which are either driven by standards or are autonomously driven:
  - **Permissioned Decentralized Autonomous Organization (pDAO)**: **Decentralized Autonomous Organizations (DAOs)** are just like cooperative organizations, where various collaborating parties provide funding. For example, funding for permissionless DAOs are arranged by ICOs and tokens. There can be a pDAO, where the governance of the consortium is set out in rules, which are embodied in the chaincode itself. In such a configuration, it is the chaincode that drives the operations of the consortium. The founders of the consortium can handle the setup and maintenance of the consortium. Operations are taken care of by the chaincode automatically.

pDAOs

pDAOs are decentralized (no single authority) and autonomous (self-sufficient). This means that they are community-based blockchain networks that are owned by participating enterprises. However, the operations, funding, and dispute resolutions are automatically taken care of by the chaincode that governs the autonomous permissioned organizations. Such a setup of the enterprise consortium will withdraw the need for a huge enterprise exercise in order to maintain and handle the operations of the consortium. All of the decisions are *democratic*, which is driven by the code that is handling the operation of the consortium. Such an enterprise consortium will define the *operation* and *maintenance* of the chaincode. Essentially, they will first define the constitution of the business network. Thereafter, the chaincode will be responsible for the automatic realization of the constitution. Every proposal, such as adding and removing a member, can be submitted as a transaction to the chaincode, which will take care of its execution on the blockchain itself. Such a community-driven blockchain network is for the blockchain, by the blockchain, and of the blockchain. Power is not in the hands of few; it is distributed, permissioned by the version of underlying permissioned network and chaincode for the specific use case, and autonomous.

I believe that pDAO might be the future for enterprise blockchain adoption. Such an enterprise consortium can be started with few participants. All of the legal certainty can be resolved with a legal structure, and differences can be resolved with arbitrators. Read my next book, *Blockchain for Solution Designers*, which extends and talks about pDAO in detail.

Business network goals and governance

The previous section outlined how to define and choose a structure of the blockchain. The next step in the design strategy should focus on establishing business network goals and governance. Defining business network goals and governance will also need analysis results, which are collected when you're defining the blockchain network. This section goes in parallel with the previous section, as the decision that was made in the previous section is cemented here.

There are various questions that need to be analyzed before a blockchain structure is chosen. Following are some of the questions that will have strong impact on choosing a specific blockchain structure:

- How can you ensure that the consortium doesn't lead to a concentration of power?
- Who controls the consortium?
- Do primary consortium members benefit more than later joiners?
- Who benefits from the already existing infrastructure? Does this create confusion and infrastructure dependency or locking for the new joiners or late joiners?
- Who decides on new member inclusion or member exclusion?
- Who decides the inclusion/exclusion of non-core members of the consortium?
- How will the operational decisions be executed?
- How will the consortium be financed?
- How are disputes realized?

Governance a wider topic and out of the scope of this book. For now, you should understand that it is an important step in defining the business network and scalability of the business network from the maintenance and operational perspectives.

Dispute resolution and arbitrators

Since a consortium includes various enterprises and discrete parties, it has its own business complexities. These complexities can lead to disputes. Hence, a consortium must have arbitrators to settle disputes. This means that there is a need for an arbitration function for a consortium, which takes care of the participation contract (via a legal document) between members of the consortium. This can be CPA authorities who handle legal documents until these documents also turn into a smart contract (chaincode), which acts as a smart arbitrator.

A consortium can engage smart contract (chaincode) auditors to verify the smart contract and verify the interface and integration of the smart contract with external applications and data sources. Such independent auditors will offer assurance to the consortium and help in surfacing vulnerabilities.

Engage, experiment, experience, and influence

Once you have explored the design strategy, it's time to engage with the *as-is* flows and define the *to-be* flows. A holistic design of the solution will ensure synchronicity between the flows, use cases, and technology. Starting blockchain solutions with a Big Bang can be a problematic approach. Choose a **minimum viable product** (**MVP**) and draw a sketch for the future enhancement. Start with a simple, clear, yet critical use case. This ensures two benefits:

- Simplicity and clarity of the processes will help you to translate the requirement into a solution, in both an effective and timely manner
- Criticality of the use case will cement the prowess of the blockchain in handling critical use cases

Start with a smaller blockchain business network. Try not to include arbitrators, regulators, and huge consortia. Design a solution that is scalable and dynamic, but build a minimum viable product to satisfy the use case's scope. Details regarding this are out of the scope of this book. You should follow the agile way to develop a blockchain-based solution. You can learn more about blockchain solution design in my next book, *Blockchain for Solution Designers*.

Blockchain properties and use cases

DLT, like blockchain, is exemplified as one of the most disruptive technological advancements of this century. Although there are many regulatory challenges that it needs to overcome before being part of the majority, there are various properties of blockchain that make it truly revolutionary. It is the properties of blockchain that offer numerous potential for various industries. In this section, we will talk about blockchain properties and the use cases that are catalyzed by those properties.

Blockchain properties

With the immense success of blockchain's first application, Bitcoin, and then the emergence of Ethereum and Hyperledger, enterprises, organizations, industry leaders, entrepreneurs, and individuals have realized that blockchain is not a quixotic dream but a true revolution that will propel today's enterprises across industries into a new era of digital enterprises. Various properties of DLT and blockchain can enable decentralized autonomous marketplaces, catalyze the reduction of friction in transactions and reconciliations, allow for the secure maintenance and sharing of decentralized records, and enable consumers and businesses to track the provenance of products, supplies, and documents.

The following is a list of the most important properties of blockchain:

- **Shared and transparent access**: This results in the consistency of data, which allows participants to access consistent data as updates are replicated across participants. For a permissioned blockchain, it allows only authorized participants to access the data. Transparency enhances auditability and trust in the system and reduces the cost of frauds and audits.
- **Immutable**: Blockchain is append-only; records cannot be altered or deleted. Immutability enhances confidence in the information that exists on the system and reduces the potential for fraud many times.
- **Validated and undeniable transactions**: Transactions are added to the blockchain in blocks only after consensus is met. Hence, the validity of the transactions cannot be denied.
- **Isolated for confidentiality**: With a permissioned blockchain, transactions can be made accessible for views and only updates authorized participants or parties.
- **Decentralized**: DLT, like blockchain, is a decentralized P2P network with no central authority controlling the network. This results in the elimination of third parties and intermediaries, which further results in the reduction of transaction costs and near real-time execution of the transactions.
- **Distributed ledger**: All of the participating nodes maintain a copy of the ledger. Hence, reconciliation is not needed as the DLT guarantees data consistency. Since data consistency is guaranteed, the need for reconciliation, dispute resolution, and delays due to dispute resolution are omitted.
- **Smart contracts/chaincode**: Business logic is authored in smart contracts or chaincodes, which are validated by and shared among the participants, resulting in a high degree of trust in the automated business processes. Any asset can be represented digitally in a blockchain, and transactions are executed as per the business logic defined in those smart contracts or chaincodes.
- **Resilience**: A trustless ecosystem, robustness, confidentiality, and availability are a few other proprieties we discussed previously.

These properties not only upheave the evolution of various use cases across industries, but also address the perceived challenges of DLT and blockchain. Beyond that, blockchain can be customized to be a permissioned blockchain such as Hyperledger. In a permissioned blockchain, only authorized parties will have access to the blockchain network and can view and update only relevant information and tasks. Although a permissioned blockchain needs meticulous planning, it takes out the apprehension that enterprises have about blockchain. Various BaaSes, such as the **Oracle Blockchain Platform** (**OBP**), offer solutions for permissioned blockchain and ease the adoption of permissioned blockchain. Hence, BaaS is essentially catalyzing the adoption of the blockchain revolution.

Properties and use cases

There are several disruptive properties of blockchain that are attractive to various industries and address a wide array of use cases for a whole spectrum of industries. Although the financial industry is continuing to be the key emerging player in exploring and implementing DLT and blockchain use cases, there are several blockchain advantages/properties that are attractive to an industry, such as immutable permanent records, repository of public records, universal formats, accessibility, and notarization with timestamp hashing, and they also address various government and legal use cases such as voting, propositions, governance services, transactional organizations, P2P bonds, land titles, IP registration, tax receipts, notary services, and document registry services.

Similarly, properties such as distributed ledger, decentralized network, consensus for transactions, and trustless counter-parties attract use cases for markets such as digital currency, payments, remittance, financial sector, banking, insurance, settlements, trading, derivatives, internal audits, and crowdfunding. Blockchain and DLT attributes such as large-scale coordination, transaction security, and communication (also known as messaging) are attractive to **Internet of Things** (**IoT**) sectors and fuel enormous chains of use cases such as smart home networks, connected cars, smart cities, personalized robots, digital assistants, drones, and sensor networks. Healthcare use cases such as digital health wallets, smart health tokens, health data analytics, heath databanks, universal EMR, and personal development contracts are possible with DLT and blockchain properties such as large-scale multi-stream integration, privacy and security, real-time accessibility, and universal formats.

The aforementioned properties also result in addressing art, science, and AI use cases such as P2P resource nets, crow analysis, community supercomputers, films, art tracing and tracking, blockchain advocates, digital mind files, and blockchain learners. The following diagram lists some of the use cases, and is just a glimpse into the possibilities and opportunities that DLT and blockchain have evoked for businesses, organizations, and individuals:

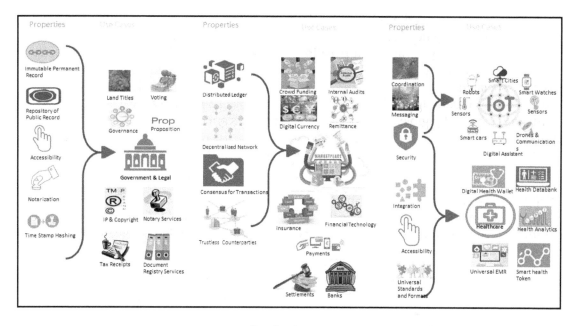

Properties and use cases

The preceding diagram shows the properties that helped realize various use cases for varied industries such as the government, legal, marketplace, IoT, and healthcare. The property columns list the properties, while the use case columns highlight the use case that's the most alluring for a given industry.

Types of use cases

Broadly speaking, blockchain is an ideal use case for the decentralized consensus on ledgers that are appended by themselves on agreed transactions that are non-commutative. In this section, I'm going to categorize blockchain use cases into a few categories; however, I believe that there are millions of use cases, which is the result of non-commutative state transition functions. The listed categorization of use cases is exhaustive.

Let's start by simply putting the definition of blockchain into an equation:

Blockchain = Who Owns - What, When, and How much

When is the timeline, while *How much* is the quantity. However, *What*, is the topic of discussion here. My efforts to categorize blockchain are centered on *What* and *Who*.

WHAT: *What* represents the assets; essentially, the scarce assets that are valuable. Assets such as identity, currency, land title, contract, vote, provenance, and payments are valuable and scarce. Let's analyze various applications of blockchain and check what they actually manage. Bitcoin manages accounts, Ethereum manages contract states, Everledger manages events associated with diamonds, and trust lines are managed by Ripple, and so on. Similarly, for Hyperledger Fabric, assets can be tangible assets such as real estate and hardware, while intangibles are assets such as contracts and intellectual property. Hence, blockchain is a potential solution for those cases where the requirement is to transact those assets while establishing decentralized consensus by recording them on an immutable ledger.

WHO: At any given point in time, blockchain is a currency, a network, a protocol, or a platform. It is a notion that is driving the world toward a world of DAO or **Decentralized Autonomous Communities** (**DAC**). I will be using these terms interchangeably throughout.

An organization or an enterprise is a set of people who are working together to achieve a certain defined set of goals and follow rules. Such organizations own assets and liabilities, which means there are sets of people and legal contracts that establish the truth in holding assets and owning liabilities. An organization acts because there is a mutual consensus between a key set of people to do so. Similarly, hiring someone means an employee has agreed to offer certain services while an employer has agreed to offer monetary and other benefits. In all of these cases, there are contracts (sets of rules).

The question is: do we really need management to execute these rules, or do we need certain jobs at certain business functions to execute these contracts? Industrialization answered this by incorporating machines at the bottom level; can DLT, such as blockchain, do it for the top levels as well? Organizations stand and operate on contracts and rules while following regulations, which are, again, a set of rules. Organizations execute these contracts and rules to generate revenue, offer services, and pay employees for the services they offer to the organization so that the organization can offer its services to their customers and pay taxes to the government. Can these not be achieved by software and, in particular, by DLTs such as blockchain and Hyperledger?

To me, the answer is *yes*, and with minimal human involvement. There can be DAOs (also referred as DACs), where asset owners are the stakeholders, and smart contract and chaincode are the rules and contracts that take care of the daily, strategic, and tactical operations of the organizations. Participating nodes are the employees themselves, who take care of validating, verifying, and reaching consensus with minimum rewards. Yes, it's too early to fully chart the upcoming future of DAOs; it is possible to have a distributed one-world government where policies and relationships are taken care of by super smart contracts.

Well, jumping back to the present and glancing back at the preceding equation, let's concentrate on the *Who*. While adopting blockchain, the key elements that you should look for are as follows: what are the assets and what is the consensus mechanism that the business will consent to when moving toward blockchain? Are you planning for a DAO or is your business planning to establish a business network where parties will interact and a consortium will be established? Here, I'm hinting toward the permissioned and permissionless world of blockchain. In either case, *Who* is important and needs to be determined. Since the world of DAOs and DACs is unwinding, I'm considering a marketplace fueled by smart contracts and chaincodes as a category of use case for blockchain. The more mature the world of DLT gets, the closer the world will move toward the reality of DAOs and DACs. Now, let's get back to the equation again and look at the other two parts of the equation, other than *What* and *Who*. These two pieces are *When* and *How much*. Essentially, *How much* is a generic term for quantity and all the other parameters for an asset. *When* helps in analyzing the timelines, the dates of the events, and transactions.

Now, the question is, how to we derive information about *Who*, *When*, *What*, and *How much*? This information is part of the blockchain ecosystem and brings the third most important category of use cases, which is the analytics. Go into design and development and try to always put forward the visibility aspect of the solution. Based on the equation and the definitions around it, there are three primary categories of blockchain use cases:

- Digital assets
- Digital analytics
- Digital platform

In this section, we will deep dive into these categories and list the subcategories of these blockchain use cases.

Digital assets

When we use the term digital assets, we are counting a plethora of assets with the following main categories:

- Tangible assets and
- Intangible assets.

Following are the subcategories for tangible assets :

- **Financial assets**: Currency, equity (public and private), bonds, derivatives, commodities, finance, micro-finance, charity, and crowd funding.
- **Records**: Records can be public, semi-public, or other types as well:
- **Public records**:
    - Financial records, such as spending records, trading records, mortgage records, and service records
    - Public records, such as business ownership records, regulatory records, business incorporation/dissolution records, health/safety inspections records, immigrant records, and government laws
    - Titles, such as land titles
    - Registries, such as vehicle registry and forensic evidence
    - License and permits, such as business license, building permits, and gun permits
    - Certificates such as birth certificates, death certificates, and marriage certificates
    - Digital identities, such as passport, SSN number, unique ID, voters ID, vote, a product's digital token, and so on

    - **Semi-public records**:
        - Certificates, that is, degree, grades, learning evaluation reports, and so on
        - Records, such as employee records, behavioral records, medical records, accounting records, business transaction records, arbitration, supply records, delivery records, and citizenship records

    - **Private records**:
        - Contracts and escrows
        - Personals, such as wills, trust, signatures, and GPS data
        - Keys, such as car keys, hotel keys, apartment and home keys, locker keys, rental car keys, and package delivery keys

Following are the subcategories for intangible assets :

- Intangible assets, such as coupons, tickets, patents, reservations, trademark, copyrights, licenses (such as software licenses, video game licenses, and movie licenses), domain, art proofs such as authorship, photo, and video or audio ownership records
- Miscellaneous, such as temperature records and sports records

Here, we have tried to enlist some of these assets. However, there are use cases to manage and record these assets on a blockchain. In addition, there is a special category of use cases that deals with the provenance of some assets and is mostly implemented in SCM cases such as tracking from supplier to shelf, tracing medicines, and the custody of pills. The following are the possible subcategories of these use cases:

- Digital identity
- Provenance
- Records

Let's talk a bit more about these subcategories.

Digital identity: Identity theft and identity fraud are common headlines from the digital world. Billions of record are stolen, lost, and exposed every year across the globe, and two thirds of data breaches are because of identity theft and identity fraud. Blockchain DNA includes immutability and native authentication, which curb identity theft and identity fraud. For example, if the identification system is based solely on biometrics, then identity verification issues are omitted. As a result, banks, governments, and organizations can use highly accurate results. Even before biometric identity verification becomes a reality (for the world, not just in specific cases), private key ownership is a highly secure and a proven way to manage identity, where keys are digital assets. Hence, user identities are managed and verified without the risk of exposing valuable information, such as personal data. Human identities, item identities, and uniqueness are verified and managed with digital tokens. A digital token is an asset that is the mapping of the physical item with a digital identity of the item. This digital token can then be used for SCM to prove provenance in order to provide the rights to intellectual property for example.

Records: Blockchain is not a decentralized database; it is a system of records. Every day, every single moment, businesses are creating transactions with these assets, where assets are exchanged between suppliers, customers, partners, and individuals. Blockchain is a system that records these transactions and the digital identities of these assets. This is immutable and enhances the confidentiality of the information that exists on the system and reduces fraud opportunities. Also, transactions are added to the blockchain in blocks after a consensus is met. Hence, the validity of the transactions cannot be denied.

Provenance: With a unique digital identity (digital token), any physical item can prove its authenticity and prove its origin. Since records are immutable in the ledger, an item can be traced from its origin to its end point. Provenance checks fake products and allows consumers to be informed before they pick the item as it now leaves the onus on the consumer because the consumer is fully informed of a product's origins, journey, temperature during journeys, farms, region, and so on. Consumers can make informed decisions. With provenance, every product will speak the truth. Companies know about the materials they're supplied with, can check whether any substandard items were used to build the product, and know about the potential issues they have.

Beyond that, blockchain will remove the cost that organizations incur due to the inspection of items and products. This is why the item to market time is reduced while trust is increased manifold. For provenance, blockchain induces transparency, sustainability, and trust in the item and product. The end consumer is well informed about the product, its ingredients, and its journey, even before they pick it up. Blockchain allows intelligence tracking and tracing of the product and manages a product's digital identity (for example, serial numbers), records the origin, and marks the authentication of constituting components and tracks the entire journey of the transformation, packaging, shipping, storage, and shelving of the product while managing regulatory compliance, and recalls and checks the authenticity of the products.

These subcategories are interrelated. For example, for provenance, the product's digital identities are a must. Transactions on that product, such as transformation, packaging, shipping, storage, and shelving are recorded on the ledger so that the digital footprint of the product can be analyzed. These digital footprints help the consumer trace and track it. However, on a broader level, we consider them as drivers for use cases such as tracking and tracing analytics, although they are primarily about the digital records of the asset.

Digital analytics

A blockchain ledger is a huge system of records that is immutable. As the world starts adopting more and more blockchain use cases, think about the immense data contained in a permissionless blockchain. Even permissioned blockchains will have consortiums or private data that will continue to grow massively. Analytics and predictive analytics on blockchain will uncover many stories, facts, and insights. Such an ecosystem will offer real-time, trusted, and unaltered information, which will empower not only enterprises but also smaller organizations and individuals to analyze information, and in permissioned blockchains, relevant (authorized) information.

Blockchain has numerous use cases in financial technologies, such as trade financing, where smart contracts and decentralized applications (dApps) can be created to enhance the speed of payments and reduce the time to execute transactions across the boarders and parties. Blockchain smart contracts, chaincode, or dApps can streamline clearing and settlement functions as well. These dApps will result in enormous transactions and trade data, contracts, and transaction data are executed against those contracts. This data is extremely useful for strategic and tactical purposes, and digital blockchain analytics will help in analyzing the blockchain data. This result in blockchain analytics use cases such as **Anti-Money Laundering** (AML) and fraud analytics, risk analysis, trade execution, operation analysis, compliance reports, and regulatory reports.

Digital platform

A consortium of organizations can build a platform to allow their customers to interact with them as a unified system. Alternatively, several individuals can vote for change from their home or smart device, and the results will be available the same day. All of this is possible with the modern array for transformative applications built on blockchain platforms. Such applications are termed dApps.

dApp offers a decentralized platform to build decentralized applications. These dApps inherit many of the benefits of blockchain, such as P2P interactions, trustless systems, and consensus for reliability. Since dApps' inherited blockchain benefits are built on a blockchain platform, data isn't recorded centrally, and it's distributed. This overrules the possibility for a single point of failure, enhances transaction speeds because no reconciliation is needed, reduces costs because third parties are not involved, and reduces fraud and its associated costs while enhancing transparency. The cost and time it takes applications to get to market is greatly reduced and blockchain is easily integrated with legacy systems, hence giving enterprises the opportunity for blockchain to coexist with their legacy systems.

Beyond dApps lies the world of DAO and DAC. Smart contracts/chaincodes can be authored in such a way that they can execute most of the functions of a business. Blockchain can run a business by executing legal contracts and rules authored as part of smart contracts or chaincode and refer to records, data, and documents that are recorded on the blockchain ledger.

The dApps marketplace is a major area where many applications are available that solve simple to complex problems, which are built on blockchain platforms such as Ethereum for permissionless applications, Hyperledger Fabric for permissioned use cases, and Hyperledger and **Internet of Things Association** (**IOTA**) for IoT-based use cases. For example, stock trading follows T+3, where trade is settled three days after it's accepted. With blockchain, trade can be settled instantly. Government regulations can be absorbed into dApps and DAO because regulatory compliance are government rules that can be coded into smart contracts or chaincodes. This will infuse regulations into dApps and DAOs/DACs. Refer to the previous section for details on DAOs/DACs.

The blockchain and IoT marriage offers an ecosystem where machine-to-machine interaction is recorded, processed, and shared. Blockchain adds immutable recording of IoT data to the blockchain ledger, which brings in trustlessness and transparency to IoT systems. With digital identities of the devices, blockchain allows authentication, verification of the identities of devices, and opens up a multitude of use cases for permissioned and permissionless use cases. IOTA is a data layer for IoT, and it relies on a DLT called **directed acyclic graph** (**DAG**), where the focus is on executing and recording transactions between machines.

The following diagram shows different use cases based on the three primary categories of use cases:

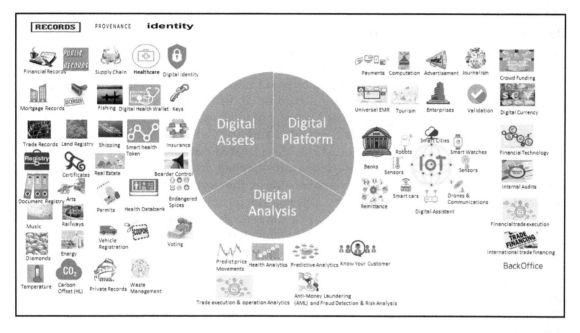

Categorized use cases

The following section explores a few of the use cases in depth.

Exploring use cases

In the *Design strategy* section, we tried to define a design strategy for a blockchain-based business solution, which has five steps: explore, engage, experiment, experience, and influence. In this section, we will concentrate on the first step. In this step, we will explore a few blockchain use cases. They are as follows:

- Real property registry and transfer of ownership
- Know your customer
- Invoice factoring

Government – real property registry and transfer of ownership

Real properties are recorded and maintained by governments, mostly at the local government level. For example, a country assessor is responsible for recording and maintaining the country's property records. Although a few countries are digitized, many countries still use traditional methods and rely on a paper-based system. More or less, recording results in legal title ownership, recording of the transaction, and checking unlawful disposal. Essentially, the record is proof of legal ownership of the title. In this recording process, the government is the trusted authority which maintains property records, assesses its values, and collects taxes. As a trusted central authority, the government body offers trust and advocates transparency. In addition, the government's central authority also offers a procedure to recognize the property rights, secure documents, display property rights as public records for transparency, and offer seamless methods to transfer ownership of these rights and records transfer transactions. In a nutshell, the public looks for records and rights maintenance, the transference of titles and rights, and the records of transfer transactions and trust.

Doesn't this sound like an effective use case that can be addressed though blockchain? In fact, many local and international governments have started adopting blockchain to digitally record land title records on blockchain. It helps in many ways, such as transparency, protecting records, checking fraudulent transfers, and recording transfers. This use case covers a simple blockchain solution for real property registry, assessment, and listing.

Challenges with the current process

Recording a deed incurs administrative costs. Usually, a deed is delivered either though eForm, post, email, or in person on paper to the recording office. Then, it is scanned and uploaded to document stores. This results in the posting of records to central storage. From that point onward, recorded information is used to determine the ownership of the record. That ownership of the record is also made available to the public for reference. Any further transaction, such as transfer of ownership, needs to happen in the same central storage. This is costly, inefficient, error-prone, and time-consuming.

Blockchain, the savior

Records will be stored on the blockchain or the government's central repository, and its references can be on the blockchain. Refer to the *Large object storage - on-chain or off chain* section in `Chapter 3`, *Delving into Hyperledger Fabric*, for more details on large object storage. Land or property titles are recorded as digital assets and are available on the blockchain for public reference. Transactions can be executed against those assets and assets can be transferred quickly. Government bodies don't need to scan documents all of the time, print labels, record files, and maintain them. All the information for that digital asset is available in the immutable blockchain. Tax transactions can be executed against those assets as well. Property values can be assessed, and that value assessment can be posted as a transaction for those digital assets (properties) on the blockchain. Everything is recorded in one place, and analytics and reports can be generated over blockchain records. Blockchain serves as a traceable and auditable history of records for all of the transactions that are performed on digital assets (properties).

Various transactions, such as the one parcel change transaction (where the digital asset is split, combined, or reclassified), can be recorded on blockchain. Various propositions, such as 58 and 193 (referring props in California), that result in real property transfer transactions between parents and children or between grandparents and grandchildren can be recorded on the immutable ledger. Various other life cycle events, such as address changes, and any property attribute changes can be recorded as well. Since data is available on the blockchain, it's easy to share it with other departments, and it also makes it easy for other departments to connect with one source to get hold of the relevant information. Various other transactions can occur on the digital asset, such as valuation, assessment, and roll corrections, which can transact on the digital asset and can be recorded for auditability and traceability.

A blockchain solution for real property (also known as *real estate* or *realty*) registry could be a **RealPropertyChain** registry. It's a blockchain solution where real property records such as land records and building records are recorded. These properties are identified as a digital asset on a blockchain, and transactions on those digital assets (records) are recorded on the blockchain platform:

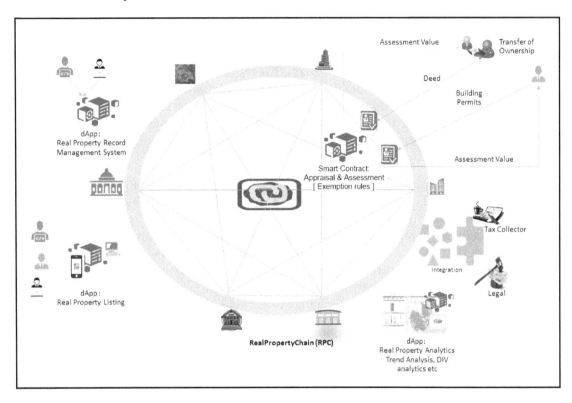

Blockchain solutions for property registry and assessment

The preceding diagram shows a simple blockchain solution for real property registry, assessment, listing, and analytics. It is a blockchain platform with the following components:

- There is a dApp to register real properties, which will also verify and associate taxpayers with it. It's called a **Real Property Record Management System**. Recorded real property will have a digital identity, and the system will recognize it as a unique digital asset with an ownership that's defined and a taxpayer that's identified. If a property is already recorded, then the property's unique digital asset ID can be used to verify it and its ownership.

- There is a dApp that allows you to list properties. Again, the property owner authorizes the listing of properties. The listing will allow you to buy and sell properties. Today, there are **Multiple Listing Services (MLSes)**, which is a real property database for which realtors pay a fee to list, buy, and sell properties. Various websites, such as Zillow, collaborate with these MLSes for residential properties, while other companies such as CoStar partner with MLSes to deal with commercial properties. For you to sell your property, you need to pay agents that are registered to these MLSes. It's sometimes 6 to 9% of the sales price. It is an expensive affair and, for you to get a better deal, you might need to work with an MLS for a wider market reach. A blockchain-based dApp is looking to list *authorized* properties on the blockchain. Buying and selling are now for everyone, and it's transparent, and transactions are immutable as well.
- A dApp can also be created to analyze real property data, which can showcase trends, assessment value changes, and transactions on a property.
- Smart contracts such as **Appraisal & Assessment** can be created, which can take care of the transfer of ownership, construction permits, and so on. For example, when a transfer occurs against a property (digital asset), the blockchain receives a copy of the deed. Smart contracts will determine whether a reappraisal is required using state law. If reappraisal is required, then a new market value of the property is determined and new assessment values are communicated to the taxpayer by the smart contracts communication services. Such a smart contracts will also take care of exemption rules such as disability exemption and veteran exemption. In addition, certain transfer of ownership, such as a husband to wife, doesn't lead to reappraisals. These smart contracts deal with such appraisal rules and can create new assessed values for the taxpayer. Smart contracts can also communicate with the taxpayer with a new assessment to let property owners appeal if they don't agree with the assessed values.
- Other systems, such as the legal and judiciary systems and tax collectors, can easily connect with the blockchain and access relevant authorized information from it.

Advantages of blockchain solutions

Advantages of blockchain solutions for property registry, listings, and assessments are as follows:

- **Efficiency**: Deeds recording is expensive today. Bringing a property registry to blockchain platforms results in **Property as an Asset service** (**PaaAS**), where it is recorded immutably. Subsequent transactions such as change of ownership, assessments, and appraisals can be taken care of by smart contract, which adds efficiency; it is less error-prone and more efficient.
- **Real time**: Property records are updated in real time. Transactions such as transfer of ownership, assessments, and reappraisal calculations can be performed by smart contracts almost immediately. Blockchain enhances the transparency and accuracy of public information in real time.
- **Immutable transactions**: Since the digital asset registry and transaction records are on DLT, it is immutable, is prone to attacks, and is tamper-proof. Natural disasters such as the one that happened in Haiti, where land records were destroyed can occur. This cannot happen on an immutable ledger such as a blockchain.
- **Trust**: Blockchain facilitates trust, transparency, efficiency, accuracy, and security to property registry and recording, records transactions on the property, listing, automated appraisals and assessments, ease of integration, and so on. This demonstrates that blockchain is a powerful alternative to centralized real property recording, ownership, and transaction systems.

Social factor

Such blockchain-based solutions for land title registry can mean a lot for countries such as Honduras, where the World Bank issued dollars to aid Honduras' government in digitizing land titles. The centralized system was not a viable solution as corrupt players could have hacked and tampered with it. The blockchain solution is the most suitable solution for such a problem as it's immutable and cannot be tampered with. Another example is India, where two thirds of civil cases are related to land and property. According to government data, there are 22 million pending cases. Of these, 6 million have been dragged out for more than five years. On a blockchain platform, land and property records are digital assets with a unique digital identity. They are stored immutably on the ledger, and blockchain system will take care of the transactions on these digital assets, such as transference of ownership, change in attributes, new constructions, and loans. Users, authorized agencies, and governments can track and trace the entire history for a digital asset almost instantly. Such a system will be a boon for highly unorganized and corrupt regions.

Crowd funding of real estate properties

Another interesting use case, which is in line with the preceding use case, is related to the crowdfunding of properties. Crowdfunding a property, where tokens represent part of the ownership of the property, has existed for a long time. However, the issue arises when you want to liquidate and your partners aren't ready at that point in time. With token-based ownership of digital assets such as a property, you can trade your tokens without worrying about issues and liquidate at your will and need. Tokens or a fixed number of digital tokens can represent the percentage of ownership for a digital asset such as property (land, a building, or an apartment). Based on the percentage, you will receive rental income or dividends. This is an open window for those who want to enter real estate and want to invest in real estate but also want to start with small investments. Now you can own a fraction of a business, a fraction of a home, or a fraction of an apartment and have potential earnings from its rental or dividends.

FinTech – know your customer

In order to check regulatory risks, money laundering, unauthorized financing, and so on, banks are spending billions of dollars in order to onboard new customers and maintain compliance for existing customers. Although opening accounts is a simple, straightforward process, it involves regulatory processes to identify and further verify the applicant. These processes are known as on-boarding processes, also known as **know your customer** (KYC). This process faces constant regulatory changes and needs to be up to date to meet compliance. It is complex, time-consuming, and costly. Roughly, each bank spends 60 to 300 million dollars annually. It takes approximately 5 to 45 days per KYC and, on average, it takes 24 days for a new account to be on-boarded. Along with that, financial institutions need to maintain their systems and processes to remain compliant with changing regulatory requirements. In addition, a customer doesn't have a unified experience because it changes from bank to bank. On top of this, banks collectively spend billions of dollars on AML yearly.

It is evident that the burden in all financial institutions and banks results in poor client on-boarding. Blockchain is a potential savior in this case because it allows financial institutions to share the burden. Also, it removes the duplication of efforts since customer details will be available at the shared distributed ledger. With blockchain-enabled KYC processes, a customer's most recent information is available on the shared distributed ledger. Participating financial institutions and banks will reach a consensus if changes need to be made to the customer data, and they will participate in a joint consensus-based approach to verify applicants.

Currently, KYC/on-boarding involves document collection from the applicant, engaging credit agencies to verify an applicant's identity, and its inclusion into AML and illegal financial transactions. This chain involves multiple parties and it's costly, time-consuming, slow, and error-prone.

Present

Currently, KYC, also known as on-boarding process, has many challenges. Firstly, there is a lack of structure as different departments such as credit, accounts, legal, and operations follow different processes. Since each department interprets regulations differently, there is a separate process per department for each financial institution or bank. Secondly, these processes need to comply with the constantly changing regulations. Thirdly, an array of documentation and various touch points are needed to verify that an applicant adds time and cost to the process.

Future

Blockchain technologies such as cryptography, security, hashing, and properties such as transparency and immutability will ensure that the records that banks are trying to access are accurate, consistent, secure, reliable, and true. As data is shared, it is neither controlled by a single entity, nor is there a single point of failure. By virtue of consensus, data is reliable as well. The availability of a customer/applicant's personal data on blockchain is a concern that can be addressed. Each financial institution and bank can maintain their secured database to host their customer's data and only share a link to the blockchain or a token to the blockchain.

For an applicant, financial institutions or banks execute the KYC process, which verifies the identity of the application. This ensures that the individual isn't indulged in any illegal financial transaction. The applicant provides certain information to the financial institution or bank, which is then used by a bank's **line of business** (**LOB**), also known as departments, to verify applicant involvement in AML and illegal financing activities. With blockchain solutions for KYC, even participating banks can share the verification of the applicant over a secure shared immutable ledger. Any faulty transaction by a customer will raise an immediate alert to the blockchain, which can be consumed by participating banks and financial institutions to flag that customer.

KYC is essentially a movement of identity that involves multiple parties. Since blockchain is shared, immutable, reliable, and secure and doesn't have a single authority or single point of failure, banks and financial institutions don't need to reconcile.

With reference to the **Pre-Blockchain KYC Process** in the following diagram, applicants submit documents, including government-issued identity documents such as SSN number, driving license, and passport, along with other information such as employment, business tax, and address proofs. Banks collect these documents and, after initiating a scan, forward it to a central intermediary to verify the person's identity. An intermediary will store such information in a central database and will incur costs to manage, maintain, and secure such data. This cost is further cascaded to banks. Also, each participating bank and financial institution repeats the same process:

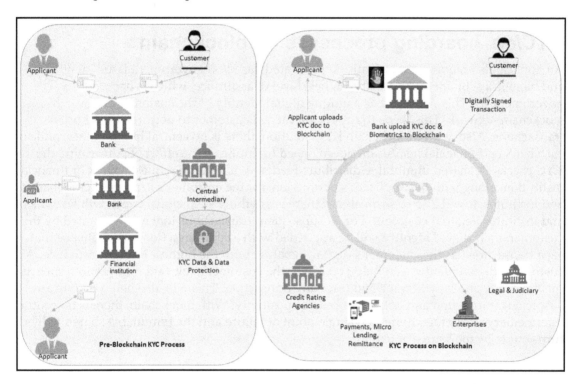

KYC use case

Although the applicant submitted government-issued identities, a challenge still lies in the level of assurance. The major challenge is to prove *who you are*. Intermediaries will check various data sources, credit agencies, and so on, but still, the assurance level is a doubtful question.

What if the applicant is a first timer and doesn't even have a credit history? The missing chain in the highest level of assurance is biometric identification and verification of the applicant. The applicant can offer government-issued identity documents such as a passport, SSN number, or driving license, along with the inherence of biometrics. The highest level of assurance is guaranteed by matching biometrics and government identity. This translates to the fact of having biometric data at the central intermediary as well. This adds data protection costs and brings in sophisticated devices into the picture in order to scan an applicant's biometrics.

KYC/on–boarding processes on blockchain

An applicant's unique digital identity is generated based on government issue identifiers and biometrics. Biometrics adds the highest level of assurance, which is backed by a government ID. This will serve as a unique digital identity of the customer on the blockchain network. This helps the applicant turned customer to perform cross border transactions. Also, with a blockchain KYC solution, there is no central intermediary, and so each bank and financial institution doesn't need to duplicate the effort of performing the KYC checks. A shared immutable distributed ledger will offer to request a bank or financial institution, along with the applicant's permission, for the customer's activities across banks and institutes. It will also raise an alert if there is anything suspicious, which will let banks and institutes flag that customer. For all subsequent transactions that are performed by the customer, their digital identity will be appended with each transaction, which means that each transaction has the customer's digital signature with the highest level of assurance. A customer's digital identity can help you access the customer's relevant information, such as their address, and let you track and trace any transaction. This will also help you flag any suspicious transaction and helps reduce false positivity. With blockchain, there is no central intermediary. Therefore, there's no single point of failure and the immutable shared ledger turns out to be the source of truth.

Process on the blockchain

With blockchain, the KYC/on-boarding process will be as follows:

1. The applicant approaches the bank with their government ID, address, and tax proofs.
2. The bank will scan the document, along with the biometrics of the applicant, and push it to blockchain (assuming that banks start using biometrics for on-boarding). Alternatively, the customer can upload his/her KYC documents to blockchain directly (as shown in the preceding diagram).

3. The blockchain network will use certain attributes of the government IDs, such as SSN number and date of birth, and, if biometrics is enabled, will use biometrics to generate a unique digital identity of the applicant. If the applicant already exists, verified information will be returned to the bank.

4. When a new applicant is added to the blockchain, a transaction is performed, which the participating banks and financial institutions verify. Hence, digital identity is highly assured and added based on consensus, which also means it's reliable. Similarly, any change that's made to an already existing customer's information can be appended to the blockchain upon consensus. All updates and new additions are accessible to participating banks and financial institutions in real time.

5. The verified applicant is added as a customer.

6. Transactions that are performed by that customer will always include their digital signature.

This ensures the creation of the digital identity of the customer and that each transaction has a verified digital signature. However, let's discuss who can access the data on the blockchain. Since data is available on a shared distributed ledger, it can be accessed by third parties for verification, but only after permissions are granted. This checks any unauthorized access to data and empowers individual users and institutional users.

When an applicant provides information to a bank, along with its biometrics, their digital identity is created by the blockchain system. However, no-one can access it until the user grants consent. The user will own the data, and others can access it only after the user provides consent. Users can grant consent by logging in to the KYC portal (the unified KYC portal as a dApp of the blockchain network) and establishing a private key to the data. Now, banks and other third parties can access the data for verification purposes, and the data is still owned by the user. In addition, each verification request and each access to user data will leave a trace, which will empower the end user and inform them about who's using their information and for what.

The KYC process can be built as a smart contract, which can then be used across industries and further induces standardization. Blockchain offers strict checks against fraud as data on the blockchain is immutable. Banks and financial institutions don't need to perform verification individually. Since data is on a shared distributed ledger, various parties can access it, although it is still owned by the end user. As transactions are signed, any fraudulent activity can be spotted and communicated across the blockchain network. Since data on the ledger is trusted, reliable, and immutable, secondary verification isn't required. Scams and fraudulent transactions can be spotted in real time, which saves time and the aftermath of undetected frauds and scams.

The KYC solution we discussed previously is a distributed digital identity solution of the customers. In addition, bringing banks and financial institutions to the blockchain eliminates redundancy. Signing transactions with the digital identity helps check against frauds and identify illegal and fraudulent transactions. However, KYC and its underlying digital identity solution on blockchain have various use cases as well. It can find solutions to use cases that need a unique digital identity; for example, membership cards, legal systems, and credit rating agencies. Along with this, all of those use cases where transactions are involved are a prime candidate for a blockchain-based KYC solution. Examples include wagers, digital rights, micro financing, P2P lending, remittance, global payments, equity, debt, crowdfunding, derivatives, voting, ownership, title records, intellectual property, and healthcare.

FinTech – invoice factoring

Small businesses usually bring their invoices to larger financing firms, such as banks, to obtain finance. Usually, business to business and business to government transactions, especially procurement, take longer for payments. Companies usually sell invoices to invoice financing companies and can obtain finance for the outstanding invoices. Usually, it's 75 to 85% of the invoice. The rest is received when the invoice financing company has received the amount, with the remaining amount having a fee deducted by the invoice financing company. The amount that's charged by the invoice financing company is usually dependent on the payment term. The longer the payment term is, the higher the fee that's charged by the invoice factoring company. Roughly, invoice factoring is a 3 trillion dollar business globally. Globally, approximately 2% of invoice financing is subject to fraud every year.

What is there today?

Banks and financial institutions do have processes to check for fraud and tackle potential risks; however, it's labor-intensive, manual, costly, time-consuming, and inefficient. The following are the main steps in invoice factoring:

1. The supplier invoices its client with payment terms (30 to 90 days)
2. The supplier is in need of cash and thereby reaches an agreement to assign an invoice to factor, which includes fee and other details
3. The invoice is sold and assigned to a factor
4. The factor will advance approximately 80% of the invoice amount
5. Upon invoice due dates, the client pays the factor the invoice amounts
6. The factor pays the supplier with the remaining 20%, after subtracting the fee

What are we trying to solve?

Mostly, firms take the invoices to multiple financing institutes or banks. Since financing firms and banks don't have an integrated communication mechanism; it's open to vulnerability, which can be the potential point of fraud. Since there are multiple places for the firm to take its invoices and since financial institutions and banks are not integrated, they don't know about the same invoice being presented to various financing institutes or banks. In addition, an invoice can be altered and presented to various parties to obtain finance. Here, we are talking about two primary challenges: first, the same invoice is being sent to various parties, and second, an altered invoice is being sent to various parties. Along with this, other risks are associated with invoice factoring, such as non-payment and late payment, to name a few. Additional risks include that the invoices could be fake, or may have been tampered with. Invoice factoring is also a use case that's used to verify the identities of the clients and their customers. Verified and established identities can reduce the risk of late and non-payment.

Bringing invoice factoring to blockchain will result in decentralizing the entire process of invoice factoring. Blockchain smart contracts will take care of the agreements and verify the credit of participants (the supplier and its customer, in terms of the previous example in this section). Since it's an immutable record of transaction, where participating parties can also analyze the past performances of the participants, it helps to reduce risk and induce transparency to the overall process. Blockchain solutions, particularly based on Hyperledger Fabric, will help to reduce fraud that occurs in invoice financing, particularly due to a lack of communication and double invoicing.

Consortium–based solutions

A permissioned Hyperledger-based solution can help companies share key information about the invoice on the ledger and not give them a detailed insight about a customer's data. Even though it's a consortium of banks, financial institutions, and so on, they are competitors. In a consortium-based solution, the invoice seller will connect with a specific factor (bank or a financial institution). The digital identity of the invoice will be verified over the blockchain network. In the case of uniqueness, that invoice will be considered by the factor (bank or financial institution) for factoring. A supplier can allow their clients to be part of the blockchain network so that clients can directly pay the factors. All of the transactions will be processed through the blockchain network, which is signed by the digital identity of the transacting party and will include information about the digital identity of the invoice (digital asset).

As you can imagine, the digital identity, also known as the digital token, of the invoice is issued by the blockchain network and will be unique. Hence, a double invoice cannot occur on a blockchain network. Besides that, all of the parties, such as banks and financial institutions, are in the consortium; hence, everyone will know about the invoice, which eliminates any communication issues. This will also check any chances of the seller taking the same or a tampered invoice to multiple lenders at the same time. If they do so, the invoice will be paid for only one request, and an act of double invoicing will be recorded permanently on the blockchain, which can hit the credit rating of the seller. As the blockchain network evolves, more emphasis can be given to the credit scores of the sellers and lenders. The better the rating of a seller is, the less they need to pay as a fee would encourage legal and trustworthy sellers. With blockchain, invoice factoring can also be taken forward to small and medium investors.

Marketplace solution

Invoice sellers can use the blockchain platform via a dApp, which will allow them to choose the invoices that they want to sell. Once an invoice is marked for sale, a verified factor can accept the invoice. If the seller approves of it, this means that the seller has agreed to the factoring agreement and fees. In this case, a smart contract will issue payment transactions to the seller and the seller will be paid. Upon the due date, a smart contract will issue a debit transaction from the client's account to credit the factor account. Upon payment to the factor account, the smart contract will take care of the remaining payment to the seller and credit the fee to factor accounts.

In this entire journey, once an invoice is pushed to the blockchain platform for trade, all of the transactions are taken care of by the smart contract itself. Supplier, factors, and clients are invoiced, credited, and debited automatically by the smart contract. Certain attributes from the invoice can be used to generate a unique hash, also known as a digital identity, of the invoice itself. Any change in the invoice attribute will result in a change in the invoice hash and can easily be spotted by the blockchain network.

Tokenized marketplace

With blockchain, invoice factoring goes beyond the boundaries of banks and financial institutions. Small and medium investors can also participate in invoice factoring. Let's say, *Invoice Buy & Sell* is a dApp built on a blockchain solution:

- The invoice seller can use that app and choose an invoice to trade.
- The seller can set the invoice amount or smart contract based on the previous scores. The credit scores of the seller will modify the price of the invoice.

- A blockchain smart contract (invoice factoring smart contract) will generate a digital identity (digital token) of the invoice and get it verified for duplicity.
- Upon verification, the invoice will be tokenized based on the percentage or fraction of the invoice amount.
- Lenders (small, medium, or big) can own those tokens. Tokens represent the part that's due to be paid to the seller. Ownership of tokens means agreement to pay the seller.
- Upon the due date, the smart contract will issue a debt transaction from the client's account to credit the factor account, based on the tokens owned by the lenders (factor accounts).
- Upon payment to lenders (factor accounts), the smart contract will take care of the remaining payment to the seller and credit the fee to lenders/factor accounts.

The following diagram shows the invoice factoring process, with and without blockchain:

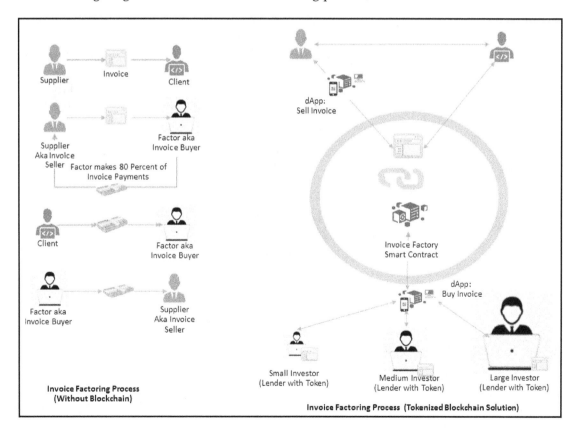

Invoice factoring use case

Since this is a token-based approach, small, medium, and big lenders can buy invoices across the border with the immutability, trust, and reliability of the blockchain network.

Engaging with a use case

In the *Design strategy* section, we tried to define a blockchain design strategy that consists of five steps: explore, engage, experiment, experience, and influence. In this section, we will concentrate on the second step. During this step, we will engage with one of the use cases we defined in previous section. Chapter 5, *Managing Solution on Oracle Blockchain Platform*, and Chapter 6, *Developing Solutions on Oracle Blockchain Platform*, take care of experimenting with the solution. There, we will define another use case and try to build the chaincode for the solution. We will also set up and configure a blockchain network to run the chaincode and use integration via REST to connect with the chaincode.

In this chapter, while engaging with the use case, we will start by defining the flow—first the *as-is* flow and then the *to-be* flow. We have covered a lot in terms of the flow in the previous section, which is why this section will be about the *as-is* flow. During the engaging process, we will learn about the art of defining a model, including assets, data models, transactions, participants, events, and access controls. Once the flow is defined and the components are identified, we will look into the integration architecture and infrastructure configuration of the use case.

The steps to engage and define a blockchain-based business network for a given use case is as follows:

1. Define the *as-is* flow to identify the problem and define a high-level flow (*to-be*)
2. Identify and define the blockchain network components:
   - Identify the participants.
   - Define the asset and data model.
   - Define the business flow in transactional details. This allows you to identify the transactions and events.

Defining the flow

This use case covers account receivable factoring, also termed as invoice factoring. It is a financial transaction that allows businesses to generate quick values out of their outstanding invoices. We will start by defining the *as-is* flow and then the *to-be* flow, which allows us to identify various blockchain components.

As-is flow

Sellers make a transaction with the customer and raise an invoice. These invoices are due in 30 days, 90 days, or whatever, depending on the business terms of the supplier and their customers. Hence, their customers don't pay the sellers immediately. In those cases, where the seller wants immediate cash to operate or generate more business, they can opt to sell their outstanding receivables. This allows sellers to meet their immediate needs. The invoice seller usually puts the outstanding invoice for sale at a discount. The buyer usually accepts the discount and immediately pays the seller. However, the buyers only pay the discounted amount, for example, 90% of the total invoice amount. Behind the scenes, the buyers check the credit history of the payer (customer) since it is the customer who will finally pay the buyer. During this process, there are three parties—the invoice seller, the invoice debtor (payer), and the invoice factor (buyer). Such invoice factoring is also referred to as account receivables financing or account receivables factoring. It is a kind of **asset-based lending** (ABL), which allows a seller's account receivables to be collateral.

To-be flow

At a high level, the supplier delivers goods to its customers—customer A and customer B. The supplier issues invoices to these customers for payments. Invoice 1 is due in 30 days to customer A and invoice 2 is due in 90 days to customer B. The supplier needs immediate cash and puts invoice 1 and invoice 2 for sale at a discount of 5% and 10%, respectively. Bank 1 and Bank 2 are also participants of the blockchain-based business network (KonsensusChainBC). They browse for the available invoices and factor them. Bank 1 factors invoice 1 and pays 95% of the invoice value to the supplier, while Bank 2 factors invoice 2 and pays 90% of the invoice value to the supplier. Factoring will result in the immediate payment of the invoice to supplier. Immediate payment confirmation will result in the customer's account receivables being updated. Now, customer 1 needs to pay Bank 1, while customer 2 needs to pay to Bank 2. The amount that's payable is updated with new payee details. Upon the due date, the account is paid from the payer (customer) account directly to the buyer's (the bank's) account, and the AP systems of the customers are updated. Upon 100% payment of the invoices by customer 1 and 2, the buyer will pay the remaining invoice amount to the seller (supplier). However, the buyers (Bank 1 and Bank 2) will pay the remaining to the seller, minus a transaction fee.

Identifying and defining business network components

The following diagram highlights various blockchain components for a business network called KonsensusChainBC. These components include assets, transactions, events, channels, and an access control list for the blockchain network. Since this blockchain business network is realized on a Hyperledger Fabric-based blockchain, it has a concept for channels as well. Although this step needs a detailed flow with transactions and events, you can jump to the transaction flow step and then come back to this section.

Based on the transaction flow, you get the following list of components on the blockchain business network:

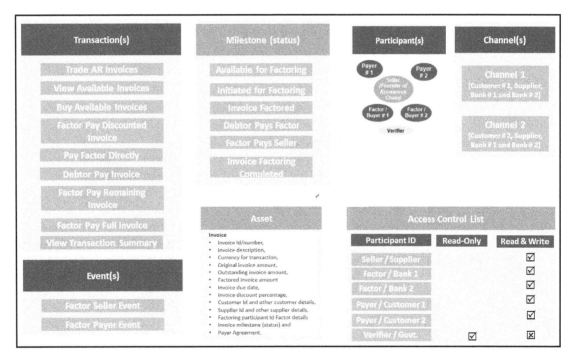

Blockchain components of KonsensusChainBC

Visit `Chapter 3`, *Delving into Hyperledger Fabric*, for details on transactions, events, channels, participants, and access control. Visit `Chapter 5`, *Managing Solutions using the Oracle Blockchain Platform*, to configure the network on the OBP.

Defining assets

Assets can be anything of *value*. Assets can be tangible assets such as real estate, and hardware, and intangible assets such as contracts and certificates. Assets can be modified using chaincode transactions. Therefore, before we identify the transactions, it is good to identify the assets that will be transacted on the blockchain network. Assets such as identity, currency, land title, contract, vote, provenance, and payments are valuable and scarce. Let's analyze various applications of blockchain and check what they actually manage. Example accounts are the assets in Bitcoin, contract states are managed by Ethereum, diamonds as assets are managed by Everledger and so on. Similarly, for Hyperledger Fabric, assets can be tangible assets, such as real estate and hardware, where intangibles can be things such as contracts and intellectual property. This means, blockchain is a potential solution for those cases, where the requirement is to transact assets while establishing a decentralized consensus while recording them on the immutable ledger.

For this business case, the primary asset is the invoice. The following are some of the attributes of the asset:

- Invoice ID/number
- Invoice description
- Currency for transaction
- Original invoice amount
- Outstanding invoice amount
- Factored invoice amount (calculated based on discount percentage)
- Invoice due date
- Invoice discount percentage
- Customer ID and other customer details
- Supplier ID and other supplier details (banks details as well)
- Factoring participant ID (banks that agree to the *to-be* factor for the invoice)
- Factor details (the factor bank's details, and so on)
- Invoice milestone (status)
- Payer agreement (true/false)

Defining participants

This subsection concentrates on defining the participants for the business network. For the use case of invoice factoring, the following parties are involved:

- Supplier, also known as the seller or issuer of the invoice:
    - The supplier is also a founder of a blockchain network (KonsensusChainBC), where various banks and customers are connected as participants
    - The blockchain network's chaincode is presented as a dApp called KonsensusChain
    - This dApp offers a solution for selling the receivables. It also comes with user interfaces, which allows the supplier (seller), buyer (factor) and customer (payer/debtor) to transact
    - The supplier's account receivables are connected with the blockchain network
- Customers (customer A and customer B) are also termed as payer/debtors:
    - The customer uses the KonsensusChain dApp to browse the milestone (status) of the invoices and checks the payee's information.
    - The customer's account payables are connected with blockchain network, where it subscribes to events that are emitted (raised) from the blockchain network. Various events allow the customer's **account payable** (**AP**) to update payee details and update their AP system with the ongoing status changes of the invoice.
- Banks are the parties that buy the invoices. They are also known as buyers. There are two banks (Bank 1 and Bank 2) in this scenario.
- Verifiers are participants that have access to the transaction summary, but don't have many details. An example of this would be a government authority, such as **Securities and Exchange Commission** (**SEC**), wanting to check fraud in invoice factoring and need access to the transaction summary.

The following diagram shows the participants:

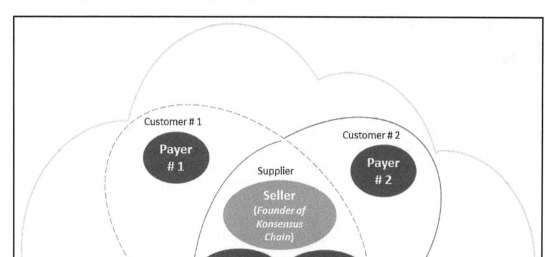

KonsensusChainBC business network participants

The circle with the dash line/blue color shows the channel between customer 1, the supplier, and all the banks, while the circle with the solid line/red color shows the channel between customer 2 and the supplier. We will be discussing channels in more detail in Chapter 3, *Delving into Hyperledger Fabric*.

Detailed flow with transactions and events

This section is the core to identifying the transactions and events, and also lays the foundation for defining the channels and access control. We will cover all the remaining blockchain components in this section.

The **Supplier** (**seller**) offers to sell the receivables at a discount of 5% the value of the invoice (invoice 1 is raised to customer A) and a discount of 10% the value of the invoice (invoice 1 is raised to customer B). Supplier's **Account Receivables** (**AR**) will automatically push invoices to the blockchain network (KonsensusChainBC). AR invoices that are pushed to the blockchain network are marked with '*Pending Approval for Factoring*' as milestone (status).

Following are the steps performed by **seller**, to ensure the availability of invoices for factoring :

1. The KonsensusChain dApp offers a user interface for the supplier (role-based). This UI allows the **seller** to approve AR invoices, which are pending for factoring (*Pending Approval for Factoring*). Upon approval, the invoice will be available for banks to factor.
2. Once approved, chaincode (the smart contract behind KonsensusChain dApps) will issue transaction *Trade AR Invoices*, and the milestone (status) of the invoice will be *Available for Factoring*.

Banks (**buyer/payer**) use the dApps (KonsensusChain) and the user interface that's meant for buyers.

Following are the steps performed by **payer** :

1. Bank 1 and Bank 2 use the dApps UI to browse the invoice, which is available for factoring.
2. While browsing, dApp issues **View Available Invoices transaction.**
3. The banks browse for invoices and choose the invoices to buy. This will result in transaction **Buy Available Invoices** and the milestone of the invoice changes to *Initiated for Factoring*:

Let's assume Bank 1 bought the invoices of customer A and Bank 2 bought the invoices of customer B. Following are the results of this assumption :

1. This status (*Initiated for Factoring*) change will result in the automatic execution of the *Factor Pay Discounted Invoice* transaction, and the milestone of the invoice will change to *Invoice Factored*.

2. The *Factor Pay Discounted Invoice* transaction generates two events: *Factor Seller Event* and *Factor Payer Event*. The *Factor Seller Event* will result in following activities:

   - Bank 1's system will pay 95% of the invoice amount to the supplier (against invoice 1 of customer A) and 90% of the invoice amount to the supplier (against invoice 2 of customer B)
   - The *Factor Seller Event* will also result in the supplier's AR system updating its records.

The **customer (debtor/payee)** account payable system will receive the *Factor Payer Event* from the chaincode. Following are the impact of *Factor Payer Event* and changes at the customer's account payable (AP) :

1. The *Factor Payer Event* will also result in the customer' account payable (AP) system updating records:

   - Customer 1 and customer 2 are subscribed to the *Factor Payer Event* with filters containing unique customer identities, invoice identifiers, and the payee's account details. This will allow the AP system to associate payee details with the invoices.
   - These events will contain details about the invoice for which they are listed as the payer/debtors. These invoices will now have the modified payee (banks) details. In this case, the bank's details and the bank's account details will be part of the event as well.

2. The customer's AP system will also invoke the *Pay Factor Directly* transaction. This is an agreement by the customer to pay the payee (invoice buyer/factor) directly. This will not lead to changes in the milestone of the invoice, but the *Payer Agreement* invoice attribute will be set to *true*.

When the invoice becomes due, that is, in 30 days for customer A and 90 days for customer B, KonsensusChain (chaincode) will automatically result in the payment of 100% of the invoice value to the payee (bank). Following occurs when the invoices are due :

1. Invoices turning due, will result in the *Debtor Pay Invoice* transaction. This will changes the milestone of the invoice to *Debtor Pays Factor*

2. Upon execution of the *Debtor Pay Invoice* transaction, chaincode will automatically result in the *Factor Pay Discounted Invoice* transaction, and the milestone of the invoice will be *Factor Pays Seller*. This will result into following :

   - This step will result in the payment of the remaining invoice by the banks (buyers/factor) to the invoice seller (supplier).
   - The factor (buyer) of the invoice will, minus a factoring fee, pay the remainder to the seller (the supplier, in this case).

- Upon payment, the seller system will automatically invoke the *Factor Pay Full Invoice* transaction. This is a final indicator to the KonsensusChain blockchain network indicating a successful payment receipt. At this final stage, the milestone (status) of the invoice will be *Invoice Factoring Completed*.

The following diagram highlights the entire transaction flow:

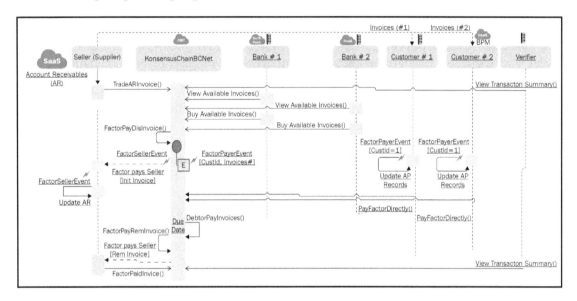

Transaction flow

Integration architecture

The following diagram shows how various systems can integrate with the blockchain business network. Applications can integrate with the blockchain network using REST, SDK, and events. This allows for simplified application development and integration with the blockchain network. Events allow SaaS, PaaS, and custom processes to subscribe to events and respond accordingly.

The business scenario that we have designed in this chapter is because all the participants are part of the KonsensusChain blockchain network and are using the dApp to execute transactions. Such dApps offer a role-based user interface, which allows participants to connect to the application and execute transactions. However, we also discussed transactions, which lead to updating account receivables and updating account payables. AR and AP are the SaaS and on-premise (E-Business Suite) applications of supplier and customer 1, respectively. Such applications can subscribe to blockchain events and act accordingly.

With reference to our business scenario, the seller (supplier) can integrate with the blockchain network (KonsensusChain) via REST and execute the *Trade AR Invoice* transaction. This transaction will result in invoice discovery at the blockchain network. The bank's application can connect their SaaS, PaaS, and custom processes with the blockchain network via REST and SDK. Customer 2 doesn't have SaaS and they build their processes and applications using BPM solutions. Such applications can also subscribe to blockchain events and connect via REST.

The verifier is using Java, Go, and Node.js for advanced integration:

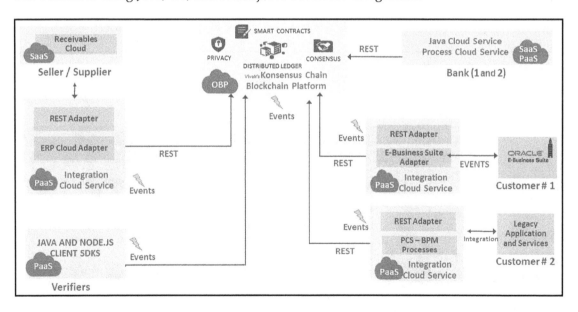

Integration architecture

Infrastructure of the business network

Up until now, we've walk though the invoice factoring use case and modeled the business network (KonsensusChain) to realize the use case. We also learned about the integration options with the blockchain network. This section is dedicated to realizing the infrastructure of the business network. The use case we've discussed so far can be realized on a permissioned blockchain such as Hyperledger Fabric. Therefore, we will try to define the infrastructure using a cloud platform that is based on Hyperledger Fabric. We had a glimpse of OBP in the *BaaS* section of `Chapter 1`, *Exploring Blockchain and BaaS*. In this section, we will try to realize the business use case over the OBP.

From an infrastructure perspective, Oracle offers a cloud hosted platform for Blockchain, and it is pre-assembled with various underlying services such as compute, storage, identity management (authentication), containers, object store (embedded archiving), log and management analytics (operations), and so on. Various SaaS applications, PaaS applications, on-premise applications, and legacy applications can integrate with blockchain using Oracle's integration cloud service and can subscribe to events that are raised (emitted) from the blockchain business network.

The following diagram shows that OBP is built on top of Hyperledger Fabric:

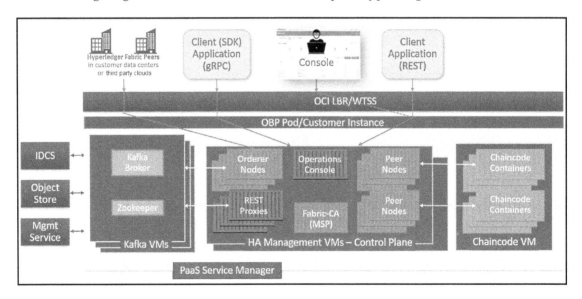

OBP Leveraging Hyperledger Fabric

The supplier's (seller) organization plans to start a consortium and decides for a founder-based consortium, thus adding a few more participating organizations to it. To do so, they set up blockchain instances on the OBP. Each blockchain instance contains managed containers, virtual machines, identity management, block and object storage, and Kafka, the Oracle Event Hub cloud service. In this section, we will walk through the business case and try to realize the infrastructure for it.

KonsensusChain is a founder-based blockchain network with a chaincode that takes care of financial transactions, invoice buying and selling, payments to invoicing sellers, and receiving payments from end customers. KonsensusChain is set up on OBP. It has a physical machine for each organization (founder and participant). Since it is a production deployment, its ordering is based on Kafka, and the ordering nodes are made with the founder organization. This infrastructure also includes one **certificate authority (CA)** for each organization. With a requirement of less than 1,000 transactions per hour, this highly available configuration will look as follows:

- Two fabric CA nodes replicated across separate virtual machines (VMs) for **high availability (HA)**.
- The supplier (founder) will have two peer nodes, while customers and banks have two peer nodes each.
- 4 TB of storage.
- A console node replicated on each VM for HA. This console can be used to manage participants, and the founder can use it to manage the chaincode.
- The identity cloud service is integrated, which allows organizations to manage roles and identities.
- There will be a container in an isolated VM for the chaincode. You can use the console to manage the chaincode.
- The REST proxy nodes will be replicated across separate VMs for HA. These nodes offer the RESTful APIs.
- A load balancer and operations management and monitoring are supplied as well.
- An object store for configuration backup and replication of blocks across regions is provided.
- The founder (seller/supplier) will have two Kafka orderers nodes, which are replicated across separate VMs for HA.

The following diagram shows the infrastructure for the blockchain business network (KonsensusChain) that we discussed in this section:

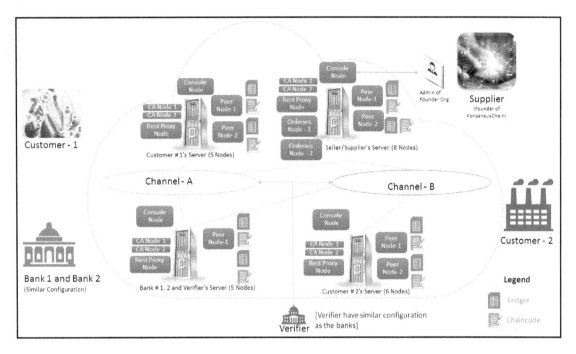

Infrastructure for the blockchain business network

Each organization will get a blockchain instance (one founder and five participant instances). Each instance will include nodes—a peer node, a console node, a REST proxy node, and a CA node, while the founder will have an orderer's node. Instances are also integrated with the object store for the dynamic backup of configurations and ledgers. The backup includes ledger blocks, channel configurations, checkpoints, chaincode, and nodes for provisioning files and log files. Backup and restore are automatic processes. It also uses the Oracle event hub cloud service for Kafka at the orderer's nodes. The REST proxy nodes will allow for RESTful APIs, which further helps SaaS, PaaS and their applications to connect and integrate with the blockchain business network. With all of these services, containers, and the infrastructure, OBP takes care of high availability, scalability, and the resilience of the blockchain business network.

Summary

This chapter highlighted the challenges and opportunities of DLT and blockchain. This chapter also drilled into various properties of blockchain and how those properties are upheaving the usage of blockchain in various scenarios. In this chapter, we also delved into modeling a use case and demonstrated the integration aspects and infrastructure for implementing a use case. The *Design strategy* section mentioned the five stages of this—explore, engage, experiment, experience, and influence. We also covered the initial two stages (explore and engage) of the design strategy. We explored the design strategy by examining various use cases, justifying the adoption of blockchain, and also tried to formulate an equation to justify/quantify the employment of blockchain for a given use case. Later, we engaged in the design strategy by defining a blockchain-based business network for a given use case. Here, we sketched flows and identified various blockchain-based business network components, such as assets, transactions, participants, events, access control, and channels. My next book, *Blockchain for Solution Designers*, covers design strategy extensively. In this edition, `Chapter 5`, *Managing Solution on Oracle Blockchain Platform* and `Chapter 6`, *Developing Solution on Oracle Blockchain Platform*, covers the experimental part of the design strategy, where you will learn to build a chaincode and run it on a blockchain platform. This allows you to experiment with the blockchain platform. From the next chapter onward, we will be exploring Hyperledger, its architecture, and other details.

3
Delving into Hyperledger Fabric

Permissioned blockchain has evolved to address the need to adopt blockchain among a set of known (and not necessarily trusted) but identifiable participants. Such participants first need to be explicitly admitted to the blockchain network. Here, knowing (identifying) participants is more important than fully trusting those known participants. These participants might not trust one another, but are known and identifiable and they are chained by a common goal. **Hyperledger Fabric** (**HLF**) (a permissioned blockchain) uses **Byzantine Fault Tolerance** (**BFT**) variant **Practical BFT** (**PBFT**), as the consensus protocol instead of **proof of work** (**PoW**). HLF offers improved functional qualities to permissioned blockchain, such as confidentiality and consistency, while also offering improved and enhanced non-functional qualities, such as performance and scalability.

This chapter focuses on the fundamentals of HLF. This will allow you to understand how business logic is implemented in HLF and learn about various transaction types that facilitate read and write operations to distributed ledgers. The Linux Foundation, in collaboration with various leading companies and some of the smartest developers, is endeavoring to solve some of the most complex challenges facing the world of IT and is also promoting the commercial adoption of open source technology. This is the largest ever open source software project in the world. The Linux Foundation is a blanket project for various open source projects. For big data and analytics, it supports R, as well as consortium projects. For networking, it powers **ONAP** (short for **Open Network Automation Platform**), OpenDaylight, and others. For cloud computing, it empowers projects such as Cloud Foundry, and cloud native computing. Similarly, for blockchain, the Linux Foundation handles the Hyperledger project.

A glance at the Hyperledger project

The Hyperledger project, initiated in December 2015, was hosted by the Linux Foundation in an effort to create advanced, cross-industry **distributed ledger technology** (**DLT**) and blockchain technologies. It hosts blockchain frameworks and supports a number of tools as well. It is an umbrella of open source projects, where some of the projects are DLT frameworks, including Iroha, Sawtooth, and Fabric.

Frameworks hosted by Hyperledger

The following are the frameworks hosted by Hyperledger. These are classified as follows:

- Hyperledger Burrow
- Hyperledger Fabric
- Hyperledger Indy
- Hyperledger Iroha
- Hyperledger Sawtooth

Hyperledger Burrow:

- **Contributor**: Originally contributed by Monax and co-sponsored by Intel.
- **Key features**: Burrow is a lightweight, fast, and efficient permissioned chaincode machine. It leverages the Tendermint protocol for consensus. The most important feature of Burrow is the speed of blockchain. Three dimensions achieve speed in blockchain. The first is the codebase's transactional throughput. The second is the block's propagation speed within the network. The third and final dimension is the time when the blocks are finalized (aka the finality of blocks). Burrow is a non-forking blockchain and transaction finality is guaranteed. Finality enhances the overall speed of the system because applications and systems can instantly rely on the information on the blockchain network.
- **Objective**: It provides a modular blockchain client with a permissioned smart contract interpreter partially developed to the specifications of the **Ethereum Virtual Machine** (**EVM**). It is a permissioned smart contract machine that provides a modular blockchain client with a permissioned smart contract interpreter incorporated, partly in line with the specifications of the EVM.
- **Consensus protocol**: Tendermint.

Hyperledger Fabric (HLF):

- **Contributor**: Initially contributed by Digital Asset and IBM
- **Key features**: Modular and pluggable architecture and permissioned with a high level of privacy and confidentiality
- **Objective**: To serve as a basis for developing permissioned enterprise applications or solutions with a modular architecture
- **Consensus protocol**: Apache Kafka

Hyperledger Indy:

- **Contributor**: The Sovrin Foundation.
- **Key features**: Built for decentralized identities. It manages keys, proofs, and other relevant information that enables trusted peer interactions between various parties.
- **Objective**: To offer tools, libraries, and reusable components to create and use independent identities to be interoperable across applications.
- **Consensus protocol**: PBFT.

Hyperledger Iroha:

- **Contributor**: Contributed by Soramitsu, Hitachi, NTT Data, and Colu
- **Key features**: Allows the manipulation of accounts and digital assets
- **Objective**: Hyperledger Iroha emphasizes mobile application development with client libraries for Android and iOS, thereby setting it apart from other Hyperledger frameworks
- **Language**: C++
- **Consensus protocol**: **Yet Another Consensus (YAC)**

Hyperledger Sawtooth:

- **Contributor**: Intel.
- **Key features**: A modular platform for DLT applications.
- **Objective**: Sawtooth creates a digital platform, enabling physical traceability in a trustless world. It is a blockchain framework that utilizes a modular platform for building, deploying, and running distributed ledgers. It supports both permissioned and permissionless deployments.
- **Consensus protocol**: **Proof of Elapsed Time (PoET)** consensus.

The previously listed Hyperledger frameworks are used to build DLT and blockchain applications, along with a list of modules (also known as tools) that facilitate the deployment and maintenance of blockchain applications, analyzing ledger data, and managing blockchain networks.

Tools hosted by Hyperledger

The following **modules**, also known as tools, are hosted by Hyperledger:

- Hyperledger Caliper
- Hyperledger Cello
- Hyperledger Composer
- Hyperledger Quilt
- Hyperledger Explorer
- Hyperledger URSA

Hyperledger Caliper:

- **Contributors**: Oracle, Huawei, and others
- **Objective**: To enable the performance of specific blockchain implementations to be measured
- **Key features**: It allows the generation of reports with various performance indicators, such as resource utilization, transactions per second, and transaction latency

Hyperledger Cello:

- **Contributors**: IBM, Huawei, and others.
- **Objective**: To allow businesses to have **Blockchain-as-a-Service** (**BaaS**), which enables quick blockchain solutions for enterprise. It reduces complexity and minimizes the efforts required to create, terminate, and manage blockchains.
- **Key features**: It offers multi-tenant services in addition to various infrastructures, such as **bare metal**, and virtual machines. It enables the creation and management of blockchain via a simplified dashboard allowing the immediate availability of the blockchain instance.

Hyperledger Composer:

- **Contributors**: Contributors from IBM and Ox-chains are the maintainer community, however, everyone is encouraged to participate and contribute.
- **Objective**: To develop a set of collaboration tools that facilitate the easy and quick building of blockchain business networks to enable developers to quickly create chaincode and applications.
- **Key features**: Built using JavaScript and tools including Node.js, npm, and CLI. Its modular language facilitates asset definition, participant definition, and transaction definitions. These three components constitute the blockchain network. It allows faster and easier development of blockchain applications.

Hyperledger Quilt:

- **Contributors**: NTT Data and Ripple.
- **Objective**: It allows interoperability between ledger systems by implementing the **Interledger Protocol** (**ILP**). ILP is a payments protocol and is designed to transfer value across both distributed and non-distributed ledgers.
- **Key features**: It allows atomic swaps between ledgers (even non-blockchain or distributed ledgers) and a single account namespace for the accounts within each ledger.

Hyperledger Explorer:

- **Contributors**: IBM, DTCC, and Intel.
- **Objective**: It allows authorized participants to explore DLT projects. It also allows the visualization of blockchain operations, which enables enterprises to extract value from data.
- **Key features**: Explorer can view, invoke, deploy, or query blocks, transactions and associated data, network information (name, status, and a list of nodes), chaincodes, and transaction families, as well as any other relevant information stored on the ledger.

Hyperledger Ursa:

- **Contributors** : Ursa contributors include Hyperledger Indy, Sawtooth, and Fabric developers, who worked on security aspects of these modules. Also, to ensure that all cryptographic algorithms meets the standards, several cryptographers are involved.
- **Key features**: A modular, flexible cryptographic library that is intended for, but not limited to, use by other projects in Hyperledger.

- **Objective**: To ensure safe and easier access to trusted cryptographic libraries to other Hyperledger projects. Its modular library will help blockchain developers to switch or change cryptographic schemes with the aid of simple configurations.
- **Language**: Rust.

HLF – features and qualifiers

Along with the Linux Foundation, various companies, such as Fujitsu, and IBM, are collaborating on the HLF project. HLF is a permissioned blockchain framework that is designed and architected to develop modular applications.

The following are the key features of the Hyperledger framework:

- HLF is governed by excellent, diverse technical steering committees from various organizations.
- HLF is modular and configurable, which makes it useful for various use cases, ranging from banking, finance, and the supply chain, to education and healthcare.
- It is a DLT where chaincode is authored in general-purpose programming languages, such as Java, Go, and Node.js, instead of programming in **DSL** (**domain-specific languages**). This also brings HLF closer to enterprises that have applications and resources built and skilled in these languages.
- HLF is a DLT that is an open source, enterprise-grade, permissioned DLT.
- HLF follows a modular component-based approach and easy-to-use APIs.
- As HLF is permissioned, it operates under the governance model to handle disputes.
- HLF supports pluggable consensus protocols, and blockchain networks can choose a consensus protocol to address their use cases. Examples of single enterprise blockchain solutions, **crash fault tolerance** (**CFT**) consensus might be more appealing than BFT, since BFT is more suited to a multi-enterprise blockchain network.
- The membership service (a key component of HLF) is plug and play.
- HLF also has pluggable identity management protocols, such as **Lightweight Directory Access Protocol** (**LDAP**) and OpenID Connect. This also makes HLF appealing to enterprises that have diverse identity solutions.
- In HLF, smart contracts, also known as chaincode, execute in a container (for example, Docker) and hence, are isolated from the ledger state.

- In HLF, ledgers can be configured to support various database management systems.
- HLF does not require cryptocurrency, which significantly reduces the reliance on cryptocurrency for a blockchain existence and reduces the risk of attack.
- An HLF service diagram shows the various components of HLF. They are integrated, assembled, and interacted with via APIs and SDKs. The major components are as follows:
  - Identity
  - Ledger
  - Transactions
  - Consensus
  - Smart contract
  - Security and cryptoservices

Why Hyperledger?

We covered DLT and blockchain in `Chapter 1`, *Exploring Blockchain and BaaS*, and `Chapter 2`, *Construing Distributed Ledger Tech and Blockchain*. In addition, we learned about various network topologies, such as centralized, distributed, and decentralized systems. We also became familiar with the structure of blockchain, transactions, and various other blockchain concepts. We carried out a detailed analysis of, and discussion on, permissioned and permissionless blockchain. Permissionless blockchain, such as Ethereum and Bitcoin, are open blockchain, where anyone can participate. On the other hand, permissioned blockchain allows a limited set of participants to administer the blockchain network, while only authorized and authenticated sets of participants are able to access it.

There are various advantages associated with permissionless blockchain, and similarly, there are advantages to using permissioned blockchain. Permissioned blockchain is cost-effective, and has low transaction overheads. As transaction verification and validation is faster, transaction costs are very low and transaction times are faster. The decision behind the choice of blockchain network depends entirely on the use case and the visibility of messages and transactions. However, in my opinion, the key difference that resonates well with enterprises is the determination as to who will participate in the blockchain business network and who is authorized to transact on the business network; another reason being the ability to empower the direct relationship between producer and consumer, and reducing or removing the reliance on middle parties or third parties (intermediaries).

We are in the era of disintermediation. It has been pioneered by Uber, Amazon, Airbnb, and others, where they own no vehicles, hold no real inventory, and have no inventory of rooms, respectively, yet they allow producers and consumers to connect and transact. Blockchain and DLT further empower producers and consumers, resulting in the disintermediation of third parties and intermediaries from the equation. Permissioned blockchain enhances privacy by means of permissioned access to blockchain networks and channeling transactions between participants to further allow the segregation of data on blockchain networks, thereby enabling privacy and the confidentiality of data. DLT, like blockchain, has the full potential to disrupt industries that have a high reliance on intermediaries, such as insurance, healthcare, transportation, retail, logistics, real estate, and education.

At a high level, with regard to an enterprise, blockchain offers the following:

- It checks for the risk of malicious nodes tampering with data in the event of transmission to ensure tamper-proof data transmission. This is ensured by securing the transaction tree, along with complexity in gaining PoW. Malicious users cannot alter/tamper with data without recomputing the PoW hash, which is a gigantic task and requires extreme computing power.
- As the HLF blockchain is permissioned, the blockchain network is operating among known participants, which offers a high level of trust in the blockchain network itself.
- Using HLF's channels, transactions between groups of participants can be secured further.
- It removes the reliance on a single, central point of failure.
- Consistency is ensured by following protocol, adopting the same rules for validation and block layout.
- All nodes will follow the longest chain, which ensures the establishment of agreement across geographies.
- Blockchain lowers uncertainty and enhances trust between parties, leading to faster and more secure transactions.

- Permissioned blockchain, chosen by enterprises, allows enterprises to define membership rules for participants by providing immutability (tamper-proof, where blockchain represents the truth), privacy, and confidentiality (the secure exchange of sensitive data with authorization), scalability, reliability, availability (to support mission-critical applications), and auditability (manage, track, trace, verify, and monitor).

In a permissionless blockchain, transactions are executed on every node (assuming the consensus is PoW). This means a lack of confidentiality because data and smart contracts, as well as transaction data, is available on every node on the network. Confidentiality and transaction data visibility is of great importance for enterprises. In the case of B2B transactions, an enterprise would not like the data on special rates that is offered to one partner being available to another partner, although confidentiality is addressed in permissionless networks by encrypting data. However, permissionless blockchain networks using PoW will lead to data being available on every node, which highlights the possibility of decrypting it, given time, and the local availability of data on the node. In HLF, along with the participants identified and encryption, channels offer the highest level of confidentiality. Here, only participating nodes will have access to chaincode and transaction data and that, too, is further controlled by access control. This introduces a high level of privacy and confidentiality to a blockchain network.

Permissionless versus permissioned blockchain:

When we enter into a discussion on *Why Hyperledger?*, it makes sense to quickly look into the differences between permissionless blockchain and permissioned blockchain, such as HLF. Let's analyze these variants of DLT in terms of execution style, determinism, and confidentiality:

- **Execution style**:
    - A permissionless blockchain, such as Ethereum, observes the sequential execution of transactions, where they abide by the *order-execute* architecture. All peers execute the *order-execute* style of transactions and this results in performance and scalability limitations. Here, the throughput is inversely proportional to latency in transaction. However, permissionless blockchain tries to handle this by orchestrating around a cryptocurrency. This ensures that a fuel/gas is included with each transaction. Hence, a gas is paid for each step of the transaction execution via a smart contract. However, such a mechanism of engulfing a cryptocurrency might not fit into the permissioned blockchain.

- A permissioned blockchain, like HLF's architecture, supports scalability and performance, along with trust. HLF's architecture is based on **execute-order-validate (E-O-V)** architecture, where transactions are executed even before a consensus is reached. Execution (**execute**) of the transaction will ensure a transaction's correctness (endorsement), while a modular pluggable consensus protocol will result in an ordering (**order**) transaction. Furthermore, just before committing the transaction, it is validated (**validate**) by an application-specific endorsement policy. E-O-V addresses the flexibility, scalability, performance, and confidentiality issues faced by the order and execute architecture of permissionless blockchain. HLF allows a subset of peers to execute transactions in parallel. Interestingly, chaincode delegates the work of endorsement to certain designated peers; hence, different chaincode can designate different peers as endorsers, which supports parallel execution. Note that Fabric executes a transaction even before it is ordered.

- **Determinism**:
  - Consensus ensures that nodes are in agreement over a transaction and, hence, the smart contract should execute transactions deterministically. If not, there is no point in establishing a consensus. In addition, such non-determinism will lead to nullifying the consensus, and this will result in forks. Hence, smart contract languages and compilers should ensure that smart contract execution is deterministic. Hence, various blockchains opt for DSL. This forces developers to learn new languages, just to ensure the determinism of smart contracts.
  - HLF's E-O-V architecture ensures that a transaction is validated by an application-specific endorsement policy. This means that it is the application-specific policy that ensures how many, and which, peer nodes will validate and ensure the deterministic execution of the chaincode. Hence, a subset of peers will execute (endorse) the transaction to meet the endorsement policy. This will filter out inconsistent results, even before ordering, and thereby eliminate any non-determinism. Because non-determinism is eliminated, HLF supports the use of a standard programming language. You can write chaincode in Go, Node.js, and Java.

- **Hybrid replication driver for determinism:**
  - HLF follows passive and active replication. Passive replication is achieved by executing (endorsing) a transaction by a subset of peers, which offers determinism and parallel execution. It also achieves active replication by committing transactions to ledger only after a consensus is reached. Hence, HLF follows a hybrid replication strategy. Again, the choice of consensus is specific to the use case, or deployment in relation to that use case, as Hyperledger supports a modular consensus mechanism. This allows implementers to choose any protocol of choice for consensus, such as BFT or CFT.

- **Confidentiality:**
  - Permissionless blockchain, which leverages PoW, executes transactions on every node. Hence, every transaction and the smart contract are visible to each node, which clearly indicates a loss of confidentiality for the gain of BFT offered by PoW. Loss of confidentiality is a challenge for enterprise customers and their use cases. For example, if a business wanted to establish certain rates with some suppliers and a different rate with non-premium suppliers, they would not be able to maintain the confidentiality of such preferred rates. If all suppliers are on the same blockchain network and access the same smart contract, it is impossible to maintain different trade relationships (rates) with different suppliers. Permissionless blockchain offers two types of solution:
    - It encrypts such preferred information. However, data and smart contracts are on every node. Encryption can be compromised and there is always the risk of losing information.
    - **Zero knowledge proofs (ZKP)** can handle a loss of confidentiality. However, ZKP's computation increases latency and consumes resources. This means that ZKP can solve confidentiality issues, even though this will lead to performance issues.

- A permissioned blockchain, like HLF, offers channels and **private data collection (PDC)** to address the confidentiality issue.

Go/No–Go for a blockchain solution

Now, every enterprise needs a blockchain solution and, at the same time, every enterprise needs a blockchain solution based on the use case. Hence, the core of identifying whether a blockchain solution is required by an enterprise is based on the use case that it is trying to address.

Now, let's list the factors that an enterprise should consider before evaluating blockchain:

- Is there a need for a common shared database?
- For a business process, do the participating parties have a lack of trust?
- Is more than one party involved in committing to a database?
- Are third parties or middlemen involved in the business processes?
- Does the business process data exist in multiple databases?
- Is there a need for the immutability of data or a log/history of transactions?
- Is the transaction frequency in the region of 10,000 transactions per second?
- Are the transaction rules changing infrequently? (Rules authored in blockchain are pre-set and, once deployed and initiated, chaincode will not change routes based on new rules). As everything on blockchain is deterministic, rule-changing applications are frequently not the right candidate for blockchain).
- Does the process not store a lot of static data?
- Does the process not have a lot of data? (As the data is replicated, a significantly larger set of data replication to all the nodes is not an efficient use case for blockchain).
- Is there not any need to retrieve data from external sources?

If the answer to any of the preceding questions is *yes*, then blockchain is the solution for the enterprise use case. Also, if there is a need for transactions to be public, then the enterprise use case requires a permissionless blockchain solution, or else it requires a permissioned blockchain solution, such as HLF.

Architecture – conceptual view

Before we jump into HLF architecture and its components, let's first walk though a conceptual view and learn a number of important terms. Read this section to grasp some basic knowledge by means of an example and, after reading the architecture and components, revisit this section to further affirm your understanding of HLF.

The KonsensusChain organization decides to create a product chain (a blockchain business network named ProductChain) to enable producers and retailers to enter into transactions. In addition, it will allow the regulatory authority to validate the legality of the products as well. Organization KonsensusChain will act as the founder organization and will not participate in any transactions. However, it will set up the blockchain network, develop user interfaces, chaincode applications, and will further maintain and operate the business network (consortium). This is a founder-initiated model of a blockchain network, based on HLF, where participating organizations have created a consortium. In this sample, a dApp is not fully offered by the founder. dApps are individually built by the organization. However, they use SDK, REST APIs, and other integration methods to connect with the business blockchain network and execute transactions.

The following are the different organizations intending to be part of the blockchain network:

- **Producer organization**: Identified as organization 1 (**O1**), this is an organization that produces certain products and sells them to retailers. The regulatory authority further verifies the legality of those products. The **certificate authority** (**CA**) for producer organization **O1** is **CA 01**.
- **Retailer organization**: Identified as organization 2 (**O2**), this is an organization that buys products from producer organization **O1** and sells them on to its consumers. The CA for retailer organization **O2** is **CA O2**.
- **Retailer organization**: Identified as organization 1 (**O3**), this is an organization that buys products from producer organization **O1** and sells them on to its consumers. The CA for retailer organization **O3** is **CA O3**.
- **Regulatory authority**: Identified as a regulatory organization (**O4**), this is a regulatory authority that verifies the products and stamps the legality of produce.
- **Founder organization**: `KonsensusChain.com` is the founding organization, identified as organization 5 (**O5**). All the retailers and producers have agreed to employ **O5** as the founder organization for the ProductChain blockchain network (the fictitious name of the blockchain network).

The following are the requirements of this blockchain-based business network (ProductChain):

- **Requirement one**: The producer organization (**O1**) wants to have private transactions and communications with the retailer organization (**O2**), as they have agreed on a specific rate for certain products and want to have transaction privacy
- **Requirement two**: Similarly, the producer organization (**O1**) wants to have private transactions and communications with the retailer organization (**O3**), as they have agreed on certain discounts and payment terms, which they want to keep secret

The following is a conceptual diagram of the business network that will be referred to in this section:

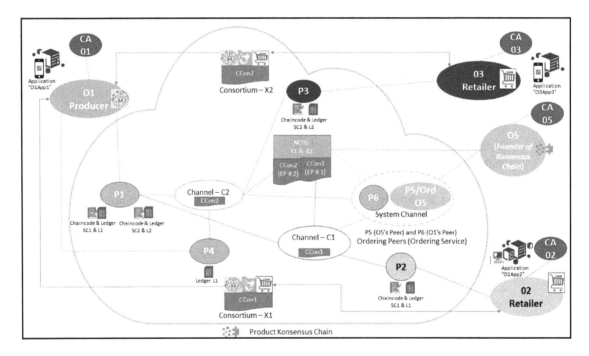

Architecture: conceptual view

Building the blockchain network

This section discusses the building blocks of the business network and covers the steps involved in forming a business network. All the terms are based on HLF. The following are the steps required to build a business network:

Step 1: **Initiating the blockchain network**: The first step in forming a network is to start an orderer. In the sample (refer to the preceding *Architecture*: *conceptual view* diagram), node **O5** is owned by organization **O5**, and it is also defined as the orderer. The founder organization (**O5**) uses network configuration, **NC05**, and configures an ordering service (**Ord05**) for the blockchain network. This setup offers full administrative rights to the founder organization (**O5**) over the blockchain network (ProductChain). The CA for organization **O5** is **CA O5**. The CA issues certificates to administrators of the network nodes of the founder organization (**O5**):

- Essentially, the ordering service is hosted on the founder organization (**O5**), or a cloud platform administrator, by **O5**, and further managed, and administered by **O5**. The network configuration file (**NC05**) defines the rights and privilege information of organization **O5** over the business network.
- CAs are central to HLF. HLF offers a built-in Fabric CA for a quick start. However, organizations can use their own CAs. Different participants use certificates to identify themselves on the blockchain network. In this fictitious blockchain network (ProductChain), we will define five CAs, one for each organization.
- Network configuration (**NC05**) uses a structure called a **membership service provider** (**MSP**) to map certificate issues by **CA05** to the certificate holder of the **O5** organization. Furthermore, the MSP name is used in policies, by **NC05**, to grant access to participants from the founder organization (**O5**) over blockchain network resources. Take the example of identifying a participant from **O5** who acts as the administrator of a blockchain network and can further add new member organizations to the blockchain network.

Other administrators being added by the founder: The founder organization (**O5**) adds a producer organization (**O1**) as an administrator by updating the network configuration (**NC05**). This modification further defines **O1** as the administrator of the blockchain network. The producer organization employs its resource (node) as an additional orderer (**O1**) to the blockchain network.

Step 2: **Defining a consortium to realize the separation and security of transactions**: Secondly, we will look at defining the consortium. It is an association of two or more organizations, which participate to achieve a common goal. In a consortium, each participating organization has its own legal status and is joined by agreed-upon contracts. This consortium formation is different from the consortium defined in Chapter 2, *Construing Distributed Ledger Tech and Blockchain*. In Chapter 2, *Construing Distributed Ledger Tech and Blockchain,* the founder organization itself defines and owns the consortium and also participates in the transactions. Here, a founder is responsible for setting up, maintaining, and operating the infrastructure of the blockchain network. It also offers a solution, where various organizations can amalgamate and form a consortium and channels, and can enter into transactions. Such a configuration can allow cloud platform providers to manage the business network, without participating in it. After all, consortia are groups of like-minded organizations, working to solve a common problem. In this process, they employ their resources in the business network. In this sample, the founder organization is employing its infrastructure and also employs a few nodes as orderers. In this consortium, the following applies:

- The founder organization is employing its infrastructure and also employs node **P5** (**Ord O5**) as the orderer node
- The producer organization **O1** (also defined as the network administrator) defines a **Consortium-X1** with two members—organization **O1** and organization **O2**
- The consortium definition is stored in the network configuration (**NC05**) file

Step 3: **Defining channels**: Thirdly, we will be creating a channel that allows members of a consortium to enter into transactions with one another securely. Generally, such channels are referred to as application channels:

- Channel configuration **CCon1** governs **Channel-C1**. **Channel-C1** is created for **Consortium-X1**. **O1** and **O2** can both manage channel configuration, **CCon1**, and they have equal rights over it.
- Channel configuration (**CCon1**) is completely separate from network configuration (**NC05**) and, hence, organization **O5** has no control over channel configuration (**CCon1**). However, **Channel-C1** is connected to the ordering service (**Ord 05**).
- Channel configuration (**CCon1**) contains policies that define the organizations (**O1** and **O2**) rights to transact over **Channel-C1**. Other organizations, such as **O3** and **O5**, cannot affect transactions over it.

Adding peer nodes to channels:

- **Adding peers to the channel, organization 1**: Peer **P1** is joined to a business network by the producer organization (**O1**). This is possible because the organization owns the peer (**O1** owns **P1**). Peer **P1** in the diagram also hosts the copy of ledger 1 (**L1**). It is clear that **P1** and **O5** (the peer and ordering service) can communicate with one another over **Channel-C1**.
- **Adding peers to the channel, organization 2**: Similarly, peer **P2** is joined to the channel by the retailer organization (**O2**), which owns peer **P2**. Peer **P2** also hosts the copy of ledger 1 (**L1**). It is clear that **P2** and **O5** (the peer and ordering service) can communicate with one another over **Channel-C1**.

The following are the lessons we can take from this configuration:

- **Associating peer with the organization**: The association of peer **P1** with organization (**O1**) can be confirmed based on the certificates. In this sample, organization **O1**'s CA (**CA O1**) has issued the X.509 identity to peer (**P1**), hence, **P1** is associated with **O1**. Similarly, the association of peer (**P2**) with the organization (**O2**) can be confirmed based on the certificates. In this sample, organization **O2**'s CA (**CA O2**) has issued the X.509 identity to peer (**P2**), hence, **P2** is associated with **O2**.
- **Associating peer with the ledger**: Peer 1 (**P1**) and Peer 2 (**P2**) host the copy of ledger 1 (**L1**). Hence, ledger 1 (**L1**) is physically associated with **P1** and **P2**, while logically associated with channel (**C1**).
- **Functioning**: At startup, peer (**P1**) sends a request to the orderer (**Ord O5**). The request from peer (**P1**) is verified by the orderer (**Ord O5**) by referring to the channel configuration (**CCon1**). This verification unlocks information about **P1**'s permissions (access controls) over the channel (**C1**). It helps in determining the operations (read/write) that peer (**P1**) can perform over ledger 1 (**L1**). The same holds true for peer **P2**.

Adding chaincode and allowing an application to access the ledger: In this sample, a dApp is not fully offered by the founder. dApps are individually built by the organization.

However, they use SDKs, REST APIs, and other integration methods to connect with the business blockchain network and execute transactions:

- Producer organization (**O1**) owns application (**O1App1**), and retailer organization (**O2**) owns application (**O2App2**). These applications are integrated with chaincode (a smart contract), defined as chaincode (**SC1**) in the diagrams. Chaincode (**SC1**) is deployed on peer 1 (**P1**) and peer 2 (**P2**) and allows dApp (**O1App1** and **O1App2**) to access ledger 1 (**L1**). All the participating entities, such as applications (**O1App1** and **O2App2**), peers (**P1** and **P2**), and the ordering service (**O5**) use **Channel-C1** for communication purposes (transactions).
- dApps (**O1App1** and **O2App2**) are also known as client applications. They, too, have identities associated with the organizations (**O1** and **O2**). Chaincode (**SC1**) defines operations, and dApps (applications) can integrate with chaincode to execute transactions that allow access to the ledger (**L1**). The applications (**O1App1** and **O2App2**) access to ledger (**L1**) is completely governed by the chaincode (**SC1**) operations.
  - Chaincode is developed by an organization's (**O1**) development team, and is reviewed and agreed by the consortium team (**X1**'s members, such as **O1** and **O2**). However, a consensus on the chaincode is required by the consortium before being deployed to the peer(s).

Chaincode and its stages

Chaincode has four stages—installation, initiation, the defining of endorsers, and allowing transactions. A detailed analysis of these stages follows. You can relate them to the example as well:

- **Installed**: In the event of consensus in relation to the chaincode (development and testing), chaincode(s) can be deployed (installed) by the organization's (**O1**) administrator on peer nodes (**P1** and **P2**). Although the peers on which chaincode is installed have full access to and knowledge of the chaincode, client applications (dApps) are limited to invoking transactions. Interestingly, just installing chaincode on the channel will not enable client applications (**O1App1** and **O2App2**) to issue transactions against chaincode (**SC1**). This can only happen when the chaincode is initiated.

ᵗᵗᵗᵗᵗᵗᵗ

- **Initiated**: So far, chaincode is only installed on peers (**P1** and **P2**). Hence, other than the peer(s) (**P1** and **P2**), other channel participants do not know about it. The producer organization (**O1**) will initiate chaincode (**SC1**) on channel (**C1**). Once chaincode is initiated on a channel, other channel participants, such as dApps (**O1App1** and **O2App2**) can invoke the chaincode (**SC1**). In addition, only peers (with chaincode installed) can access the chaincode logic. However, the chaincode logic remains inaccessible to other components, but operations can be invoked on the chaincode.

- **Endorsement**: Referring to the preceding *Architecture: conceptual view* diagram, it is clear that organizations (**O1** and **O2**) are part of **Consortium-X1**. They have defined channel (**C1**), where it is governed by the channel configuration (**CCon1**). Having said that, an endorsement policy (**EP #1**) is also part of channel configuration, **CCon1**. Endorsement policy (**EP #1**) gets attached to channel configuration (**CCon1**) when the chaincode is initiated. It is the endorsement policy that dictates the acceptance of transactions on ledger (**L1**). And transactions can only be accepted when the organizations (**O1** and **O2**) on the channel (**C1**) approve it.

- **Invocation**: Only after instantiation will client applications be able to send transaction proposals to the peers (**P1** and **P2**). Transaction proposals are like inputs to the chaincode (**SC1**), which will result in an *endorsed transaction response* by peer nodes **P1** and **P2** being sent back to the client applications, **O1App1** and **O2App2**, respectively. This will be discussed in further detail in the *Transaction flow* section of this chapter.

Referring to the diagram, organization 1 (**O1**) and organization 2 (**O2**) have chaincode installed on peers **P1** and **P2**, which are owned by **O1** and **O2**, respectively. However, as chaincode is initiated by **O1**, organization **O2** need not initiate the chaincode as it is already initiated by **O1**. In addition, the gossip protocol allows peers to communicate with one another.

Types of peers

Peers can be subdivided as follows:

- **Mandatory peers**: Endorsing peers, and non-endorsing peers, also known as committers and leader peers.
- **Option peers**: Anchor peers. These are optional, and a blockchain network can function and exist without them.

The following are the different types of peers available:

1. **Endorsing peers**: The preceding section covered endorsing peers in detail. Referring to the *Architecture*: *conceptual view* diagram, peers (**P1** and **P2**) have chaincode installed by administrators of organizations (**O1** and **O2**). Hence, they can endorse transactions, and are referred to as endorsing peers.

2. **Non-endorsing peers** (also known as committing peers): Referring to the preceding diagram, peer **P4** (owned by organization **O1**) does not have chaincode installed. The administrator of organization 1 (**O1**) chose to install chaincode only on **P1**, and not on **P4**. This highlights two points:
    - Firstly, organization administrators can selectively choose to install chaincode on peers.
    - Secondly, peers with chaincode installed are termed endorsing peers, and peers that do not have chaincode installed can exist on the channel. Such peers (**P4**) are non-endorsing peers (called committing peers). Every node on the channel is a committing peer:
        - Peers such as **P4** (non-endorsing peers, also known as committing peers) cannot generate transactions. However, they can accept or reject transactions to ledger (**L1**).
    - Peers with chaincode installed can generate transactions and also endorse transactions.
    - Committing peers receive blocks of transactions (transactions initiated by endorsing peers) and are validated before being committed to a local copy of the ledger (**L1**). Such a commit to the ledger copy (**L1**) by the peers (endorsers and committers) constitutes an append-only operation to the ledger.

Remember that the endorsement policy (**EP #1**) for chaincode, existing in channel configuration (**CCon1**), dictates which peers of an organization should digitally sign transaction before being appended to the ledger (**L1**) of the channel.

3. **Leader peer**: Organization **O1** has two peers (**P1** and **P4**) on the channel (**C1**), where **P1** is an endorser and **P4** is a committer. Hence, transactions need to be distributed to all peers (committers) in an organization (**O1**). The distribution of transactions means distributing from orderers to committing peers of the organization. To ensure a transaction distribution, a peer can be defined as a leader peer (statically), or any peer can assume the role of leader (dynamically). Hence, in our sample network, for **Channel-C1** and organization **O1**, peer **P1** is dynamically defined as the leader peer, which will distribute transactions to all peers of organization 1 (**O1**) that are attached to **Channel-C1**.

4. **Anchor peer**: For inter-organization, peer-to-peer communication, a channel requires an anchor peer. This is an optional peer and is only required when cross-organization communication is required.

 A peer can be all four. Example **P1** of **O1** is an endorser, a committer, a leader, and can be an anchor peer as well. In addition, for a channel, there will always be one endorser, one committer, and one leader.

Evolving the network

In this section, we will evolve the network further to realize requirement #**2**. Requirement #**2** wants the producer organization **O1** to execute private transactions and communications with **O3** (retail organization 3), as they have agreed on certain private discount rates and payments terms.

Administrators from the founder organization (**O5**) define a new consortium between the producer organization (**O1**) and a second retail organization (**O3**). Consortium definitions are defined in the network configuration (**NC05**). One of the organizations (**O1** or **O5**) can define a new channel (**C2**) for the new consortium (**X2**). Channel (**C2**) configuration resides in the channel configuration (**CCon2**). You may observe that the channel configuration for **C2** resides in **CCon2**, and is separate from **Channel-C1**'s configuration (**CCon1**). Both channel configurations are separate from the network configuration (**NC05**). Hence, only **O1** and **O3** have rights over **C2**, and **O5** has no rights over **Channel-C2**. **O5** only offers a resource (orderer service – **Ord O5**) to channel (**C2**).

The organization (**O3**) adds a peer (**P3**) to the channel (**C2**) and has a different ledger (**L2**). The scope of the ledger is confined to the channel, hence, **Channel-C1** has ledger **L1**, and **Channel-C2** has ledger **L2**. Chaincode **SC2** is installed and initiated on **Channel-C2**, and organization **O3**'s application (**O3App3)** uses **Channel-C2** to invoke transactions against chaincode **SC2**.

Physical realization of network configuration and channel configuration

This section walks though how configurations are physically realized in a blockchain network.

Logically, channel configuration (**CCon1** and **CCon2**) seems to be a single configuration for the channels (**C1** and **C2**, respectively). In practice, peers of the channel host a copy of the channel configuration. Logically, the network configuration, **NC05**, appears to exist as a single file for the blockchain network. However, in reality, it is replicated on all of the ordering nodes of the blockchain network.

When administrators configure networks and channels, they issue configuration transactions to the blockchain network. Such transactions are digitally signed by the organization (organization administrators), as defined in the policy files called modification policy (`mod_policy`).

`mod_policy` files are the policies within the network and channel configuration. For example, as you add more organizations to a blockchain, those organizations and their permissions are modified to `mod_policy` within the network configuration for the blockchain network.

Ordering service

Each ordering node maintains a copy of the network configuration and uses a system channel to execute configuration transactions and maintain a consistent copy of the network configuration. In the diagram, we have two ordering nodes—**O5** and **O1**. The founder organization (**O5**) added producer organization **O1** as the administrator by updating the network configuration (**NC05**). This modification further defines **O1** as the administrator of the blockchain network. The producer organization (**O1**) employs its resource (node) as an additional orderer (**O1**) to the blockchain network. Orderer **O5** is employed and maintained by organization **O5**, and its certificate is issued by **CA05**. While orderer **O1** is offered and maintained by organization **O1**, its certificate is issued by **CA01**. Network configuration (**NC05**) defines the exact permissions for the participants from the configured organizations (**O5** and **O1**).

The ordering service also collects endorsed transactions from client applications (dApp) and orders them in blocks. These blocks are then distributed to each committer node on the channel. When a consensus is reached, each committing peer will record and append the local copy of the ledger. Interestingly, you will notice that the ordering service has meticulously taken care of the distribution of transactions. Even though the same ordering service is used over multiple channels (**C1** and **C2**), it handles the distribution of the right transaction to the right channel. This is controlled and defined in the network configuration (**NC05**) and channel configurations (**CCon1** and **CCon2**).

Ordering nodes maintaining a consistent copy of network configuration

To understand how ordering nodes maintain a consistent copy of network configuration, we need to look at channels.

We know that there are two types of channels:

- **Application channels**: Channels **C1** and **C2** are examples of application channels.
- **System channels**: Ordering nodes are connected by a system channel, which allows them to distribute configuration transactions among themselves. Hence, when administrators try to configure the network, they issue configuration transactions on this system channel. The system channel (depicted in the diagram as **System Channel**) will then ensure the distribution of these configuration transactions across ordering nodes on the blockchain network.

In this configuration, applications **O1App1** and **O2App2** will transact on **Channel-C1**, based on chaincode **SC1**, and will use **Channel-C1** to communicate with peers **P1**, **P2**, and orderer **O5**. Application **O3App3** will effect a transaction based on chaincode **SC2**, and will use **Channel-C2** to communicate with peers **P3** and orderer **O5**. This clearly demonstrates precise decentralization, where different organizations can execute their specific transactions and store blocks on their own ledgers.

A node's behavior when part of multiple channels

The producer organization (**O1**) wants to have separate application channels, **C1** and **C2**, for consortia **X1** and **X2**, respectively. This will allow **O1** to enter into private transactions with organizations on these channels. Hence, the diagram shows **O1**'s peer, **P1**, and also hosts chaincode **SC2** installed on **P1**. Organization **01**'s client application (**O1App1**), to which **P1** belongs, will now be able to transact on **Channel-C2** based on logic defined in chaincode **SC2**.

Node behavior, which is an element of multiple channels, is controlled by the channel configuration for that channel. Channel configurations, **CCon1** and **CCon2**, define the operations available to a node (**P1**) when it is part of multiple channels, **C1** and **C2**, respectively. Similarly, application **O1App1** can now execute transactions on channels **C1** and **C2** based on chaincode **SC1** and **SC2**, respectively, which is again dictated by the channel configurations, **CCon1** and **CCon2**.

Hyperledger architecture (layered view) and components

This section will cover the Hyperledger framework architecture layer and components. As shown in the following diagram, the HLF architecture is divided into four major layers, and each layer has its components working in concert. Together, these layers, components, and their interactions constitute a permissioned blockchain network, as shown in the following diagram:

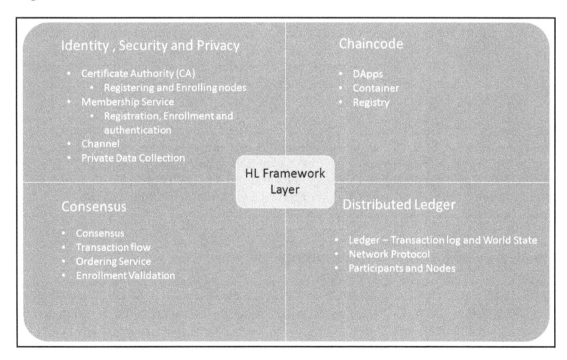

Architecture: Layered view

Identity, security, and privacy

This section covers aspects of blockchain architecture that are specific to identity, security, and privacy. There are various participants in a blockchain network, such as nodes (committers, endorsers, and suchlike), dApps and client applications, and network and channel administrators. Each of these participants needs to have an identity established, because it's the identity of these participants that determines their access permissions on the blockchain network and its resources. Principle is a set of identities and properties, where identity is a user ID, and properties include the organization it belongs to, the roles it is a member of, and suchlike. Hence, it's obvious that the permissions are determined by the properties of the identities.

HLF uses X.509 certificates for identities. However, the MSP validates identities and determines whether those identities are permitted in a blockchain network. At a high level, remember that MSP has the rules, which enables identities in the blockchain network. However, those identities must be trusted and verified by the public key infrastructure.

A permissioned HLF blockchain network tightly controls the identities of the participants. This is a mandatory two-step process—establishing the participants' identities and secure communication.

Public key infrastructure

Public key infrastructure (**PKI**) ensures secure communication in the blockchain network between various participants, and also authenticates the messages sent to the blockchain network. PKI comprises CAs, who are responsible for issuing digital certificates to participants (users, nodes, and so on). Participants are authenticated based on these certificates, and messages are then sent to the blockchain network.

In the Hyperledger framework's distributed blockchain network, root CA is an HLF CA, which is configured as a trust anchor. It is a self-certified root CA that also signs and certifies the leaf certificates of the intermediate CAs. In addition, these intermediate CAs can sign and certify other leaf intermediate CAs. Hence, for the given digital certificate, trust can be traced back to the root CA. This is termed a chain of trust. The HLF, and particularly HLF membership services, have a Fabric CA and intermediate CAs for secure functioning of the blockchain network.

The following are some of the key elements of PKI:

- Digital certificate
- Keys
- CAs
- **Certificate revocation list (CRL)**

Digital certificate

A digital certificate is a document comprising various properties of the certificate holder. These certificates are standard-compliant, and, in the case of HF, this is the X.509 standard.

Here are a few brief details regarding certificates:

- What is in a certificate? A certificate is like an identity card, and includes certificate data that consists of the following:
  - Algorithm information (such as SHA256)
  - Issuer information, including the validity of the certificate (time)
  - Subject information, including the following:
    - Subject details, such as the organization unit
    - Subject public key and signature algorithm details
- The subject of a certificate (the user or node) can use that certificate to prove their identity.
- To prove their identity, the subject can use a private key to sign any communication (transaction and suchlike) that is sent to the blockchain network. A subject's public key is in the certificate itself. However, the subject's private key is secret and private.
- All the information contained in the certificate is encrypted in such a way that any change to it will mark the certificate as invalid.
- The subject signs using their private key and uses this certificate to prove their identity. As other parties trust the identity provider, also known as the CA, the interacting party can trust the subject. Parties trust the CA and believe that the certificate shown by the subject has not been tampered with.

Keys

In this section, we will cover digital signatures and public and private keys. In the preceding description, we saw that messages are signed by the subject. Signing a message is termed the digital signature of the message. It is the digital signature that guarantees message integrity and authentication. Authentication ensures that parties involved in a transaction are sure about the identity of the message sender or creator, and integrity affirms that the message was not modified/tampered with during transit. Hence, it is the digital signature that guarantees integrity and authentication. The transaction (message) sender will sign the message using their private key and send it to the recipient. The recipient will use the sender's public key (widely known) to verify the integrity and authenticity of the message. This means that the recipient will use the sender's public key to ensure that it was sent by the sender who is claiming to be the sender, and who is the expected sender. A combination of keys, both public and private, ensures secure communication over the blockchain network.

CAs

CAs are mostly included in a Docker image with HLF release and are released as an HLF CA component. In the case of a blockchain network, a CA has the following purposes:

- Registering nodes
- Enrolling nodes

In HLF, Certificate Authority is a CA service that creates and issues certificates (enrollment certificates) to participating nodes, allowing them to join and participate in the blockchain network. These certificates (enrollment certificates) are in the standard X.509 v3 format. However, an HLF CA can be extended by enterprises and they can even replace it, if needed. CAs issue X.509-compliant certificates to participants (user, groups, and nodes). It is these certificates that enable participants to transact and interact on the blockchain network. CAs issue certificates to participants, and these certificates include various pieces of information pertaining to the subject (participant), as shown previously. CAs only issue those certificates after signing those certificates with their private keys. Hence, the certificates issued by the CA are signed by CAs and, since these CAs are trusted, the participant is also trusted. In addition, the information included in the certificate is trusted, as it's signed by the CA. As long as the recipients have the public key of the CA, they can trust the certificate.

In addition, when the subject (participant/sender) signs any transaction, the recipient can use the subject's (sender/participants) public key to ensure the authenticity and integrity of the message. Trusted CAs include DigiCert and Verisign. These certificates do not have any private keys—either of the CA or of the participant. In a blockchain network, every participant (subject/actor) needs to have a digital identity that should be issued by the organization's CA, which actually means that the CA facilitates a verifiable digital identity for the participant.

The following types of CA are available:

- Root CAs are biggies, like Symantec, who self-sign their own certificates and then issue those certificates to other CAs. Intermediate CAs are CAs that have a certificate issued by the root CA or by another intermediate CA. This results in a *TrustChain* (chain of trust) of certificates. Organizations that use CAs can use intermediate CAs with confidence, since the *TrustChain* will allow them to trace the certificate back to the root CA. Also, the *TrustChain* limits the root CA's exposure, which is paramount from the security perspective of the *TrustChain*. Also, various organizations participating on the blockchain network can use different intermediate CAs and may have different, or the same, root CAs.
- HLF offers an inbuilt CA called Fabric CA, which is a root CA for that HLF blockchain network. It is a private CA for the Fabric blockchain network; it cannot offer SSL certificates for use in browsers. Hence, organizations can use commercial public root and intermediate CAs for their HLF blockchain network. The capabilities of the HLF CA, also known as the Fabric CA, are as follows:
  - The HLF CA can either register identities or can be configured to use existing enterprise LDAPs as a user registry
  - For member organizations, users, and administrators, the HLF CA can issue, renew, and revoke enrollment certificates and root certificates for the blockchain network
- The HLF CA generates self-signed X.509 certificates, and there can be one or more Fabric CAs, where there will be one root CA and the remainder are intermediate CAs, and where the chain of trust is followed by virtue of PKI.

CRL

CAs can revoke certificates, and such revoked certificates do not constitute expiring certificates. In the case of compromised identities, certificates can be revoked, and put into a list called a CRL. It is recommended that any party who wants to verify the identity of any other party's (the subject party) should first refer to the CRL to check whether the party (the subject party's) certificate is included in the revoked list.

The membership service

We now know that PKI offers verifiable identities to participants. However, how can these participants represent themselves as trusted participants from a participating organization on a blockchain network? Every organization manages its participants under a single MSP. However, organizations can have multiple MSPs if they want to manage a participant's different **organization units** (**OU**), such as financial and legal units. If you check the certificate issued to a subject from a CA, it will include OU information. This allows further control of the access to channels based on OUs.

The membership service manages a participant's identity and is used for the validation of participants and their authentication. Specific privileges on system resources (a network, channel, or suchlike) are controlled in the access control list of the blockchain network. The membership service code is executed on peers and orderers. It is responsible for authenticating, authorizing identities, and managing those identities on the HLF blockchain network. The participants of the HLF blockchain network have identities where the PKI generates certificates that are linked to the participants (such as network components, organizations, dApps and client applications). This facilitates the creation of an access control rule for participants at the network level, as well as at the channel level, where a channel is a subset of a blockchain network where participants conduct private transactions. Access controls and channels in a blockchain network together address confidentiality and privacy challenges:

- **Authentication**: HLF uses PKI to verify the identities of users and devices.
- **Authorization**: HLF uses **role-based access control** (**RBAC**) to control access to an entity example controlling an identity's read and write access to an entity (for example, a ledger). Access control to identities for given resources is based on RBAC, where identities are assigned to roles, authorization policies are defined for resources, and rules are defined that determine which roles are authorized to access what on that resource.

MSP

This is the identity management solution for the HLF blockchain network. MSP performs the following tasks:

- It registers and enlists network and channel participants
- It maps certificates to members or participating organizations
- For an organization, MSP identifies the roles (administrative and suchlike) a participant can play

- It defines the participant's network and channel, and access privileges, such as read and write

Its principal activities are as follows:

- MSP identifies the root CAs and intermediate CAs who can further define the members of a domain, also known as an organization, either by listing the identities of their users, or by authorizing CAs to assign valid identities to their members
- MSP represents an organization, and is also responsible for RBAC on a network, and channels of the member of that organization
- An organization can have one or more OUs, and enrollment certificates (X.509 certificates) include an OU attribute in the certificate to define that organization's area of business

Types of MSP

In this section, we will cover the types of MSP. Broadly speaking, there are three—network MSP, channel MSP, and local MSP:

1. **Network MSP**: An MSP at the network level is used to define the blockchain network that is authorized to perform administrative tasks at the network level, such as maintaining networks and creating channels:
   - **Scope**: Network level
   - **Duties**: Administrative activities, such as defining channels

2. **Channel MSP**: A channel (also known as a global) MSP is defined in the channel configuration. However, each node has a local copy of the channel/global MSP, which is kept in sync by consensus. Each participating organization on the channel has an MSP defined, and all the nodes on that channel will share the MSP and, hence, will be able to authenticate the channel participant using the same single source of truth for authentication. Hence, any new participating organization first needs to add its MSP to the channel configuration to participate in transactions on the channel. A channel MSP is mostly used for identity validation, and does not need to sign transactions. All the members of a channel are familiar with the configuration of an MSP, where members of that organization participate. This is termed a channel MSP:
   - **Scope**: Channel level
   - **Duties**: Establishes a chain of trust by defining administration and participation rights to members of entities at the channel level

3. **Local MSP**: MSPs authenticate nodes and users. Each node and user has a local MSP in their local filesystem. To authenticate member messages, and to define permissions outside the channel context, peers, orderers, and clients maintain an instance of a local MSP:

- **Scope**: Each node has a local MSP that defines that node's permissions
- **Duties**: To authenticate member messages and define permissions outside network and channel levels and maintain a local copy of the MSP as configurations are applied locally
- **Facts**:
    - Nodes such as committers, endorsers, and orderers, are termed local MSPs. Examples include defining peer admins and suchlike.
    - Users such as client users use local MSPs to authenticate themselves in relation to the transaction performed on the channel.
    - A participant's membership in an organization is determined by the root or intermediate CA that is part of the local MSP.
- **Structure**: The following list defines the various elements that constitute the MSP structure. For each type of element, there is a sub-folder and a local MSP is stored in the local folder as a file folder, inside that particular sub-folder.
    - Structure-wise, various elements constitute a local MSP, including the following:
        - **Root CA and intermediate CA**: The root CA contains self-signed certificates (X.509 standard) of the root CAs that are trusted by the organization represented in the MSP. The intermediate CA contains a list of intermediate CA certificates that are trusted by the organization.
        - **Organization unit**: This is an optional element that contains a list of OUs and is used to restrict organization members.

- **Administrator:** This contains the identities of the actors who are administrators for an organization. It is like defining the role. However, access privileges (such as adding a new organization and suchlike) are determined by system resources, such as channel configuration or network configuration policies. The role attribute in a CA issue certificate also defines a participant's role in the organization and not on the blockchain network. It is the system resource (channel, network, and suchlike) policies that define that role's privileges on the blockchain network's system resource.

- **Revoked certificates list**: Logically, this optional list is the same list as CAs and the CRL. However, it also defines the revocation of membership of the participant from the organization.

- **Node identity**: This is a mandatory element and defines the identity of the node. One should exist in the local MSP, along with the KeyStore (private key) and the node identity, allowing a node (a peer such as an endorser) to authenticate itself in the message that the node sends on the network or channel; for example, the certificate that the endorser sends as part of the response to a transaction proposal.

- **KeyStore**: This mandatory element is a node's key that a node (committer, orderers, client node, and suchlike) uses to digitally sign a transaction. It is only part of a local MSP and not part of a channel MSP, since the channel MSP does not send transactions and, hence, is not required to sign transactions.
- **TLS root CA and TLS intermediate CA**: TLS communications are sent when a node wants to connect to another node, example the committer peer and connects with orderers to get a ledger's recent updates. This element contains self-signed certificates of the root CA/intermediate CA.

 All MSPs (network, channel, and local) should identity and interact with root or intermediate CAs to ensure the establishment of a chain of trust.

Referring back to the diagram in the *Architecture – conceptual view* section, the network configuration (**NC05**) uses the MSP of organization **O1** to ensure the association of participant **P1** with organization 1 (**O1**). The network configuration (**NC05**) then uses the MSP name defined in the access policies to further grant privileges to **O1**'s participants (**P1**, **P4**, and **P6**); for example, defining **P1** as the administrator from organization 1 (**O1**) as the administrator of the blockchain network. Referring to the following MSP diagram, each peer has its own local MSP copy in its filesystem. Also, each peer keeps a copy of the global MSP of the channels it belongs to; for example, peer **P1** belongs to **Channel-C1** and **Channel-C2**. Hence, although it has its own local MSP, it also contains a copy of the channel configuration, **CCon1** and **CCon2**, for channels 1 and 2, respectively. A local copy of the channel configuration also means a local copy of the global MSP. Hence, **P1** has a copy of the global MSP for **Channel-C1** and **Channel-C2**.

For each peer, the trust domain is the organization to which it belongs, which is part of a peer's local MSP. However, to allow that organization (and also its peers) to transact and communicate on a channel, an organization's MSP needs to be added to the channel configuration:

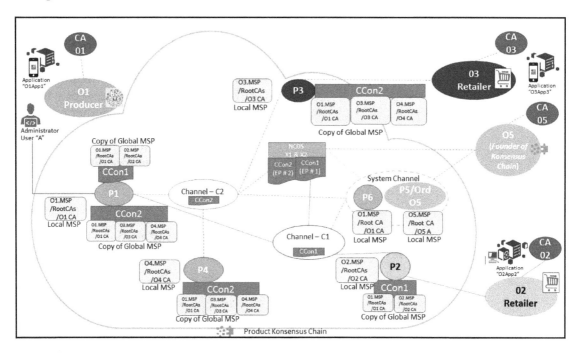

Membership service provider

The diagram also shows that user A belongs to organization 1 (**O1**), and that user A's identity is issued by **CA01** (CA of organization 1). A local MSP copy of peer 1 (**P1**), which belongs to **O1**, contains the identity information of user A. Depending on the type of operation requested by the user (local or channel-level), peers will verify user A's identity. Given that peers **P1**, **P3**, and **P4** are on **Channel-C2**, they have a copy of the global MSP. The global MSP will contain the certificate and other details of all the members (**P1**, **P3**, and **P4**) of the channel (**C2**). Also, each peer has its own local MSP.

Local-level transaction: Referring to the following diagram, it is evident that MSPs can be found in two places—channel configuration (as a channel MSP), and as a local peer (local MSP). Local MSPs are for applications, users, peers, and orderers, and they define the privileges (permissions), such as the administration of the peer, for that node. Every node and user has a local MSP. For example, a user's local MSP allows the user to authenticate themselves on the transaction, as well as defining a node's participatory rights and suchlike. When user A tries to execute a local-level transaction (such as installing chaincode), peer **P1** verifies the identity of user A by referring to its local MSP copy. By means of verification, **P1** ensures that user A belongs to organization 1, and has the privileges to perform that transaction. Only upon verification can the installation transaction be completed successfully.

Channel-level transaction: Every organization that is participating on the channel must have a channel MSP. All peers and orderers on the channel have the same view of the channel MSP. When user A tries to execute a channel-level transaction, such as initiating chaincode, which requires the agreement of all the participating organizations, then peer **P1** will check the channel MSP before executing the transaction. Administrative and participatory rights in the channel are defined as the channel MSP.

Channel (privacy provider)

Confidentiality in blockchain business networks is achieved with segregated communication between network participants, which is achieved by using HLF channels. Transactions in a blockchain business network are executed on a channel, where transacting parties are authenticated and authorized to effect transactions on that channel. By default, all participants in a network are part of a channel. However, for private transactions, organizations need to create separate channels and authorize members to that channel. Ledgers are separated from channel to channel and, hence, ledger data cannot move between channels. The separation of ledger data and peers by channels allows private and confidential transactions between organizations that are still part of the same blockchain network. Data separation between channels is achieved by configuring membership services, chaincode, and the gossip protocol. Here, data includes transaction information, the state of the ledger, and channel membership. This data is restricted to just those verified peers who are members of the channel.

A client SDK passes parameters, such as the MSP ID (unique within a channel), policies, and members (organizations) to the network configuration chaincode. This invocation creates configuration transactions on the network configuration chaincode. These versioned configuration transactions (configtx) result in the creation of a genesis block on the channel's ledger. This genesis block records information such as the channel configuration. As soon as a member is added to a channel, it gets access to relevant information on the genesis block.

Participants can deploy chaincode once the channel setup is complete. Then, participants can propose transactions, endorse, order, and validate transactions. Access rights are granted to participants by their MSP, and these rights define the limits of a participant on a channel. Participants outside the channel do not have access to any transactions or messages on the channel. Hence, segregating transactions based on their channels enhances the privacy offered by the blockchain network.

PDC

We know that channels facilitate private and confidential transactions between organizations. However, what if you want to have a few organizations on a channel, but still want to keep some of the data private to a subset of organizations participating in that channel. Channels have advantages. However, if you keep creating multiple channels between organizations that require private communication, then you might end up with channel-explosion, which will lead to maintenance overheads. You have to maintain MSPs, policies, and chaincode versions, and this does not allow us to address the use case of having private data for a subset of organizations in a channel. To address the challenge of allowing private data for a subset of organizations in a channel, HLF (from v1.2 onward) offers the facility to create PDCs.

PDC – more privacy in channels

With PDC, subsets of organizations can query, comment, and endorse private data, inside a channel without creating a separate channel.

Referring to the following diagram, peer **P1** belongs to organization **O1**, **P3** belongs to organization **O3**, and Peer **P7** belongs to organization **O4**. Here, **P1**, **P3**, and **P7** are all on **Channel-C1**. However, organization 1 (**O1**) wants to have a private data exchange with **P3**, and also wants a separate private data exchange with **P7**. If only the channel concept is followed, then the system will have multiple channels. Organization **O1** (**P1**) and organization **O3** (**P3**) will have a separate channel, while organization **O1** (**P1**) and organization **O4** (**P7**) will have a separate channel. Another way of handling this requirement is to allow private transactions between channel members in PDC:

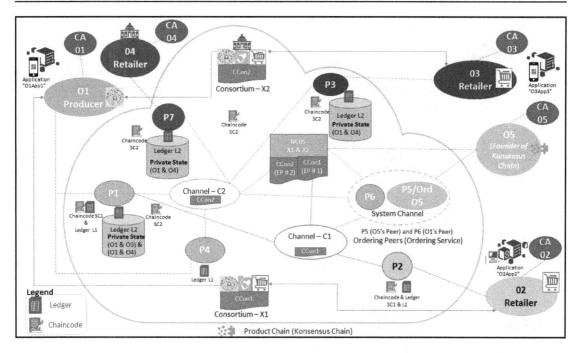

Ledger and private data

From the ledger perspective, each peer has a ledger comprising states—the current state and the transaction log. We will be covering ledgers in detail in subsequent sections in this chapter. The diagram shows the current state as the ledger state, and shows the transaction log in the ledger. Here, organization 1 has peer **P1**, organization 3 has peer **P3**, and organization 7 has peer **P4**. As **P1** and **P3** are sharing private data, the diagram shows the private state (**O1** and **O3**) at peers **P1** and **P3**. In addition, since **P1** and **P7** are sharing private data, the diagram shows the private state (**O1** and **O4**) at peers **P1** and **P7**. Chaincode (**SC2**) is *instantiated* on the channel (**C2**); hence, all the smart contracts within the chaincode (**SC2**) are available for applications on the channel (**C2**). This private state will be replicated to all the peers from an organization that wants to have private communication. Those authorized peers will be able to see the hash of the data, which is located in the main ledger, and the real private data will be on their private database. As private data is not synced with unauthorized peers, they will never be able to see the private data. However, the main ledger's data hash is accessible to them.

PDC is an excellent way to comply with the **General Data Protection Regulation** (GDPR). One such regulation stipulates that data owners can delete private data. However, we know that blockchain is immutable and, once data is recorded to the ledger, it cannot be deleted. With PDC, private data remains in your private database. It is not written to the ledger. Only the hash of the data is written to the ledger.

Technically, PDC is supported by two key elements:

1. **Private database**: This is also known as the SideDB on each peer, and participates in private data communication. You will recall the anchor peer discussed in this chapter. Since ordered nodes are not involved in private data communication, anchor peers need to be set for P2P communication via the gossip protocol.
2. **Data hash**: Hash is on the current state, the main ledger. It serves as the transaction evidence, cannot be removed, and is accessible to all peers from the channel, irrespective of whether they are into a PDC.

Distributed ledger

This section covers aspects of blockchain architecture that are specific to the ledger. It also covers nodes, such as peers and orderers, and, while defining the orderers, we will also cover the transaction flow process.

Nodes

The deployment view of HLF comprises nodes that are connected as P2P networks with a distributed edger that is shared among these nodes. Nodes can have different roles in the HLF—peers and orderers.

Peers: These propose transactions, save/apply and commit transactions, and maintain a local copy of the ledger.

The types of peers are as follows:

- **Endorsing peers**, also known as endorsers: These obtain a transaction proposal from the client/apps, verify the client signature, get the RW state of the world state to be affected by the transaction, and send these states to orderers.
- **Committing peers**, also known as committers (non-endorsing nodes): Following endorsement and ordering, these validate the transaction, applying the result of the transaction to the local ledger. This is committed to the ledger and the transaction becomes immutable.

> In HLF, every endorser node is also a committer node. However, not every committer needs to be an endorser node.

- **Orderers:** At least one orderer should exist in a blockchain network. Orderers ensure the correct ordering of transactions.

Peers

Peers constitute a blockchain network and host ledgers and chaincode. We saw in the conceptual view of architecture that each peer has a copy of the chaincode and ledger. Peers offer APIs, which allow applications to interact with them and also to start, stop, configure, delete, and reconfigure the peers. A peer can host a ledger and chaincode, and it is feasible for peers to host only ledgers and not chaincode (application chaincode). Peers usually always have system chaincode. The HLF SDK offers APIs, which allows applications to interact with peers, since it is the peers to which applications connect if they need to query a ledger or invoke a transaction on the ledger. Then, in turn, the peer invokes the chaincode to effect the execution of that transaction.

Along with orderers, peers ensure the synchronicity of ledgers on every peer. We will walk through the transaction flow in subsequent sections, which will highlight peer involvement. Here is a brief synopsis of that:

- The application (the party that wants to execute a transaction) connects to a peer. Where the application and peer are from the same organization, certificates are issued by an organization's CA.
- The peer invokes the chaincode, which results in the generation of a proposal response. The response depends on the transaction request from the application. For instance, if the application requested a query to the ledger, then the proposal response will have a query result or, if the application requested an update to the ledger, then the proposal response will include the proposed ledger updates.
- The application receives a proposal response from the peer:
    - If it was a query (*ledger-query-transaction*), then the process is completed as the application has received its response
    - If it was a ledger update (*ledger-update-transaction*), the request then proceeds to the next step
- For a ledger update request (*ledger-update-transaction*), the peer cannot send the response as the update to the ledger first needs to be agreed by all the participating peers. This agreement to change the ledger is termed a consensus.
- As a consensus is required for the *ledger-update-transaction*, the peer returns a proposed update response to the application, which is actually a snapshot of the change that the peer is proposing. This is similar to a change being performed on the ledger only once a consensus is reached.

- The application receives responses. The application will build a transaction from all the responses and send it to the orderer's node.
- Orderers will collect this transaction and various other transactions from the blockchain network and compile them into a block.
- Orderers will then distribute this block to all the peer (committer) nodes, which also includes the peer to which the application (in this sample) sent the initial request.
- All the peers, including the peer in this context, will validate the transaction.
- Upon successful transaction validation, the peers will update the local copy of the ledger.
- Once the ledger is updated, the peer to which the initial request was sent will generate an event.
- This event will be received by the application, which marks the completion of the update transaction.

We saw in the *Architecture – conceptual view* section that peers are owned and contributed by various organizations, and this group of peers forms the blockchain network. Applications that are developed by an organization usually connect to the peers of that organization.

 A blockchain network does not literally depend on the organization and its contributed peers. However, there should be at least one organization existing with one peer. Interestingly, organization peers (belonging to any organization) host the same ledger; however, every organization is free to use its own code language for building application and presentation logic.

From the *Architecture*: *conceptual view* diagram, we know that peers are connected to channels. Channels also have channel configuration and contain the global MSP. This global MSP helps to map peers to their organization, as the certificate issued to the peer emanates from the CA of that organization. By way of an example, refer to the *MSP* diagram in this chapter. Here, peer **P1**'s certificate is issued by the CA (**CA O1**). The channel configuration (**CCon1**) determines that the identities (participants such as **P1**) are issued by the CA (**CA O1**), which is from organization 1 (**O1**). This is defined in **O1**. The MSP is contained in the global MSP of the channel configuration. This helps in associating a peer with an organization.

 Each peer has a digital certificate issued by the organization's CA. This digital certificate acts as the identity of the peer.

At a given point in time, a peer can only belong to/be owned by one organization. A peer can reside anywhere; on a local machine, in an enterprise on premise, on the cloud, and suchlike. It is the certificate (identity) of the peer that maps and associates that peer with an organization. This mapping is provided by the MSP. Along with the authentication of the user via the MSP, channel configuration also involves access policies, which determines the privileges assigned to a peer (the peer's identity). Details of this can be found in the *MSP* section. However, in short, the mapping of an identity to an organization is defined by the MSP, along with the roles assigned to the peer in that particular organization, and also the rights (privileges) assigned to that identity.

Orderers and transaction process flow

In a blockchain network, orderers maintain a ledger's synchronicity and consistency. We have seen details pertaining to a *ledger-update-transaction*, which needs all the participating peers in the network to reach an agreement in order to approve an update to the ledger. The agreement process of receiving approvals from other peers to update the ledger is called a consensus. Once a transaction is approved by all the peers, it is committed to the ledger and the client application is further updated with the success of the commit (an update to the ledger). The following are the stages of a *ledger-update-transaction:*

- **Proposal**: This is the stage where the transaction proposal is sent by the client application to the channel's peers
- **Endorsement**: This is the stage where the transaction is simulated
- **Packaging proposal response**: At this stage, each endorser will return its signed endorsement back to the client
- **Verify and send for ordering**: At this stage, the client application then verifies the proposal response and sends the transaction message for ordering
- **Distribution:** At this stage of the transaction process, orderers will distribute the block to peers
- **Validation and tagging**: At this stage, peers will receive a block from the orderers and they will tag it as valid or invalid
- **Notifications**: When the ledger is appended, client applications are notified at this stage

> We will be talking about transaction flow in detail in the *Consensus everywhere* section later.

Ledger

As we discovered in `Chapter 1`, *Exploring Blockchain and BaaS*, accounting ledgers have transaction history recorded as credit and debit transactions, while a statement shows the current balance. All the credit and debit entries lead to the current balance. Now, let's build the analogy, where the current balance is the current state of the ledger, and credit and debit entries are the transaction log entries. Current state and transaction logs, together, form a ledger; a blockchain ledger. To interact (also known as transact) on a distributed ledger, chaincode needs to be invoked:

- **Current state**: Also termed *world state* or just *state*, this is a key-value pair that shows the current value of the ledger states, and it changes frequently as states are created, appended, or erased.
- **Transaction log**: This is the set of changes that leads to the current world state. Transactions that are ordered and sequenced in blocks are appended to the blockchain. Sets of transaction lead to the current value of the world state. These transactions, once ordered and sequenced, cannot be modified and, hence, the block and blockchain, also known as the ledger, become immutable.

 The ledger is distributed; hence, it is on all the peers. We have seen in transaction flows that a consensus is required before a transaction is committed to the ledger. Hence, the ledger is kept in sync with participating peers.

Each peer node has a copy of the ledger. This copy contains the transaction log and world state results, stored as key-value pairs in the database. DLT in HLF has two aspects; a world state, and a transaction log. A ledger state comprises a key-value pair. The world state is an aggregated state of the distributed ledger at a given point in time. The world state allows consumers to get the current state of the ledger. The equation for the ledger is as follows:

$$distributed\ ledger = world\ state + transaction\ log$$

The following diagram shows a ledger consisting of the world state and transaction log. The transaction log comprises various blocks, with each block containing one or more transactions:

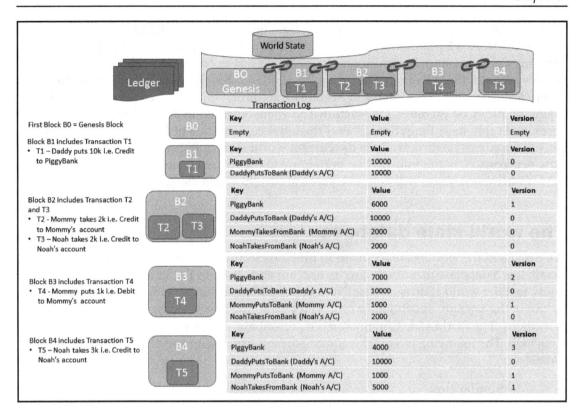

Ledger state and the transaction log

This example shows the **PiggyBank** of a boy named **Noah**. The world state and the transaction log are empty at the start. This is represented by the **Genesis Block (B0)**. **Block B1 includes Transaction T1**, where **Daddy puts 10k i.e. Credit to PiggyBank**. This is like a debit to daddy's account. The first transaction is represented by block 1 (**B1**). Block 1 represents the ledger state, with **Key** as **PiggyBank** and a **Value** of **10000**. Also, it has ledger state with **Key** as **DaddyPutsToBank** and a **Value** of **10000**. Both the ledger states are at **Version 0**. **Version 0** indicates that it is a starting version number and that they have not been updated since they were created.

Applications invoke the chaincode, which actually accesses the ledger states via APIs to perform operations such as get and put on states using the **state** key.

Noah's mommy and Noah take money from the **PiggyBank**. Block **B2 includes Transaction T2 and T3**. Here, **T2** represents the transaction where **Mommy takes 2k i.e. Credit to Mommy's account**, and **T3** represents a transaction where **Noah takes 2k i.e. Credit to Noah's account**. **PiggyBank** is debited by 4k. Similarly, **Block B3 includes Transaction T4**, where **Mommy puts 1k i.e. Debit to Mommy's account**, which is 1k credit to **PiggyBank**. Likewise, **Block B4 includes Transaction T5**, where **Noah takes 3k i.e. Credit to Noah's account**. At this state, **PiggyBank** shows the latest current state of **PiggyBank**, which is 4k. Hence, the current state represents the current world state of **PiggyBank**. Even if the world state gets corrupted and information pertaining to the current state is destroyed, replaying the transactions in order will help to create the current world state.

The world state database

We discussed the world state database in previous sections. Here, let's examine it in more detail. It is a database that offers queries and appends itself to the states of the ledger. We know that the world state is modeled as a key-value store that is versioned. Here, the values of the keys are appended or retrieved by applications via simple `put` and `get` operations. The world state is maintained in a database, which could be either LevelDB or CouchDB. The following is a quick comparison and lists recommendations for this database:

- **Similarities**:
    - Both can store binary data.
    - Both support chaincode operations, such as `get` and `set`. This is where `get` and `set` are essentially getting and setting the asset (the key's value).
    - Both support range queries, where keys are queried by range.
    - Both also support composite keys; for example, a combination of asset ID and owner ID can be used to get all the assets a particular owner owns.
- **Differences**: Business applications today model assets as JSON. Hence, CouchDB allows applications to perform rich queries to chaincode where assets are JSON modeled, using CouchDB's JSON query language:
    - LevelDB is the default database, and is collocated with a node, mostly embedded in the same operating system process.
    - CouchDB runs on a separate operating system process. However, it maintains a one-to-one relationship with network nodes and CouchDB instances.

- **Recommendations**:
    - LevelDB is recommended when the states are simple key-value pairs.
    - When the state structure is JSON, then CouchDB is recommended.
    - It is possible to start with LevelDB and later move to CouchDB. However, I personally recommend modeling assets' data as JSON and therefore use CouchDB.
    - Indexing is recommended for CouchDB, where indexes can be packaged alongside chaincode in a different directory. The moment chaincode is installed and initiated on peers, indexes also get deployed to channels and the chaincode's database for states also known as CouchDB.
- **Key Feature-Pluggable**: HLF has various components that are pluggable, and a database is one of them. Businesses can have a relational database, a graph store, or a temporal database as the database of choice for the world state.

Chaincode

In `Chapter 1`, *Exploring Blockchain and BaaS*, we learned about ledgers. There are different ledgers, for example, sales ledgers to store financial transactions, purchase ledgers to record spending and purchasing, while general ledgers record accounts, liabilities, expenses, income, and suchlike. Similarly, in HLF, transaction logs are the ledgers that record activities. These activities are also termed *transactions*. A ledger's world state tracks the transactions, which changes the world state of the ledger. The world state is a key-value pair, which is versioned, and, along with the transaction logs, it constitutes the ledger, which is available on all the participating nodes on the blockchain network. Now, the question is: who proposes changes to a ledger's world state? Well, the answer is dApps. Client applications issue transactions to the blockchain network via the execution of business logic in the chaincode, which are comprised of smart contract(s).

 All the nodes are coordinated in terms of the latest copy of the smart contract.

Now, refer back to the diagram in the *Ledger* section earlier in this chapter. In that **PiggyBank** sample, the account balance of **PiggyBank** and Daddy, Mommy, and Noah's account shows the world view of the asset transfer (also known as transactions) that happened between various parties and the **PiggyBank** account. When Mommy and Noah take from **PiggyBank**, it is represented in block **B2**, as transactions **T2** and **T3**. Here, the **PiggyBank Version** changes from **0** to **1**, as it represents a change in value for the key, **PiggyBank**. Whenever there is a change in value, a new version is created. All those transactions are executed against the chaincode, which results in state changes in the work state. So, what is chaincode?

Chaincode (and its smart contract): This is a distributed computer program that is available across the HLF blockchain network. In the PiggyBank sample, it's the chaincode that enables the movement of assets (dollars) between accounts without the involvement of a third party or an intermediary. Daddy, Mommy, and Noah were able to perform transactions without a third party's involvement.

Chaincode, a computer program, is compiled and deployed across the blockchain network. Upon approval, chaincode is deployed to the distributed blockchain network. It runs in isolation from ordering services or peer processes, inside a Docker container. dApps logic is implemented in chaincode, where chaincode is used to initialize the ledger state and then manage it, which is handled by the SDKs. Chaincode can be invoked by client applications. Hence, two types of transactions are performed for chaincode—deploy transactions and invoke transactions.

- **Chaincode deploy transaction**: Users, via participating nodes, author a chaincode (in Golang and similar) and use HLF SDK to issue a deploy transaction to the blockchain network. The permission to deploy chaincode is defined as access control and an ECert is issued by the HLF CA. Chaincode runs in a secure Docker container.
- **Chaincode invoke transaction**: The dApps/client application will use SDK to propose a change to the world state of the ledger by issuing a transaction that results in an invoke to chaincode. Chaincode's `invoke` function is called by the application by passing the function name and transaction parameters defined in the chaincode function. Using the command line or via the SDK, query transactions can be executed against the `invoke` function of the chaincode. However, in this `invoke` function call, there is no proposal to change the world state of the ledger.

Peers execute the invoke transactions, and each committing peer commits a transaction by updating the local copy of the world state. We will get into a detailed analysis of chaincode, the registry, and suchlike in subsequent chapters. Hence, this chapter is limited to an introduction to chaincode.

Consensus everywhere

The agreement process of receiving approvals from other peers to update the ledger is called a **consensus**. A consensus ensures the following:

- It ensures that ledger transactions are synchronized throughout the blockchain network
- It ensures that only valid and approved transactions are appended to the ledger
- It ensures that when transactions are appended, they follow the same sequence as is set by the orderers

For a consensus to work, it is important that the transaction order is established and maintained and that there is an effective way to reject invalid transactions from becoming appended to the ledger. This can be achieved by PBFT, which ensures file replicas to keep each copy consistent. Bitcoin uses mining for ordering, where each computing node will solve a puzzle and define the order. HLF offers various consensus mechanisms to choose from—SOLO or Kakfa.

A consensus goes beyond just establishing the order of transactions. In HLF, a consensus plays an important role in the transaction flow—from proposal to endorsement, to ordering, validation, and appending. Throughout the transaction flow, identity verification happens at various stages. It is an ongoing process. Payloads are signed by endorsers, and peers, and the payload gets verified and authenticated repeatedly, throughout the transaction flow. To achieve a consensus, it is important to ensure that the order of the transaction is met and that transactions have gone through the endorsement policy. Before committing, it is important to ensure that sufficient endorsements are achieved and that the transactions have passed the versioning checks, where the current state is agreed before committing to the ledger. A versioning check is a check against double spending and other data integrity threats.

 The transaction flow diagram and process flow are the representation of an ongoing consensus process.

To me, the whole transaction flow is a consensus process. If you check the following transaction flow, peers reach agreement regarding the order of the transactions and the content of the transactions. This is achieved by going through various stages of the transaction flow. Under the hood, SDK manages the whole consensus process and the client is notified at the notification stage when the process is concluded.

The channel (application channel) contains details about the consensus options and orderer organizations. For example, the channel configuration has a parameter called Kafka broker. If it is set with `ConsensusType` as Kafka, then it's set for the channel's orders as the consensus algorithm. It is generally established during the bootstrapping of the blockchain network and, once configured in the channel configuration and the blockchain network, is bootstrapped; then, it's impossible to change it via configuration. Also, note that the MSP is synchronized via a consensus, too. The consensus is the ordering service, and you will get this clarified when you walk through transaction flow in the following section.

BFT versus CFT: Consensus algorithms (protocols) are pluggable in HLF, allowing designers to choose a consensus algorithm based on the use case. For cases when a blockchain business network is composed as a single enterprise, or all the participating organizations are fully trusted, then BFT is not the ideal consensus algorithm as the trust already exists. CFT algorithms can be used as they are more performant and offer better throughput. However, for decentralized distributed use cases, which include multi parties, BFT is the most suitable consensus algorithm.

Transaction flow

Ledger's synchronicity and consistence is maintained by the orderers. Consensus is met, before an update to the ledger is approved. Ledger is updated only upon approval by all the peers. This is part of transaction flow; and will be covered in detail in this section.

The following diagram shows the transaction flow :

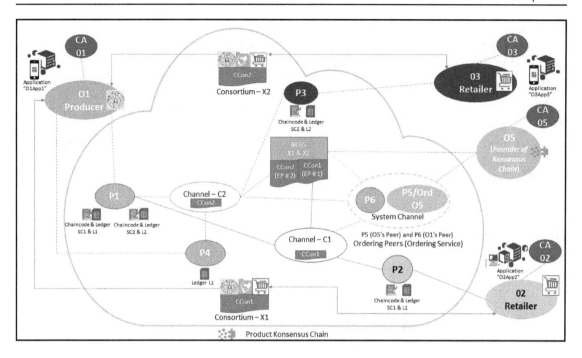

Transaction flow

The following are the stages of a transaction flow:

Proposal: The client application sends *ledger-update-transaction* to the peers on the channel. Referring to the preceding diagram, the client application, **O1App1**, sends (proposes) a transaction on **Channel-C1**. When the chaincode is installed and initiated, an endorsement policy is added to the channel configuration (**CCon1**). The endorsement policy for the channel (**C1**) defines that organization **O1**, and organization **O2** must approve the transaction. Hence, when a transaction is proposed, it goes to the endorsing peers on channel (**C1**), which belongs to organization **O1** and organization **O2**. Referring to the diagram, it goes to **P1** and **P2**, as the peers are also endorsing peers for organizations **O1** and **O2**.

Technically speaking, the application uses APIs, which result in the transaction proposal. The transaction proposal is akin to a request to execute the chaincode's functions so that ledger data can be read/updated. Here, applications use an SDK (Node, Python, or Java) and one of the APIs to propose such transactions. The SDK will take care of packaging the transaction proposal in an architecture format (such as a protocol buffer over gRPC) and applies a user's private keys to add a digital signature to the transaction proposal.

Endorsement (**simulating the proposal**): The client application sends a *ledger-update-transaction* to the peers on the channel. Such peers are the endorsing peers. Note that a peer can be an endorser as well as a committer. At this stage, orderers' nodes are not consulted and are not involved. The following are the steps involved:

1. The application generates a transaction proposal and sends it to the endorsing peers.

2. The channel will consult the endorsement policy to identify the endorsing peers and then route that transaction proposal request to the *chosen* endorsing peers:

   > I have used the word **chosen**, since chaincode's endorsement policy will dictate whether all endorsing peers on a channel need to endorse a transaction proposal request.

3. Each endorsing peer has a local copy of the ledger and chaincode. They will execute the chaincode based on the transaction proposal request, and will generate a transaction proposal response.

4. Each endorsing peer verifies that the transaction proposal is well formed and has not been submitted in the past.

5. The submitter's signature is verified by the MSP and authorizations are checked to ensure that the client application is authorized to perform a transaction (read/write) on the channel. Policies such as the write policy are defined during channel creation and help to determine a user's entitlement to perform/submit transactions to a channel.

6. Each endorser will generate a transaction proposal response. They will also sign the transaction proposal response with their private key (signing the response digitally). At this stage, there is *no* update to the ledger.

7. Each endorser will then send the proposal response to the application. For a transaction, the application will receive multiple proposal responses.

8. There may be inconsistency in the transaction proposal response sent to the application by various chosen endorsing peers, perhaps because different endorsing peers generated responses at different times, and the ledger state was different during those instances. In this case, the application can do the following:
   - Accept the responses to allow the transaction process to proceed to further steps
   - Reject the response and terminate the transaction process
   - Send another request for a more recent transaction proposal response

Technically, each endorser will use the transaction proposal inputs as input arguments to the chaincode. Each endorser takes the transaction proposal, and executes the proposed transaction using the chaincode present. These chaincode executions will not result in ledger updates. They just simulate the transaction. The endorser, while simulating the transaction, will get a current list of keys and values (the current state of the ledger) and a simulated list of keys and values (the to-be state of the ledger), which will be written to the ledger. Hence, there are two sets of keys and values (read and write sets). These sets of values, along with the endorsing peer's signatures, are added to the proposal response sent to the SDK, which will further parse the payload for the applications to consume.

Packaging the proposal response: The client application will receive endorsements from all the endorsers and, upon accepting the transaction proposal response, will send it to the orderer's nodes:

- From an orderer's node perspective, many applications will send it their respective transaction proposal responses.
- Orderers will sequence and package those transactions in blocks. It is these blocks that are the blocks in blockchain:
    - Orderers will wait for a certain amount of time to package all transactions within that time frame into a block, or, if the desired size of the block is satisfied, then the block will be ready for distribution.
- Orderers also don't have a local copy of the chaincode and, hence, they don't refer to chaincode (being judgmental) in defining blocks.
- **Note**: In HLF, the ordering of transactions is not important. However, whatever sequence they are added to the block in, they will be executed in that order.
- **Note**: A transaction in HLF is only present in **one** block, and not in multiple blocks. This means a transaction's position in the block is final and is assured at this stage.

Technically, each endorser will return its signed endorsement back to the client (through the SDK). We know that the endorser has obtained read and write set(s). These read and write sets are part of the signed proposal.

Verify and send for ordering: The client application will again participate in the transaction flow and will perform two activities—verify the proposal response and, for a *ledger-update-transaction*, the client will connect with an ordering service for further processing.

Verify the proposal response: The client application will verify the proposal response:

- If it was just a *ledger-query-transaction*, the client application will verify the proposal response and will collect its responses. It will not send it on to ordering services.
- If it is a *ledger-update-transaction*, then the application will verify whether all the endorsing peers, as specified in the endorsing policy, have endorsed the transaction, and whether they are all valid. The sequence is as follows:
    - The client application will first verify the endorsing peer signatures
    - Then, it compares the proposal responses from each of the endorsing peers to check whether the proposal responses are the same

> Even if the client application chooses not to inspect the proposal response, the endorsement policy will still be executed by the peers and will be used in the final commit of the transactions.

Send for ordering: At this stage, the client application sends the transaction message as a bundle (transaction proposal and a response) to the ordering service. This transaction message contains the following:

1. The two sets of keys and values (read and write sets)
2. The signatures of the endorsing peers
3. The channel ID for which the transaction is meant to be committed

Referring to the preceding diagram, **O5** and **O1** are orderers, and they are configured for **Channel-C1**. Hence, transaction messages meant for **C1** will be broadcast to the **O5** and **O1** orderers. They will sequence the transaction message, order them, and create blocks of those transactions.

Technically, the ordering service receives such transaction messages from all the channels to which it is connected and configured. The ordering service will sequence and order these transactions (chronologically by channel) and will create transaction blocks (per channel). Orderers will never create a transaction, and will ensure that they offer guaranteed delivery. The orderer's class offers capabilities for the client applications to interact with the orderer's nodes. The orderer's nodes have two exposed APIs—broadcast () and deliver (), and its bidirectional streaming API with a gRPC streaming connection between the client application and orderers. The broadcast() API enables clients to send transaction messages to orderers, and the deliver() API allows clients/consumers to check with orderers regarding channel information and channel configurations.

Distribution: At this stage of the transaction process, orderers will distribute the block to peers. Peers are connected to orderers in the blockchain network. Orderers will distribute the block to each connected peer via P2P communication based on gossip protocol.

Gossip protocol: I would like to talk a little bit about the gossip protocol here, as distribution is the stage where the gossip protocol is used. Orderers need to distribute the transaction message to all peers. However, it is a burden to orderers and it sounds almost impossible to reach all the peers when a network is huge in size. The HLF framework has a solution for this. Orderers do not deliver messages to each peer. Orderers only deliver messages to peers that are configured as leader peers. For each organization, on a channel, there is a leader peer identified. Those leader peers will distribute those messages to other peers and suchlike. Peers then forward these messages to a randomly selected number of peers. This random number of peers is predetermined, and this forwarding continues until the message reaches all the peers. This entire process is defined as a broadcast, and the broadcast process relies on the gossip protocol to distribute transaction messages.

 Broadcast is a push method to distribute messages. However, peers use pull methods to remain up to date if they are reincarnated from a *dead* to an *alive* status.

Peer bootstrapping: We just read that peers send messages to a predefined or predetermined list of peers. How does this determination happen? This happens via peer bootstrapping (also known as bootstrapping). When the blockchain network is established, each peer gets a bootstrap set of peers. After that, peers check for the *alive* status of the peer. If the bootstrap peer is *dead*, it will mark it as dead. However, it will check periodically whether it's alive/dead. If a peer is dead, and later becomes alive, it will have missed messages from the broadcast process. Hence, to get up to date, that peer will pull information, such as membership data (the *alive* and *dead* status of peers) and ledger data (blocks of transactions).

Validation and tagging: At this stage of the transaction process, peers will receive blocks from the orderers. They will validate them and tag them as valid or invalid:

- The peer will pick and process transactions from the block. The order of picking and executing transactions is the same order in which transactions are sequenced by the orderers. Peers do not execute chaincode for this step. Chaincode is only executed at the endorsement stage, which corroborates the fact that chaincode should only exist on endorsing nodes.

- When processing a transaction, each peer will verify that the transaction was endorsed according to the endorsement policy defined in the chaincode, which actually generated this transaction. This ensures that all the organizations that are meant to endorse a transaction have endorsed it, and have generated the same output.
- If it is verified, this means that it was endorsed correctly, and then the following happens:
  - The peer performs a consistency check. This check is to verify whether the current ledger state is compatible with the state of the ledger when the peer generated the transaction proposal update. If it is consistent, then the transaction is marked as valid. If it is not consistent, then it is not applied and the transaction is marked invalid and defined as a *failed* transaction. For example, a digital asset against which a transaction was proposed and a proposal response was generated was updated by another transaction. In this case, the state of the ledger at proposal response time and consistency time are different and, hence, it cannot be applied and is therefore marked as *failed*.
  - Once a peer validates all the transactions in the block, then all the transactions in the block that are not failed are committed to the ledger:
    - Failed transactions are not committed to the ledger, yet they are considered successful and are available for audit.

Technically, each peer will append the block to the chain of the channel, and only valid transactions are appended to the peer's local copy of the ledger (it's an append to the current world state).

Notifications: When a block gets committed to the ledger, peer, and chaincode, it generates the following events:

- The peers and chaincode generate the following events:
  - **A peer generates**: A block event and a transaction event. A block event contains the entire block content, while a transaction event highlights whether a transaction was validated or invalidated (marked as *failed*).
  - **Chaincode generates**: A chaincode event.
- Applications can subscribe to interesting events and can receive notifications. These notifications help applications to know about the final stage of the transaction.

The transaction flow defined previously clearly displays various participants involved in the transaction, from client applications to endorsers, orderers, committers, and leaders. This section also clearly highlights the powerful role of orderers in the blockchain network. Each peer validates the transaction and follows the sequence and order defined in the block by the orderers. Hence, it is the orderers that ensure consistency in the blockchain network. In addition, it ensures that the position of the transaction in the block never gets changed and, hence, induces immutability to the ledger in the blockchain network. If you re-read the transaction process defined previously, it is evident that all peers agree about the transactions and their contents. Orderers mediate this agreement process, which is called a consensus.

Large object storage – on-chain or off-chain

This section discusses the storage of large objects on or off the blockchain network. This section is part of the design strategy. However, it was more relevant to position this topic here, as it is an extension of PDC and helps to realize it.

Rationale for on-chain/off-chain architecture

Data storage and retrieval is at the heart of blockchain, where assets, accounts, permissions, and transactions are treated as data. But what about documents such as evidence files, X-rays, image scans, videos, and legal contract documents in PDF form? Where should a blockchain application store these documents? What is the architecturally correct approach to storing documents? This chapter will discuss document storage approaches and how blockchain properties, such as immutability, can be preserved even for off-chain storage.

There are arguments for storing images, PDF files, and other objects on-chain as part of the payload of a blockchain transaction. The reasons for doing so are to ensure that non-repudiation and immutability apply to these objects as they apply to any other blockchain data. If you store documents off-chain and simply include URLs or other reference information, there's a possibility and risk of tampering. Of course, images can be encrypted in off-chain storage. However, the possibility of undetected tampering exists, as does reliance on a centralized third party managing the documents.

The arguments against directly storing images and large files on-chain relate to significantly impacting performance due to large transaction payloads. There are three areas of concern to consider:

- Network latency, as large (multiple MB or even GB) payloads have to be sent across the network to multiple participants

- Compute costs, as digital signature hashes of these message payloads have to be computed when signing the message and verified when the message is received
- The cost of TLS channel encryption when sending the messages
- Storage costs, as blocks containing large transactions are stored across multiple blockchain nodes

In short, the performance and cost impacts of including large objects in transaction payloads should be a significant consideration in the design of your blockchain application. There are also potential confidentiality concerns that might apply, particularly in regulated contexts, such as US **Health Insurance Portability and Accountability Act** (**HIPAA**) regulations for healthcare data, EU GDPR for **personally identifiable information** (**PII**), and similar regulations in many countries. Even though, in permissioned enterprise blockchain stacks such as HLF, the scale of the network in terms of the number of peers is smaller, and compute power, network bandwidth, and storage might be more readily available, thus making the acceptable payload size higher, confidentiality concerns tend to be even greater due to the nature of enterprise applications.

Ultimately, the answer will depend on the use case, the nature of the data being shared, and empirically determined performance impacts for a certain payload size. While, with HLF and Oracle Blockchain Platform, it is technically possible to store documents on-chain, let's compare this with similar arguments about whether to store documents in a relational database.

A database primarily stores text strings, numbers, and date values. Using `int` or `float` data types will let you store numbers, `var` and `varchar` will allow you to store string and text, and a `blob` type column (binary large object) will allow you to store binary objects, such as images, or document files, such as PDFs or others. However, the key purpose of the database is to provide quick and performant insertion, retrieval, and data management. While you can store blobs in a database for convenience, storing documents off-database has numerous advantages. Performance is superior multi-fold when the documents are stored off-database, since the storage and the retrieval of a document from the filesystem is far more performant than a database. In fact, some databases handle blobs by storing them in a filesystem with only relevant pointer and metadata information in the actual database column, and implement this under the hood of actual database storage functions so that it's completely transparent to database users and applications. However, there is still some added cost, and so, in some cases, it may be better for applications to handle file storage off-database directly.

Coming back to the blockchain, sharing images and files as part of the blockchain transaction payloads raises various limitations, such as bandwidth, latency (to store and retrieve images), the duplication of information among various nodes, and burdening the consensus process due to the large size of the blocks. In fact, due to the distributed and replicated nature of the blockchain architecture and the critical dependency on network latency and PKI encryption (used for digital signatures and their verification), the argument against burdening the blockchain with large-size images and documents is even stronger than one against doing so with database blobs. So, the argument ultimately is not about whether to store documents on-chain, but about the size limits when it becomes necessary, and application considerations to ensure that on-chain and off-chain storage are consistent and that the application can still benefit from non-repudiation and immutability properties, even when off-chain storage is used.

In the HLF transaction flow, a transaction payload is signed by the client and sent to one or more peer nodes to be executed. After delivering the payload to chaincode execution containers, peer nodes capture the **read-write sets** (**RWSets**) of the chaincode, which will include the objects from the payload if they are to be stored on-chain. The RWSets are then signed by the peers, which involves calculating hashes over the data, and are sent to the client. The client has to verify the signatures, and, in the case of multiple endorsers, compare the results to ensure they match. Then, an encrypted result and all the signatures are sent to the ordering service, where the messages are stored in Kafka topics. **Ordering service nodes** (**OSNs**) then have to reach a consensus on sequencing these transaction messages into blocks, which are sent to the peer nodes for transaction validation and ledger updates. Peer nodes go through each transaction, validating the signatures of the other endorsers, and verifying versions of all read-set data fields against those in the current world state database before declaring the transaction valid, appending the block to the ledger, and updating the world state database with the write-set values.

Since, on a blockchain network, multiple parties (client, peer nodes, and OSNs) need to ensure that a transaction is accurate and valid, and reach a consensus, any transaction that involves storing images or documents on-chain will slow down the blockchain network. All the message transfers, storage and retrieval, signing and signature verification operations, and field validations will also consume significant resources from participating nodes.

Key design principles

What options and approaches are recommended to address these limitations? How can it be ensured that documents remain immutable and that non-repudiation still applies even when documents are stored off-chain? A fundamental best practice is for applications to capture an immutable document hash, which essentially fingerprints the document, storage location (a URL in a content management system, object store, and suchlike), and related metadata, including the timestamp, user credentials, and version number. This data then becomes a document record, which can be stored on-chain, even as the document itself is stored off-chain. The document record is immutable, and the document hash it contains can be used to verify the integrity of the document or image object when these are retrieved from the off-chain storage.

The other important practices to apply in this on-chain/off-chain design pattern are the following:

1. Ensure that you have received a confirmation that the document has been stored successfully off-chain before updating the document record on-chain
2. When retrieving the document, first retrieve the document record from the blockchain, use the location information to retrieve the document itself, and then calculate and verify its hash against the hash included in the blockchain record

While it's possible to handle these tasks in a client application, it would be more beneficial to use an off-chain storage solution that provides built-in anchoring to the blockchain; that is, a solution that automatically creates and updates records on the blockchain whenever any document is created, accessed, updated, or deleted. Depending on the nature of the documents, this could be a specific content management/document storage solution, or a generic object store solution providing undifferentiated blob storage in its containers. Thus, transactions that involve off-chain documents would be handled by this storage solution, which, in turn, would create immutable document records on-chain. This leverages the immutability of the blockchain network using small document records, while documents themselves are stored off-chain in the document storage service.

Integrated blockchain – an anchored document storage solution

Blockchain anchoring would be beneficial for documents such as ownership titles, educational certificates, regulatory compliance reports, contracts, physically signed or notarized documents, purchase orders, invoices with tax implications, bills of lading and other shipping materials, and trade agreements.

Storing document records, including the cryptographic hash, location, and other metadata, on a blockchain network would complement typical document storage/content management features, such as versioning, searching, tracing documents, and document-level access control.

Such a **Blockchain-anchored-Document-as-a-Service** (**BaDaaS**) would manage two types of artifacts—an actual document or image file stored off-chain, and document attributes, such as a unique document ID, content hash, document version, and other metadata, recorded and posted to a blockchain network as an immutable record. Any activity that involves these off-chain documents will be stored on-chain as a blockchain transaction, while related document attributes will be stored as its payload on-chain.

Essentially, BaDaaS offers the following types of API:

1. An API to upload a document by invoking a POST call, or replace a document with a new version by means of a PUT call. Each folder or container could be mapped to a separate blockchain channel for sharding purposes.
2. An API to retrieve documents using GET APIs, which allow authenticated users to download or view the document, but only after its hash has been verified against the one stored in the blockchain record.
3. An API to retrieve the document history based on the blockchain transaction history, with all the relevant versions and other metadata changes, timestamps, user identities, and so on.
4. An API to retrieve metadata for the latest version and verify that the document content matches the hash stored on the blockchain without downloading the document itself.
5. APIs for managing access permissions and granting new ones. These changes should also be stored on-chain to ensure their immutability as a series of **access control list** (**ACL**) records linked to the document records via a document ID.

This is an example of an approach that would solve the on-chain/off-chain storage requirements for certain classes of use cases. It would not burden the blockchain with large-size payloads, but would, at the same time, ensure that document integrity and transaction history is maintained on-chain in an immutable manner.

So far, we've discussed large unstructured objects, such as binary image data, and PDF files. Could this be applied to large-size structured documents? For example, in supply chain collaboration demand forecast and planning, documents can contain hundreds of MBs of structured data, which is impractical to share as a payload of blockchain transactions. The good news is that an approach similar to the one described previously with unstructured documents can be used. Only selected data is extracted for blockchain records, and the entire document is hashed to ensure that its integrity can be verified on the other end. The documents can be transferred using traditional means (for example, EDI, and B2B file transfer) but, on both ends of the transfer, the blockchain is used to store (when sending) and retrieve and verify (when receiving) the relevant metadata fields, including using the hash to verify the integrity of the transferred document.

Storage option selection for blockchain applications

An enterprise can opt for one of the following options to store documents off-chain:

1. A relational or document database—on-premise or in a cloud (for example, Oracle or MongoDB)
2. A document management or content management system (for example, Oracle Content and Experience Cloud)
3. A distributed filesystem (for example, NFS) or a distributed object store service (for example, Oracle Cloud Object Storage)
4. A distributed database (for example, Apache Cassandra wide-column NoSQL database)
5. A P2P filesharing network (for example, **InterPlanetary File System** (**IPFS**) or Storj)

This section is not intended to constitute a detailed review of each of these data storage solutions, but rather a guide to evaluating them as an off-chain storage solution for blockchain applications. To begin with, you can store documents or image data in a traditional database, such as Oracle, or a NoSQL database, such as MongoDB, which offers stronger query capabilities and a lower cost; however, it comes with low transparency, a single point of failure, and the strong presence of a central authority.

Document or content management systems provide additional capabilities specifically tailored to documents—such as folder structure, versioning capabilities, document-centric access control, UIs, REST APIs that are tailored for working with documents, and suchlike. However, they have similar drawbacks as databases in terms of being a centralized solution with a single point of failure. When deployed in a cloud environment, single points of failure can be mitigated by appropriate design.

Distributed filesystems or object storage provide other options, which are more barebones and cheaper, and better suited to storing images and other binary objects than actual documents. Note that while these can provide asynchronous distribution to avoid a single point of failure, the latency associated with the asynchronous replication of the stored data needs to be considered when deciding whether to submit a blockchain transaction when the object has been stored initially, or wait until it's been replicated. The answer will likely depend on a use case and the ability to deal with various failure modes.

A distributed database, such as Cassandra, can have nodes that follow the topology of the blockchain and remove the centralization concern. Each Cassandra node can be co-located within a blockchain node. When a document is created or updated to a new version, the local Cassandra node is the first one to store it, and then it replicates to other nodes. The blockchain record update transaction can be submitted to the local node at the same time, but will eventually be available on other nodes as well. The key benefit of using a distributed database is the possibility to achieve local affinity between the database node and the blockchain node for updates and document retrieval. However, the replication in both Cassandra and blockchain operates under eventual consistency rules, but at different speeds (considering that the document is likely much larger than the associated blockchain record) and with different failure modes that need to be taken into account.

A P2P file share network, such as IPFS, which evolved on the basis of P2P concepts from BitTorrent and Git, but which is built upon **DAG** (short for **directed acyclic graph**) architecture, enables the exchange of versioned objects in a decentralized network of storage nodes. Each object (file/document) has a hash—a unique signature/ID that's used as its address. IPFS retrieves objects based on their hashes—each node is asked to search for a file based on its hash. So, storing the IPFS hash together with a file hash and related metadata in a blockchain record provides the core anchoring capability we discussed earlier. IPFS offers historical versioning of the content and high availability across the network of nodes. Similar to Cassandra, IPFS provides a decentralized topology, though it is much more scalable since it is filesystem-based rather than a database. However, latency of distribution and potential failure modes still need to be accounted for in the application's design.

Summary

This chapter focused on illustrating HLF, its architecture, and its components. During this chapter, we looked at the Hyperledger project and walked though the qualifiers for the Hyperledger project. This chapter followed an example-based approach in illustrating HLF's architecture. We explored peers, nodes, algorithms, consensus, the membership service, and orderer services, as well as master identity, security, and privacy. The chapter also construed channels and PDC to allow private transactions between organizations. It concluded with design strategies for storing large objects—on-chain or off-chain. From the next chapter onward, we will delve into creating an HLF network and authoring chaincode to address a specific use case.

4
Engage in Business Case on Blockchain Platform

The preceding chapter explored Hyperledger's architecture and showed you how to assemble an example Hyperledger-based business network. It provided an explanation of founder-based and consortium-based business networks. It illustrated business network components, adding peers to channels, and working with chaincode and smart contracts. It also covered identity, security, privacy, membership services, channels, ledgers, and transaction flow. In this chapter, we'll learn how to design the solution in line with the constructs of the **Oracle Blockchain Platform** (**OBP**). This chapter has two parts: the first part focuses on defining a use case around certificate issuance and sharing certificates with trusted parties on a Blockchain network. The second part covers the **Blockchain-as-a-Service** (**BaaS**) platform, which offers an effective, efficient, and economical avenue to realize the potential of blockchain technology.

BaaS is a catalyst for blockchain adoption. BaaS provider ensures the installation and maintenance of your blockchain network, allowing your business and IT to focus on chaincode and dApps. The entire blockchain ecosystem will be managed, administered, maintained, and supported by the cloud service provider. Many top vendors, such as Oracle, have a managed **Platform-as-a-Service** (**PaaS**) product for BaaS because BaaS allows customers to take their SaaS, **business process management** (**BPM**) processes, custom applications, and so on, to harness the power of blockchain in a cost-effective and efficient way. This chapter also explores Oracle's BaaS by exploring a use case in the education sector, showing you the ease of using the blockchain platform.

Understanding the business scenario

Education is the foundation-building sector of human society. It also facilitates continuous upskilling of the workforce with new knowledge areas as per the needs of the changing times. Despite being one of the oldest sectors, it is still plagued with inefficiencies:

- Multiple manual processes cause administration delays
- Administration delays cause verification delays
- Manual processes always introduce some doubt over the authenticity of a student's credentials

To construct a solution implemented on OBP, we have chosen a scenario in this business process that deals with the approval of qualification certificates, issuing them to students in a secure manner, and sharing them with other stakeholders (such as employers and other educational institutions) in a trusted manner.

Introduction to the use case

The use case includes a typical setup of the interactions and process flow associated with the life cycle of the educational credentials/qualifications of an individual. In this book, we will consider the aspects of the use case that involve the following scenarios:

- Issue/approval of certificates by a competent authority
- Availability of certificates to the owner (that is, the student)
- Verification of certificate by third parties such as employers or other educational institutions

In a real-life scenario, there are too many stakeholders involved in this scenario, such as specific school of studies, examination controller, the issuing institution, students, other institutions, and employers. For the sake of simplicity, we will consider the following stakeholders:

- **Oracle Red School** (**ORS**): Certificate creator (school of studies)
- **Oracle Empire University** (**OEU**): Certificate approver and issuer (university)
- **Student, employer, other universities**: Certificate viewer/verifier

Let's take a quick look at an existing real-life process in this use case:

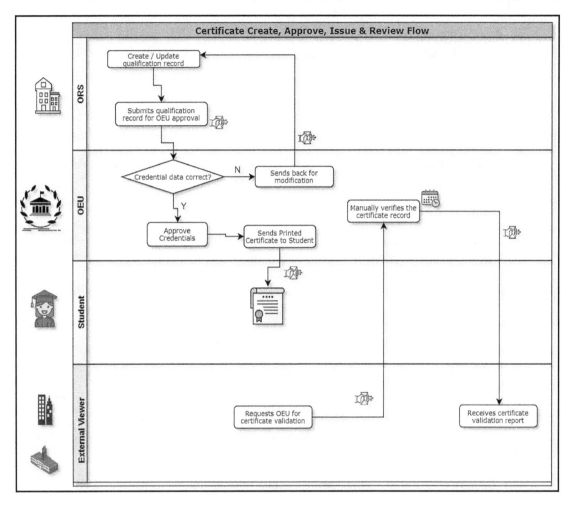

Certificate Creation, Approval, Issuing, and Review Flow

The existing process has the following inefficiencies:

- The manual process of verification makes it slow
- The verification process is slow at ascertaining fraudulent claims
- It requires external background verification services
- Paper-based certificates are prone to loss or damage
- Faking paper certificates and gaps in the verification process makes certificates trustworthiness questionable

Criteria for use case qualification

Before proposing a blockchain-based solution to our business scenario, let's first evaluate and see whether it qualifies for a blockchain solution. How can we be sure that the application of a blockchain-based solution for a use case would really solve the challenges facing the current process?

Let's ponder over some of the characteristic aspects and constraints of the use case that blockchain technologies can overcome. The following considerations are not exhaustive; instead, it's an indicative approach toward trying to come up with a blockchain solution.

The following are some of the characteristic aspects and constraints of the use case that blockchain technologies can overcome:

- Could the use case be solved with a centralized solution? A centralized solution managed by OEU would speed up certain aspects compared to a purely manual process (if it exists), but it would impose other challenges without providing a solution that overcomes all the existing inefficiencies. The challenges of a centralized solution are as follows:
    - A centralized solution would not guarantee synergy of the business processes at ORS and OEU. Hence, the disconnect between the offline and online processes would not provide much improvement in system efficiency.
    - There would be a single point of failure from a system or trust perspective.
    - It requires other parties to trust one single entity (OEU) with no validation or mandate from other stakeholders.
    - It does not provide an effective solution for fake certificates being issued.

- Is there a digital asset that multiple stakeholders share? Considering that the educational certificate is the digital asset in this use case, it will indeed be shared between ORS and OEU for generation, processing, and granting, as well as for validation.
- Does the digital asset need to be stored and accessed in a secure manner? As the certificates will be shared assets and will be accessed by different stakeholders, a secure mechanism is of prime importance. Considering the nature of the asset, security is very important for the following:
    - Any kind of access to it should be appropriately tracked
    - Any updates to certificate data should have the endorsement of both ORS and OEU

- Certificates should be protected against any kind of tampering and unauthorized access
- Are there trust issues between the organizations potentially involved in the use case? It is the establishment of trust among ORS, OEU, and certificate viewers that is needed. The solution for the use case should ensure the automatic establishment of trust by design.

Blockchain solution benefits

The use case necessitates a need for a digital asset (education credentials) that should be shared among stakeholders and exhibits the following characteristics:

- Shared asset state
- Mutually endorsed and validated data workflow
- Transparent yet secure access to all authorized stakeholders
- Untampered, perpetual proof of existence, and proof of approval

Considering the required characteristics of the solution, a blockchain-based solution is an apt fit. With its inherent support for immutability, a shared ledger, secure access, and transaction endorsement properties, a blockchain-based solution would be able to fulfill all the use case requirements. Additionally, it would open up possibilities for further automation and process efficiency by way of involving more stakeholders and the application of smart contracts.

The following key benefits would be realized by a blockchain-based solution for our use case:

- A trusted, tamper-proof digital repository for educational certificates
- Eliminates the risk of loss or damage
- Streamlined (almost real-time) verification procedure, because the educational credentials are persisted on a trusted, immutable, shared ledger with appropriate authorization

Further possibilities are as follows:

- Large-scale, collaborated, complete educational credential history of an individual
- Using a source of truth such as this as a prerequisite for any further approval, such as research grants and industrial collaboration
- Tokenizing educational qualifications as a common, industry-accepted representation (for example, EduCoin)

Designing the solution

Now that we have qualified our use case for a blockchain-based solution, let's get down to designing the solution in line with the constructs of OBP.

 There is no fixed sequence of steps for the design process. It is up to the solution designer's discretion. The primary objective should be to achieve clarity on various aspects of an OBP solution, from a logical view to deployment aspects.

Business network topology

As we mentioned previously, for our use case, we are considering three stakeholders. These are OEU, ORS, and **certificate viewers/verifiers** (let's give this an acronym of **CVs**). We need to determine the roles of each of these stakeholders based on their function:

- OEU is the university or governing body with which different schools (colleges) are affiliated. It is this entity that has the final authority to approve an educational credential of a student submitted by their school.
- ORS is one of the schools where a student is enrolled and completes their education. On completion, ORS would evaluate and submit the student's educational credential to OEU. In the larger context, ORS could be categorized as part of a representative blockchain entity called *schools*. It depends on the business requirements and the implementation context.
- CVs such as students, employers, and job agencies are primarily the consumers of the data (educational credentials) and hence would have read-only access to the network.

Based on this premise, the following table provides a depiction of the entities:

Organization	Entity Type	Access Type
OEU	Founder	Read/write
ORS	Endorsing participant	Read/write
CVs	Participant	Read

Channel association

In our use case, a single type of asset will be shared with all stakeholders, that is, certificate data. This necessitates everyone to have access to the same ledger data. Hence, it will be a single channel network organization where all stakeholders will be connected with varied access roles, as listed previously.

The following diagram depicts a logical view of how the OBP nodes will be created for the solution:

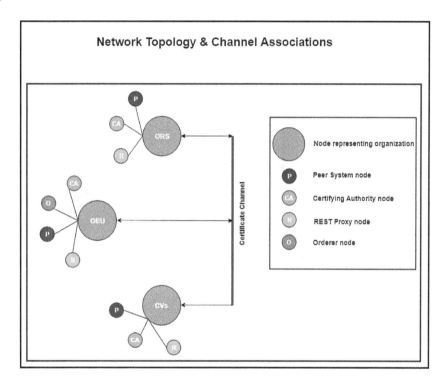

Network topology and channel association

This diagram shows the association of the various stakeholders with the single channel.

Network artifacts

After determining the network topology and stakeholders, let's define the shared asset and operations that will be performed on it over the network.

Asset model

For the given use case, we primarily have two types of object to store on the ledger:

- **Student** (**Receiver**): Basic information
- **Certificate**: Certificate data

The following diagram depicts the asset structure and the relations between them at a high level:

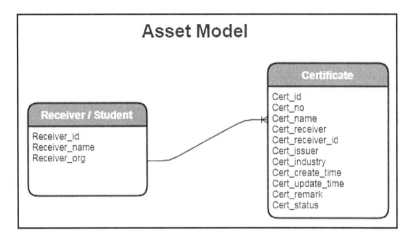

Asset model

Chaincode transactions

The use case requires the following transactions to be performed by the stakeholders at various stages of a certificate's life cycle:

Transactions	Actor	Description
CreateReceiver	ORS	Create a new receiver or student
AddCertificate	ORS	Insert a certificate for a receiver
ApproveCertificate	OEU	Approve a certificate
Search operations		
QueryByCert_id	All	Query a certificate
QueryByRecev_id	All	Query a receiver by ID
GetCertificateHistory	OEU/ORS/receiver	Query history of one key for the record
QueryAllCerts	OEU/ORS	Query all certificates of all students

Solution operational flow

So far, we've identified the OBP stakeholders, their associations, the ledger data model, and chaincode transactions. This section will help you visualize the changes that an OBP-based solution can make to the existing business process and consequently overcome the inefficiencies and challenges currently faced.

The following diagram shows the solution flow of the qualified use case:

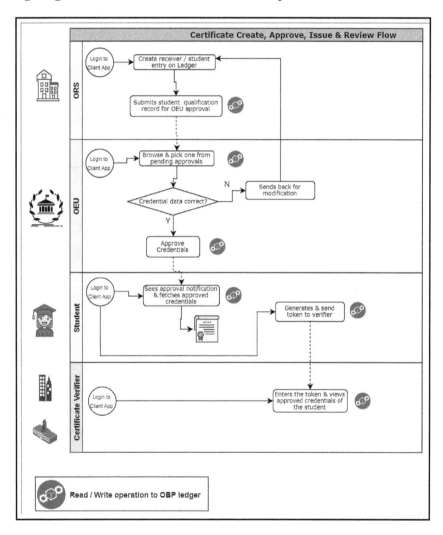

Solution flow

Solution architecture

As part of the solution architecture, this section covers a holistic high-level component view and a run-time deployment view of the OBP based solution, its components and instances.

High–level architecture

Let's determine the solution's components and the interactions between them that are required to implement the OBP-based solution. The following diagram depicts the high-level solution architecture:

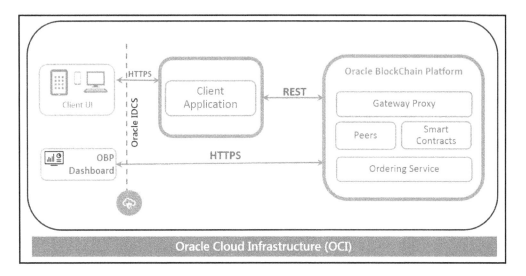

Solution architecture - high-level

These are the solution's components:

- **OBP Dashboard** provides an interface for OEU and ORS administrators/operators to perform OBP administration and configuration tasks.
- Different sets of client applications would be needed for each of the stakeholders:
    - **ORS**:
        - To create a student entry and insert certificate data for the student on the ledger
        - To be able to search student and certificate data
    - **OEU**:
        - To be able to search student and certificate data
        - To approve/reject students' certificate data

- **Student (CV)**:
  - To be able to view their approved certificates
  - Generate a token for a certificate verifier to verify their academic credentials stored on an OBP ledger
- **Certificate verifier**:
  - To be able to verify a student's academic credentials using the token generated by the student using the OBP solution

Deployment architecture

The following diagram depicts how all the pieces of OBP and the constituent solution components would run on top of an Oracle Cloud instance. Oracle Cloud bundles OBP services and solutions on top of its robust and scalable **Oracle Cloud Infrastructure (OCI)** availability domains. The whole cloud apparatus is secured through the integrated Oracle **Identity Cloud Service (IDCS)**:

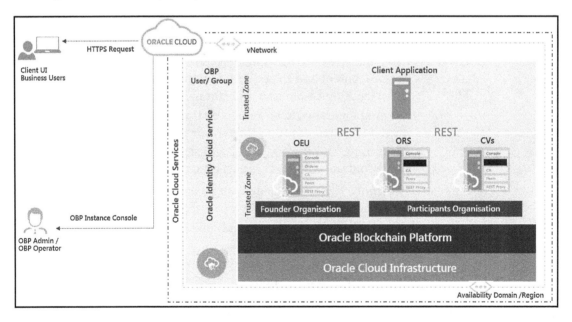

Deployment architecture [Oracle Image]

Document storage – recommended approach with OBP

Like our use case, many scenarios relating to today's enterprise business processes involve the exchange of a document object. In terms of practicality, for many cases, the document in itself is just a direct adoption of a physical process. It primarily provides a perception of the trusted physical asset in the hands of transacting stakeholders. Technically, it is a logical grouping of data values related to business transactions such as agreed terms and conditions, contracts, and transaction data.

With blockchain-based trusted solutions such as the one we're building on OBP, we can in fact do away with many such needs of a document object. Still, for the sake of practicality, documents could co-exist and may gradually fade away into irrelevance (not necessarily in all cases) as the adoption increases.

Currently, the following approach can be adopted for storing business documents along with core OBP solution (ledger) data:

- During write transactions on the OBP ledger:
    - Generate a hash of the document, record the hash on the ledger (on-chain) and store the document off-chain
    - Off-chain storage of documents could either the cloud-based Oracle Content and Experience Service or other Oracle Cloud storage options, such as object storage or file storage
    - Hashing logic should be agreed by transacting stakeholders and must be secured appropriately
    - Performing hashing and document storage operation outside the smart contract would reduce its execution time
- During read transactions (that is, while fetching a document asset):
    - Fetch the document from the chosen document storage.
    - Get a hash of the document and send it to a smart contract for comparison and validation.
    - On a positive match, the document can be read. Otherwise, an unexpected situation should be reported.

For more details on this aspect, please refer to the document storage section in the previous chapter.

So far, we have walked through the business scenario and defined the use case. We have analyzed the use case to justify the need for a blockchain solution by walking through the use case qualifications. Once we decided that the use case qualifies for a blockchain solution, we covered designing the blockchain-based solution. The next half of the chapter concentrates on exploring OBP and its architecture, and setting up an OBP network instance.

Exploring OBP

As we already know, OBP is based on the open source Hyperledger Fabric. But for enterprise, Fabric is not enough because it is not pre-assembled. Here are some of the high-level requirements for building a working blockchain network for an enterprise from the ground up:

- Set up all the prerequisites, configurations, and containers.
- Set up container life cycle management to manage all the containers of peers, channels, chain codes, and so on.
- Install security such as user management, which is one of the most important components for enterprise.
- Manage the system upgrade plans and patches to align with the rapid changes. As Hyperledger Fabric is open source, there will be continuous evolution in technology, so you need to continually manage the system upgrade plans and patches.
- Ensure high availability and scalability of all the resources.
- Offer security to data and provide integration endpoints such as REST APIs to connect with other products, such as SaaS applications, ERP, or any third-party applications.
- Work with various tools for monitoring and handling operational tasks, such as checking the health and utilization of the nodes, channel activities, peer activities, channel management, peer management, chain code management, and network management.

To structure a blockchain network from foundation to production, you need skills, resources, and time (maybe months) to set up and maintain all of these requirements. Oracle takes responsibility for all of these requirements and provides a service in terms of OBP. In this section, we will delve into OBP's architecture and will learn to set up an OBP instance and blockchain network.

Overview of OBP's architecture

OBP provides a pre-assembled platform for building a blockchain network, deploying and running smart contracts, and maintaining a distributed ledger. Once the service has been provisioned with a few clicks, administrators can use the web console to dynamically update blockchain configuration and monitor its operation. Developers can deploy smart contracts and integrate applications using REST APIs or client SDKs. OBP enables distributed P2P transactions in real-time and allows applications (new or existing) to transact and share data between trusted business partners over a blockchain network.

 For the latest updates from OBP product perspective, please refer to
`https://www.oracle.com/cloud/blockchain/`.

Because OBP is part of the Oracle Cloud platform, it's pre-assembled with underlying cloud services, including containers, compute, storage, identity cloud services for authentication, object storage for embedded archiving, and management and log analytics for operations and troubleshooting. You can configure multiple peer nodes and channels for availability, scalability, and confidentiality, and Oracle Cloud will automatically handle the underlying dependencies. The following diagram explains the architecture at a high level and explains how OBP adds value to the open source Hyperledger Fabric:

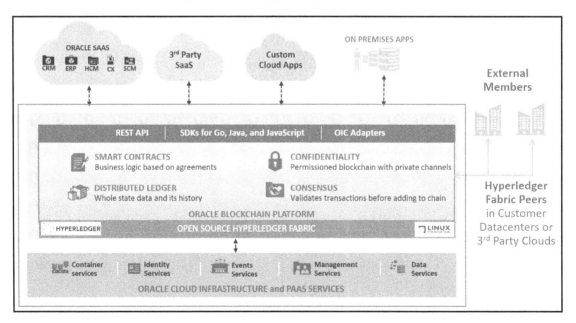

OBP high-level architecture

OBP is a permissioned blockchain, and it leverages the built-in Oracle IDCS to the Hyperledger Fabric to provide the following:

- User and role management
- Authentication for the OBP console, REST proxies, and **certificate authority** (**CA**)
- Identity federation and third-party client certificate support to enable consortia formation and simplify member onboarding

OBP is running on the OCI and it is a PaaS service. Hence, storage, scalability, high availability, and infrastructure will be taken care of by Oracle. Using the adapters of Oracle Integration Cloud Service, it can be integrated with Oracle SaaS, PaaS, and on-premise applications with blockchain transactions, events, and queries. As OBP is based on Hyperledger Fabric, it also allows us to connect external member nodes that use Hyperledger Fabric. These external members can be in customer data centers or third-party cloud services. The following diagram depicts the OBP service-level architecture on OCI:

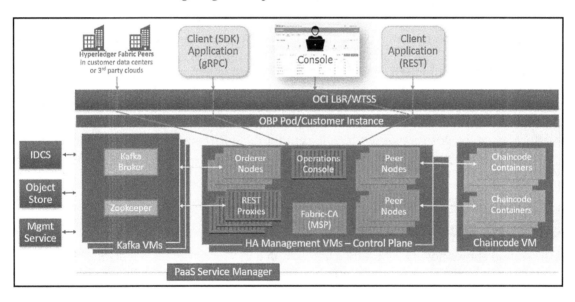

OBP service-level architecture

Oracle has made many enhancements to Hyperledger Fabric to make OBP an enterprise-grade service. Each blockchain instance contains managed containers, virtual machines, identity management, block and object storage, and Oracle Event Hub cloud service, which is a dedicated Kafka connect.

Blockchain instance

An OBP instance (aka blockchain instance for this book) is a collection of containers that includes peer nodes, an orderer, an operation console, a CA, a REST proxy, and chaincodes. OBP instance is integrated with identity management to manage users and roles. It also integrates with Oracle object storage to dynamically back up configuration changes and the ledger and restore when required. The Oracle object storage takes a backup of all the components in the blockchain instance, which includes all the block files of a ledger, which also includes the data in the system channel and customer channel, the list of channels, the latest checkpoints, the source code of chaincodes, configuration files, and the provisioning files of the nodes and log files. This backup and restore process will be done automatically in OBP without giving the user notice. So, there is no need for the user to worry about data backup. OBP uses Oracle Event Hub cloud service as dedicated Kafka for the orderers. Default REST proxies are available to integrate OBP with any other applications, such as SaaS, PaaS, on-premise, or other third-party applications.

By now, you should know that blockchain is very resource intensive because it requires many containers with lots of storage. Since OBP is running on the Oracle Cloud, the storage, scalability, and high availability of the services will be taken care of by Oracle.

OBP is available in two ways. One is by installing a pre-built VM provided by Oracle, and the other option is to create an account in Oracle cloud and provision the blockchain platform from the portfolio of services. Except for the initial steps to access and create a blockchain instance, all other features and navigation are the same. Let's see each one these ways of provisioning OBP.

Setting up the OBP SDK

This section shows how to set up the OBP SDK in a in a laptop or local machine. This is just for reference; however, there are alternative ways, such as setting up in cloud infrastructure such as OCI. Here is the process of setting up the OBP SDK.

Prerequisites

These are the prerequisites for setting up the OBP SDK:

- Oracle Linux version 7.3 or higher (OBP runs on any Linux with Docker, but Oracle Linux is recommended) with internet access, and the Linux kernel version must be greater than 3.10.

- Disk space depends on the number of instances planned to deploy.
- For the application, 4 GB memory per instance is recommended.
- There are multiple Docker containers running after provisioning, and each container's access to the host machine's CPU cycles should be unlimited. To ensure that each container runs smoothly, two CPUs are the recommended minimum.
- A hostname is required.
- An Oracle user is needed because the processes run in Docker containers (such as peer and orderer).

 Hostname should be a resolvable name when accessed from the browser. In case of setting up OBP locally, the hostname must be the name of your VM runtime. When creating multiple organization within the same OBP VM, the hostname will remain the same (i.e. the VM name) but the port range for each organization will be different

```
#create user oracle
sudo useradd oracle
sudo passwd oracle
<newPassword>
```

Prepare the Docker environment

To build and install OBP SDK, the latest Docker Engine and Docker Compose need to be installed:

1. Docker Engine installation: The OBP SDK requires the latest version of Docker Engine. Execute the following command to find out the Docker Engine version:

   ```
   docker --version
   ```

2. If the version is not `Docker version 17.05.0-ce` or higher, then install/update the latest version of Docker with the following instructions.

3. Use the following command to replace OS (operating system) version with your specific OS version using docker `yum` repo command :

   ```
   $ sudo tee /etc/yum.repos.d/docker.repo <<-EOF
   name=Docker Repository
   baseurl=https://yum.dockerproject.org/repo/main/oraclelinux/7
   enabled=1
   gpgcheck=1
   gpgkey=https://yum.dockerproject.org/gpg
   EOF
   ```

4. Install Docker Engine:

```
$sudo yum install docker-engine-17.05.0.ce
```

5. Check the Docker Engine version:

```
$docker -version
```

The following screenshot shows the version:

```
[███████████████ local]$ docker --version
Docker version 17.05.0-ce, build 89658be
```

Docker version

6. Start Docker Engine:

```
sudo systemctl restart docker
```

7. Authenticate the user to the Docker daemon:

```
sudo usermod -a -G docker $USER
```

8. Unpackage and deploy the **blockchain cloud service** (**BCS**) SDK and unpack it with the help of the following code fragment:

```
As opc user switch to
/usr/localcd
/usr/localsudo
mkdir bcssdk
cd bcssdk
```

9. Copy the OBP SDK from the web or a local source.
10. Unzip the build package to the bcssdk directory by executing the following command:

```
sudo unzip obcs-sdk-19.1.3-20190129043733.zip -d /usr/local/bcssdk
```

This book used OBP SDK version 19.1.3 in which the Hyperledger Fabric version is 1.3.

11. Now we need to install images and start provisioning the console. As **root** user, run the `build` command to load and install Docker images:

    `./build.sh`

    The following screenshot shows the output of `build.sh`:

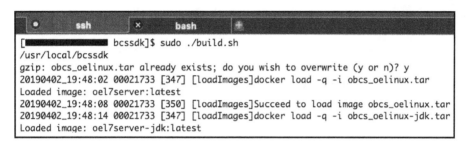

run build.sh

12. Wait until the docker loads:

```
20190402_19:57:23 00021733 [347] [loadImages]docker load -q -i bcs-prometheus.tar
Loaded image: bcs/prometheus:latest
20190402_19:57:53 00021733 [350] [loadImages]Succeed to load image bcs-prometheus.tar
provision port doesn't set, use default value 3000
provision workspace doesn't set, use default value /root/obcs_workspace
firewall is active, do you want stop firewall and restart docker(Y/N):
```

docker load

13. Confirm with `Y`, then the console will be started automatically after the images are installed:

```
Starting Provision...
46525ba502e9ea220cd65e1a18dc071bb4b79c680aae8834c4cd6ab8f6008e03
Starting Provision successfully
The provision console URL is: http://███████████:3000
```

Starting provisioning

There are certain points that you need to keep in mind:

- If the firewall is active, `build.sh` will prompt the user to stop the firewall and restart the Docker daemon.
- Please use `build.sh` to start provisioning the console. If the user doesn't choose to stop the firewall, there will be problems when provisioning or after provisioning. So, in this case, we recommend using the root user.
- If the firewall is down, user `oracle` already exists, and the non-root user has Docker access permission, we can use this user to run this command.

Provisioning

As the OBP SDK is only for development purposes, each provisioned instance can live for only 60 days. Once expired, the instance will not work anymore. You need to provision a new instance to continue your testing or prototype if you need to.

Perform the following steps for provisioning:

1. Please use the following command line to start provisioning the console (if it's not started yet):

```
./build.sh [-d <package directory>, default is current path] [-w
provision workspace directory, default ~/obcs_workspace] [-p
provision console port, default 3000]
```

2. The following message will be observed:

```
Starting Provision...
46525ba502e9ea220cd65e1a18dc071bb4b79c680aae8834c4cd6ab8f6008e03
Starting Provision successfully
The provision console URL is: http://███████████:3000
```

OBP console URL

3. Now you are able to access the console from your local machine using `ssh` and port forwarding. On a Linux/mac system, open a Terminal window and enter the following:

```
ssh -L <localPort>:<remoteIP>:3000 opc@<remoteIP>
```

4. Then, from your local web browser, just enter `http://localhost:3000` and you should see the console's UI:

OBP console

Creating blockchain instance using the SDK

The process of creating blockchain instances using the OBP SDK is as follows:

1. Open the login URL of the VM, for example, `http://studentvm2:3000/`.
2. The Oracle **Sign In** page will be opened. A user needs to be created for the first time.
3. Enter the **Username** and **Password** (remember these credentials for future use).
4. Click on **Sign In**.

5. If the user doesn't exist, a dialog window with the title **Create User** will be opened, as shown in the following screenshot:

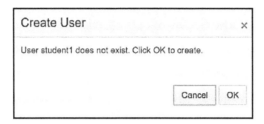

OBP SDK login

6. Click **OK** to create the user.
7. Once the user is created, the OBP **Instances** page will be opened, as shown in the following screenshot. Use this page to create an instance and list all the created instances:

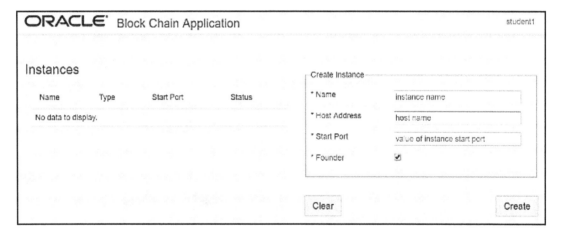

OBP SDK console

Creating a founder instance in the OBP SDK

To create a founder instance, provide details in the **Create Instance** section and make sure the **Founder** checkbox is ticked:

1. **Name**: As shown in the following screenshot, the name of the instance to be created can be set, for example, `detroitauto`.

2. **Host Address**: As shown in the following screenshot, enter the host address of the VM for which the SDK is set up. The instance will only be accessed using this host address.

3. **Start Port**: Referring to the screenshot, enter a port (or a range of ports) to access the console once the instance has been created:

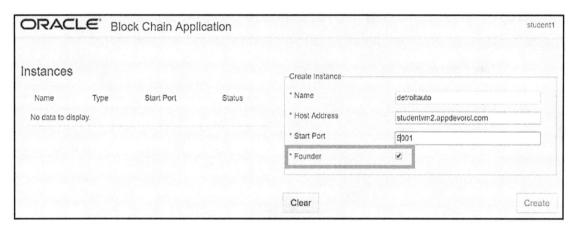

OBP sdk founder 1

4. Click on the **Create** button and wait for some time to see the created instance as multiple containers and VMs have to be created and make them up and running.

5. When the instance has been created, it will be visible under **Instances** on the left-hand side:

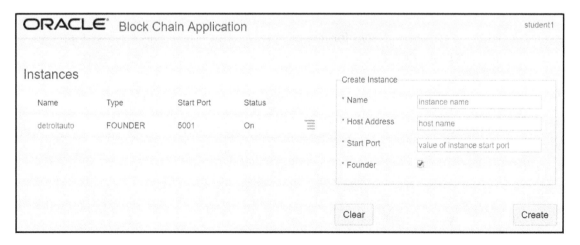

OBP SDK founder

6. On clicking the instance name, the blockchain console of the instance will be opened.

Let's now create a participant instance in the OBP SDK.

Creating a participant instance in the OBP SDK

To create a participant, follow the previous procedure, but uncheck **Founder**:

1. Check the following screenshot for reference:

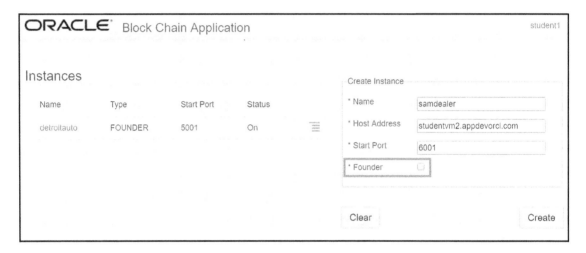

OBP SDK participant

2. Click on **Create** and wait for few minutes (in my case, it was 4 mins); then you will see that a new participant instance has been added to the **Instances** list, as shown:

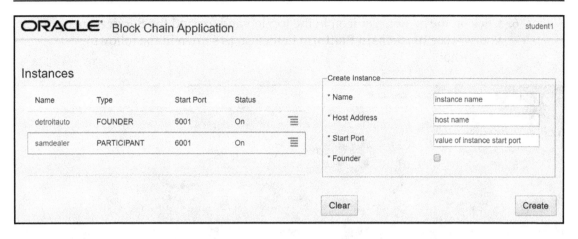

OBP SDK participant

Refer to the *Features and components of OBP* section to find out what the OBP console looks like and explore its features.

Provisioning OBP on Oracle Cloud

The procedure to access OBP in the Oracle cloud is as follows:

1. Open `https://cloud.oracle.com`.
2. Click **Sign In** in the top-right corner.
3. Enter your **Cloud Account Name** and click **Next**.
4. Enter your username and password and click on the **Sign In** button.
5. The **Cloud My Services** page will open.

6. Click on the hamburger icon in the top-left and expand the **Services** menu. Then you will see **Blockchain Platform** in the list, as shown in the following screenshot:

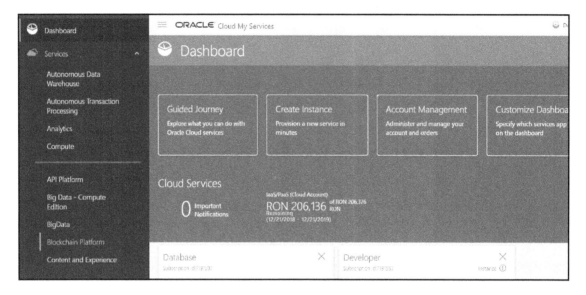

OBP cloud my services

7. Click on **Blockchain Platform**. It will open the OBP console. This is where you can create a new OBP instance or see the list of instances created in an account. You can also see the history of the activities of the instances:

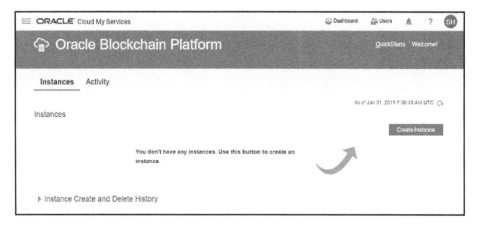

OBP cloud console

Creating a founder instance on Oracle Cloud

Once you open the OBP console as shown in the previous section, click on **Create Instance**:

1. The **Create Instance** page will open:

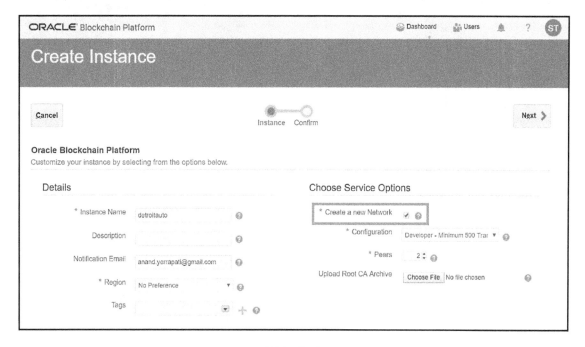

OBP cloud founder

2. Fill detail in the form as shown in the preceding diagram.
3. Make sure that the **Create a new Network** checkbox is enabled. This is very important when creating a founder.

4. Click on **Next**. A page with the details you have provided will appear for confirmation, as shown in the following screenshot:

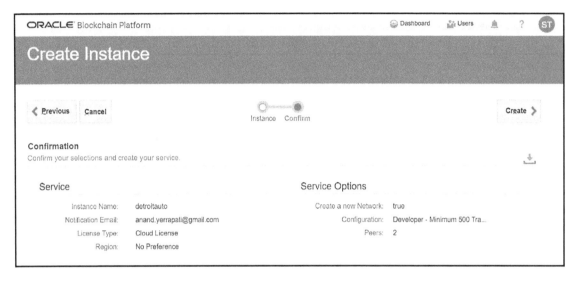

OBP cloud founder

5. Verify all the details and click on **Create**.
6. Wait for a while. The following screen will appear after successful creation of the instance. An email confirmation will be sent to the email addressed provided:

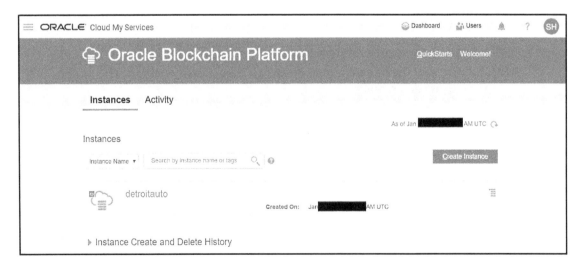

OBP cloud founder

7. Next to the instance name, click on the hamburger icon. A menu will be shown. If you click on the **Blockchain Console** option, the console of the instance will open.

Creating a participant instance on Oracle Cloud

To create a participant, follow the earlier procedure mentioned in *Creating a founder instance on Oracle Cloud* section but uncheck **Create a new network**:

1. Check the following screenshot for reference:

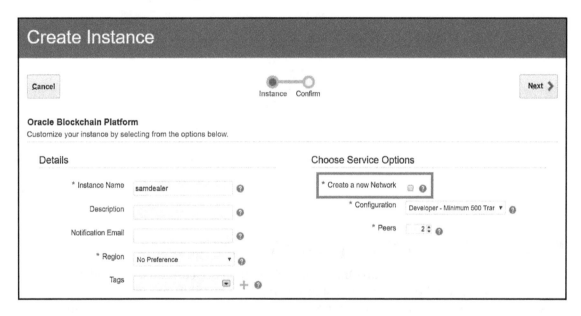

OBP cloud participant

2. After the participant instance has been created, you can see the list of instances on the **Instances** tab in the OBP console, as shown in the following screenshot:

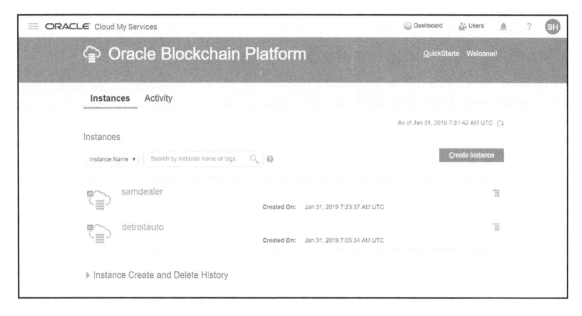

OBP cloud instances

Features and components of OBP

In this section, we will see how an Oracle blockchain instance console looks and examine its features. If you create the blockchain instance using the OBP SDK or through Oracle Cloud, the console of an OBP instance will be the same, as shown in the following screenshot:

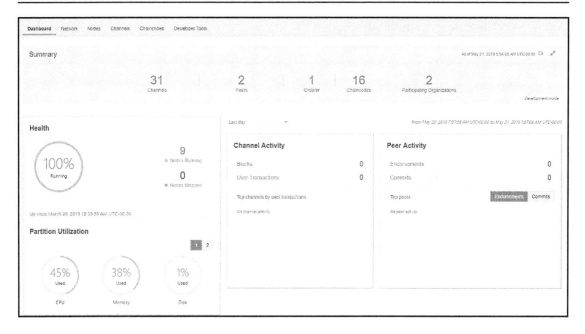

OBP instance dashboard

The console has multiple tabs, and we will explore each of them in the following sections.

Dashboard

This is the first tab, which shows the summary of the following:

- The number of channels the instance has created or is part of
- The number of peers the instance is using
- The number of chain codes deployed and running on the instance
- Activities of channels, such as the number of blocks created and number of user transactions on the channels
- Activities of peers, such as endorsements and commits
- The health of the instance, such as the number of nodes running and stopped
- Metrics of CPU, memory, and disk utilization

Along with these data on the dashboard, if the instance is a founder, then it also shows the order and the number of organizations participating in the network.

 There will be only one orderer per blockchain network, and it will be with the founder in OBP.

Network topology

This tab shows everyone who is participating in the network. Also, it shows a topology view of the network:

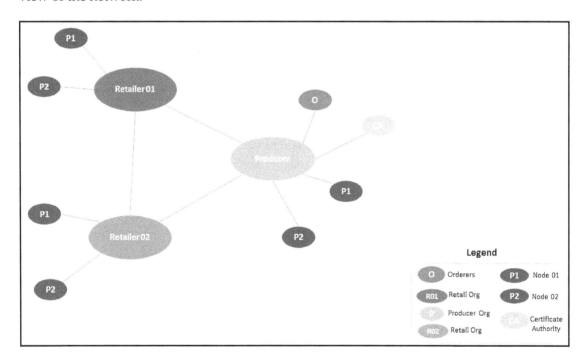

OBP network topology

The preceding diagram shows the network's structure and the relationship between organizations and nodes.

Nodes topology

This tab shows all the peers, including self peers and remote peers, who are all part of the network, and a CA node. If it is the founder, it can see an extra node for orderer. It also shows a topology view of the nodes and peers of the network:

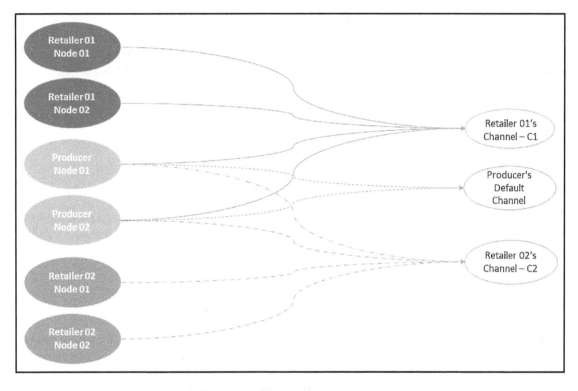

OBP nodes topology

The preceding diagram shows the relationship between peers and channels.

Channels

This tab is for managing the channels of the instance. It will list all the channels that the instance is part of. A new channel also can be created from here. Channel-level policies can be managed, new peers can be added to the channel, and organizations can be added to or removed from the channel. Each channel will have its own ledger and it will show all the blocks and transactions of a ledger. Once a channel has been created, it cannot be deleted.

Chaincodes

This tab is for managing the chaincodes and lists all the chaincodes of all the networks in the instance. The deployment, initiation, and instantiation of a chaincode can be done here. This chaincode can write to and update the ledger of the channel. Once the chaincode is deployed, it cannot be updated. A chaincode can be instantiated in multiple channels. Only one instantiation of a chaincode is allowed per version per chaincode in a channel, which means that if a chaincode is instantiated on a node in a channel, then the other nodes in the channel need only to deploy the chaincode, and instantiation will be reflected automatically on them. Each chaincode has its own logs and private data collections, which are also accessible from this tab.

Developer tools

This tab allows us to visit the OBP documentation and provides the download links for SDKs, tools, and pre-built sample chaincodes from Oracle.

We will see how to create a blockchain network and invite organizations to participate in the network, create and deploy chaincodes, use chaincodes, test the ledger, use REST proxy, and more, in the coming chapters.

Rich history database with OBP

OBP uses the Hyperledger Fabric history database to manage the ledger and present ledger transaction information in the console. Only chaincodes can access this history database and it cannot be exposed to any external applications to query for analytics. Analytics cannot be ignored in any business, even if they provide blockchain services. Hence, OBP integrates the rich history database to fulfill this requirement.

The rich history database is external to OBP and contains data about the blockchain ledger's transactions on the channels you select. You can integrate the rich history database into the OBP instance console and select the channels whose data needs to be captured in the database. Once the rich history database is enabled on a channel, then all the transactions on the channel sync to the database. This level of data collection makes the rich history database an excellent data source to generate analytics and visualization reports of the ledger activities. You can use any analytics tool, such as Oracle Analytics Cloud or Oracle Data Visualization Cloud Service, to access the rich history database and create analytics reports or data visualizations.

OBP only supports an Oracle database such as Oracle Autonomous Data Warehouse or **Oracle Database Cloud Service** (**ODCS**) with OCI to create your rich history database.

Create the ODCS connection string

OBP can be integrated with ODCS in OCI as a rich history database. However, it must also be enabled access to the database through port 1521.

Fetching ODCS information

The process of creating a connection to ODCS in the OCI console is as follows:

1. Log in to Oracle Cloud, and the **My Services** page will open.
2. Click on the hamburger icon in the top-left corner, expand the **Services** menu, and select the **Database** option.
3. Under **DB Systems**, locate the database to be connected and record its public IP address.
4. Click on the name of the database and capture the values of the following fields:
    - Database Unique Name
    - Host Domain Name
    - Port
5. Find the username and password of a database user with read permissions for this database.

Enabling port 1521 to access the database

The procedure to enable port 1521 on the ODCS is as follows:

1. As shown earlier, navigate to **DB Systems** and click the database to be connected.
2. Click on **Virtual Cloud Network**.
3. Under **Security Lists**, navigate to the corresponding subnet.

4. Click **Default Security List For <Target Database>**. The security list page will be displayed.

5. Click on **Edit All Rules**.

6. Add an ingress rule to allow any incoming traffic from the public internet to reach port 1521 on this database node with the following settings:

   - **SOURCE CIDR**: `0.0.0.0/0`
   - **IP PROTOCOL**: `TCP`
   - **SOURCE PORT RANGE**: `All`
   - **DESTINATION PORT RANGE**: `1521`
   - **Allows: TCP traffic for ports**: `1521`

Creating a connection string

After enabling access to the Oracle database, use the information collected to build the connection string in the **Configure Rich History** dialog. Construct the connection string as follows:

```
<publicIP>:<portNumber>/<database unique name>.<host domain name>
```

The following example shows what a connection string looks like:

```
123.213.85.123:1521/CustDB_iad1vm.sub05031027070.customervcnwith.oraclevcn.
com
```

Configuring the rich history database in OBP

Each blockchain network instance can configure its own rich history database, and here is the procedure to do this:

1. Open the console of the blockchain network instance.

2. Click on the option button (the hamburger icon in the top-right corner) and click on **Configure Rich History**. A configuration dialog will open:

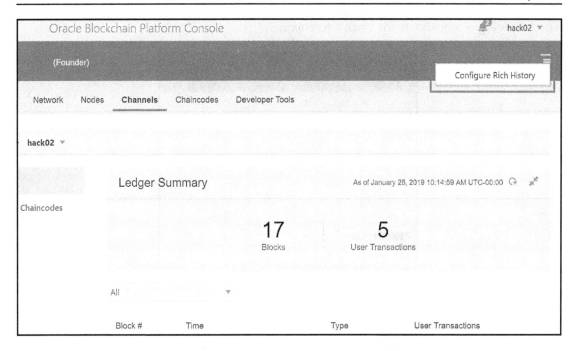

Configure rich history

3. Enter the **User Name** and **Password** of the database to be connected.

4. In the **Connection String** field, enter the connection string of the database in which the rich history data will be stored. This input depends on the Oracle database being used:

   - If the database is Oracle Autonomous Warehouse, then the connection string is like `<username>adw_high`.
   - If the database is ODCS with OCI, get the connection string as discussed in the *Create the ODCS connection string* section.
   - If you are using a non-autonomous database and want to use the `sys` user to connect the database, then you must append `?as=sys[dba|asm|oper]` to the connection string, for example, `123.123.123.123:1521/example.oraclevcn.com?as=sysdba`.
   - If you are using Oracle Autonomous Database, then instead of connection string, you can also use wallet file. This file contains client credentials and is generated from the Oracle autonomous database.

5. Click on the **Save** button.

6. To update this configuration, repeat the same procedure.

The following screenshot is for your reference:

Configure Rich History

Enabling channels that write data to the rich history database

Before enabling a rich history database on channels, it must be configured in the instance. Follow these steps:

1. Open the console of the blockchain instance and go to the **Channels** tab
2. Locate the channel and click on the **More Options** icon
3. To add the channel to the rich history database, click on the **Configure Rich History** option from the menu
4. A **Configure Rich History** dialog will open with an **Enable Rich History** checkbox
5. Click on the checkbox to add the channel, and uncheck it to remove the channel
6. Click on the **Save** button

Rich history database tables and columns

When the rich history database is configured on a channel, three tables will be created in the database for the channel: history, state, and latest height. To create analytic reports, the history and state tables will be queried:

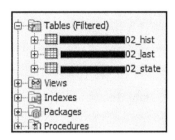

Rich history tables

Let's see each table and its columns.

History table

The name of this table is similar to `<instance name>_<channel name>_hist`.

This table contains the history of the ledger of the channel. Here is the list of columns and their datatypes:

Column	Datatype
chaincodeId	VARCHAR2 (256)
key	VARCHAR2 (1024)
txnIsValid	NUMBER (1)
value	VARCHAR2 (4000)
valueJson	CLOB
blockNo	NUMBER NOT NULL
txnNo	NUMBER NOT NULL
txnId	VARCHAR2 (128)
txnTimestamp	TIMESTAMP
txnIsDelete	NUMBER (1)

Note that the `value` and `valueJson` columns are used in a mutually exclusive way. That is, when a key value is valid JSON, then the value is set into the `valueJson` column. Otherwise, the value is set in the `value` column. The `valueJson` column is set up as a JSON column in the database, which means that users can query that column using the usual Oracle JSON-specific extensions.

State table

The name of this table is similar to `<instance name>_<channel name>_state`.

This table replicates data from the state database. Here is the list of columns and their datatypes:

Column	Datatype
chaincodeId	VARCHAR2 (256)
key	VARCHAR2 (1024)
value	VARCHAR2 (4000)
valueJson	CLOB
blockNo	NUMBER
txnNo	NUMBER

The `value` and `valueJson` columns are used in a mutually exclusive way, as in the history table.

Latest height table

The name of this table is similar to `<instance name>_<channel name>_last`.

This table is used by OBP internally to track the block height recorded in the rich history database. This table cannot be queried for analytics.

Here's a screenshot for your reference to see these earlier tables when the rich history database is connected to the **SQL Developer** tool:

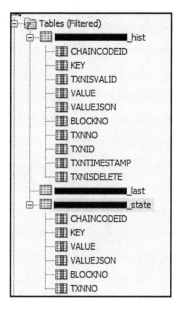

Rich history tables with columns

Summary

Businesses are constantly looking for effective and efficient ways to leverage blockchain technology, along with their SaaS, BPM, and other applications. BaaS allows them to realize it. This chapter offered a glimpse at OBP. This chapter was focused on designing a solution in line with the constructs of OBP. This chapter covered the sample business network topology, network artifacts, and solution and deployment architecture. This chapter also delved into defining and creating an instance of a founder-based business network and adding participants to it. The knowledge gained through this chapter will help you manage the blockchain network in the next chapter, and acts as a foundational milestone for developing solutions on OBP, as described in the previous chapter. The following chapter allows you to deep dive into the administration aspects of OBP and teaches you to translate network topology on OBP. It delves into peers, orders, and channel configurations. It also provides details on REST configuration and the administration of REST interfaces. Subsequent chapters will cover more on OBP and highlight the power of Oracle BaaS Platform.

Managing Solutions on Oracle Blockchain Platform

5

The previous chapter covered the business scenario and allowed us to explore **Oracle Blockchain Platform** (**OBP**). Managing solutions using OBP is a cinch; it allows you to experiment with the doing rather than reading about the doing, as it effectively demonstrates the doing with samples. This chapter offers in-depth facts on OBP and allows you to graduate with the practical knowledge of OBP. With this chapter, you'll get into the practicality of translating the network topology onto OBP, creating network stakeholders, and configuring OBP instances. This ledger of knowledge illustrates setting up transaction infrastructures, joining participants to business networks, access control, adding smartness (chaincode) to business networks, and using the REST proxy configuration to expose chaincode to dApps. For the most part, the OBP SDK and OBP on Oracle Cloud are similar in features, except for the steps that let you create OBP instances. The differences between the two options are not large and are also self-explanatory. This chapter primarily covers translating the network topology on OBP, adding business smartness to the OBP network and using the Administration REST Interface.

Translating the network topology onto OBP

This section describes how to create network instances on OBP. As described in the *Designing the solution* section of `Chapter 4`, *Engage in Business Case on Blockchain Platform*, a blockchain network requires the following business entities:

- **Oracle Empire University** (**OEU**) as a founder entity
- **Oracle Red School** (**ORS**) and **Certificate Viewer/Verifier** (**CVs**) as participant entities

Creating network stakeholders with OBP instances

The foundational step toward building an OBP solution involves the creation of OBP instances for the stakeholder entities. Perform the following steps in order to create the necessary OBP instances for the use case:

1. Launch and log in to the OBP provisioning console. Refer to the *Setting up OBP SDK* section of `Chapter 4`, *Engage in Business Case on Blockchain Platform*, to get the OBP provisioning console details.
2. After logging in, start creating OBP instances by filling instance details.
3. The following screenshot shows the sample values for creating an instance. Note these two important points:
   - The **Founder** checkbox must only be selected for Founder instances.
   - Provide values of different OBP instances for **Start Port**. Make sure that these port values are considerably far apart as OBP assigns multiple values consecutive to the start port internally, as shown in the following screenshot:

Creating an instance

4. Once all the OBP instances for our use case are created (and activated), they will show on the provisioning console, as shown in the following screenshot:

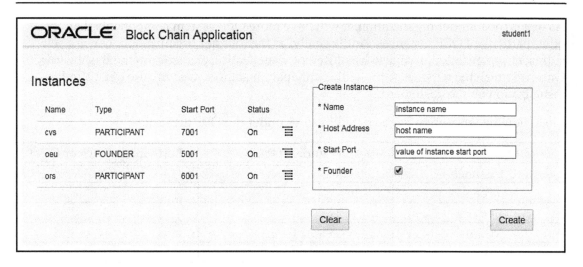

Summary of the FOUNDER and PARTICIPANT instances

5. Click on the context menu for each of the OBP instances and select **Console URL** to navigate to the OBP dashboard of the respective instance. The next steps for the OBP network creation of our use case are done through the OBP dashboard:

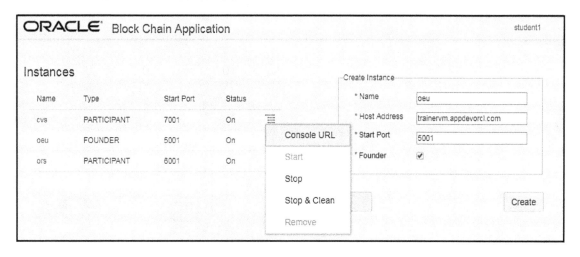

Context menu for the OBP instance

As **oeu** is the founder organization, it will have more OBP system components than the other participant OBP instances. Additionally, as the founder organization, **oeu** is a self-sufficient organization, so it also has different visualization elements on the dashboard. Once we finish the network setup with participant instances, we will also get a similar visualization on the dashboard.

The following table gives us the default values under the OBP artifacts:

OBP artifacts	Founder (OEU)	Participant (ORS or CVs)
Channel	1	0
Peers	2	2
Orderer	1	0
CA	1	1
REST Proxy	2	2

The following screenshot shows the **oeu** dashboard, which is the dashboard for the founder organization (**oeu**):

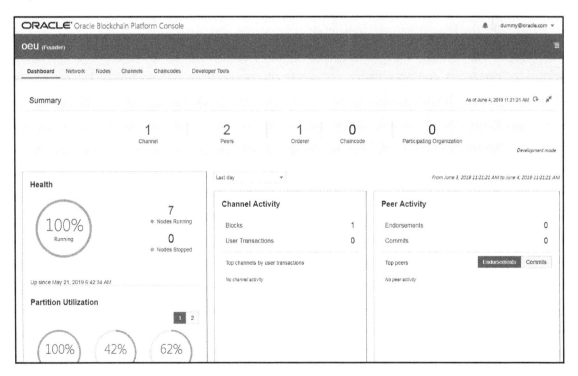

OBP founder dashboard

Take a look at the **ors** dashboard. The **ors** and **cvs** dashboards have a similar appearance:

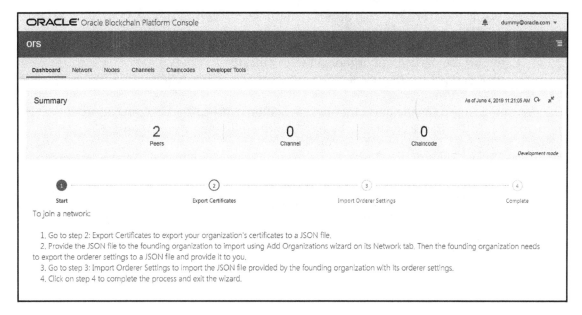

OBP participant dashboard

Configuring the OBP network infrastructure

After creating OBP instances, the next step in building the OBP solution is to establish a blockchain transactional network between these instances. This section will take you through the steps to connect all OBP instances in a network and enable an underlying shared ledger infrastructure.

The following sections lay out the steps.

Exporting/importing participant certificates

Export the participant (**ors** and **cvs**) organization/instance certificates and import them to the founder OBP instance. The steps are as follows:

1. Export the participant organization certificates
2. Import the participant organization certificates to the founder organization

The first step is to export the participant organization certificates. You can export a participant's OBP instance certificate by either of the following two options:

- **Option 1**: Using the dashboard wizard, as shown in the following screenshot:

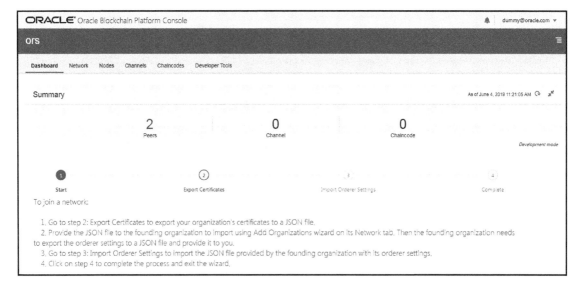

OBP participant export certificate flow

- **Option 2**: From the organization's context menu under the **Network** tab of the OBP dashboard for the participants (**ors** and **cvs**):

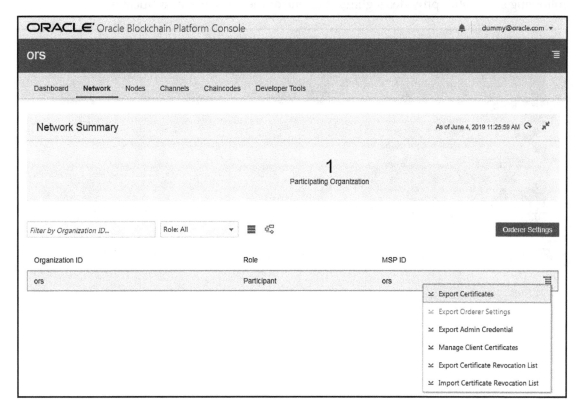

OBP participant network summary

A participant certificate is a JSON file containing its certificate keys for admin, **certificate authority** (**CA**), and **Transport Layer Security** (**TLS**), along with its signature. The following screenshot provides a glimpse of one of the participant certificates:

OBP participant certificate snapshot

The second step is to import participant organization certificates into the founder organization. Follow these steps to import the participant certificate into the founder organization:

1. Move over to the founder dashboard (**oeu**) to import these participants' certificates. This can be achieved by selecting the **Add Organizations** option under the **Network** tab on the **oeu** page. These steps are depicted in the following screenshot.
2. Add an organization by importing the participant certificates of **ors** and **cvs**:

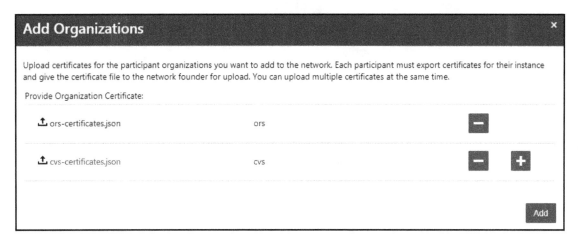

Importing the participant certificates

The **Network** tab for the founder allows us to import the participant certificate:

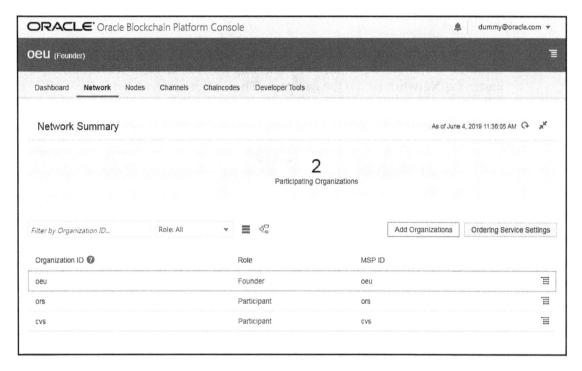

Founder network summary

Orderer configuration

The next set of steps for setting up the OBP network is importing the orderer configuration from **Founder** to **Participant**.

Since the orderer is associated with the founder instance at the infrastructure level, it becomes imperative to perform this setup. It ensures that any blockchain proposals (transactions) submitted by **Participant** peers are taken up by the same orderer for validation, as well as ordering of ledger blocks, before finally being written to the shared ledger.

The following steps provide step-by-step instructions on how to complete the orderer configuration setup:

1. Export the orderer settings of the **Founder** instance by using the **Export Orderer Settings** option, which is under the **Network** tab:

Export the orderer settings of the Founder instance

Technically, the orderer settings in OBP are also represented and stored as a JSON file and contain founder certificates, signatures, and orderer endpoints. You will also get a similar JSON file for the orderer, as shown in the following screenshot:

```
{
  "mspID": "osu",
  "certs": {
    "admincert": "-----BEGIN
CERTIFICATE-----\nMIIB8DCCAZegAwIBAgIUYkZjrgRiuFx6XFGr6lVT/6rLfYUwCgYIKoZIzj0EAwIw\nHDEMMAoGA1UEChMDb2V1MQswCgYDVQQDEwNvZXUwHhcNMTkwNjA0MDUxNzAwW
hcN\nMjAwNjAzMDUyMjAwWjBEMRswDQYDVQQLEwZjbG11bnQwCgYDVQQLEwNvZXUxIjAg\nBgNVBAMMGNN1c3RvbWVydGVuYN5OQG9yYWNsZS5jb20wMTATBgcqhkjOPQIBBgqq\nhkjOPQMB
BwNCAAQgxMBV/0HA1MOO4XSgiXbz4MAYHsi5UiHwU7d6kWymfX5QN1zC\nRataYEMCnNcXONEjVio/juV1gJuteyYpYrLpo4GRMIGOMA4GA1UdDwEB/wQEAwIH\ngDAMBgNVHRMBAf8EAjAAM
B0GA1UdDgQWBBQzFTnxvbQO5GRgAstKm5NghF4IhTAf\nBgNVHSMEGDAWgBTgpkXfe21S82Y1+Y0Nsp8aDp596jAuBgNVHREEJzAlgglsb2Nh\nbGGhv3c38CGHRyYW1uZXJmb8hcHBkzXZvcm
NsLmNvbTAKBggqhkjOPQQDAgNHADBE\nAAiB6YeBe2dfagDXi6S1nR0YEfrKj6ZmrKzu7wASPOE3GOQIgEKPS13tR8Ewy1rQG\n9YJJ7X8CsyemgfkCzJ/EUcjtzWE=\n-----END
CERTIFICATE-----\n",
    "cacert": "-----BEGIN
CERTIFICATE-----\nMIIBfsCCASNgAwIBAgIUc84gjsJWBW4qzbVdmSuppOGUe2IwCgYIKoZIzj0EAwIw\nHDEMMAoGA1UEChMDb2V1MQswCgYDVQQDEwNvZXUwHhcNMTkwNjA0MDUxNzAwW
hcN\nMzQwNTMxMDUxNzAwWjAcMQwwCgYDVQQLEwNvZXUxDDAKBgNVBANTA291dTBZMBMG\nByqGSM49AgEGCCqGSM49AwEHA0IABJnBL1+YURXmZ8j2ub1qpW/eqdqMyY/YxqM3\ncyoRWj0T
E9JRVyA+5LXcRrWrr5dMXL5eFnFu3V4yxLfGoqqm9pWjRTBDMA4GA1Ud\nDwEB/wQEAwIBBjASBgNVHRMBAf8ECDAGAQH/AgEBMB0GA1UdDgQWBBTgpkXfe21S\n82Y1+Y0Nsp8aDp596jAKB
ggqhkjOPQQDAgNIADBFAiEA6GarIsGNtr9jYdljqo8a\n3FJq9BT4xxD1XgWoIG4GVDgCIEFsK6MYXD1bLghHBzTzLCkf197UaRRzA6cBiuD2\n226K\n-----END
CERTIFICATE-----\n",
    "tlscacert": "-----BEGIN
CERTIFICATE-----\nMIIDcsCCAlugAwIBAgIJANE+81ouq1G5MA0GCSqGSIb3DQEBCwUAMFAxDTALBgNV\nBAMMBE15Q0ExCzAJBgNVBAgMAloxMQswCQYDVQQGEwJaMjEYMBYGCSqGSIb3D
QEJ\nARYJenpAenouY29tMQswCQYDVQQKDAJaMzAsFw0xODExMjMwOTA1MzdaFw0yODA4\nMjIwOTA1MzdaMFAxDTALBgNVBAMMBE15Q0ExCzAJBgNVBAgMAloxMQswCQYDVQQG\nEwJaMjEY
MBYGCSqGSIb3DQEJARYJenpAenouY29tMQswCQYDVQQKDAJaMzCCASIw\nDQYJKoZIhvcNAQEBBQADggEPADCCAQoCggEBAOEb23eBCoKJ+YC5mlbNQ10N10+N\nznNKGCm0TVAcaV8P6Cqd8h
Vz5ZeRt3s1amtv3TFCS8Pd+BiCXDqFyYmlQdRiOgp2N\n11JCDZwGnASCNp1Hqw3LTU1GrHu1W3/+DO5YGEoYDbJiZjKv4rmLT1BYI4qIY1Ga\ntnTnPXoIKmjYJDZ818NQM2ejjiC+nBVRHyqy
Flku2exz26AiZ7tUxxxir/WTssMFET\nnXSybGI4aqgL3VM8zo9knzz9nCSrQ/8dZWe9882Yg/j1EUQQUIew5as7gHAUYEke/\nnFFkmvpNHXpcqUW8mtypCxudK2k7e+w2uSoRfBWUFR8b/E23N
oR1/AYOzPaBsCAwEA\nAaANQME4wDAYDVR0TBAUwAwEB/zAdBgNVHQ4EFgQU7276E00A6EDvzfZbtoGWuagS\nnjc4wHwYDVR0jBBgwFoAU7276E00A6EDvzfZbtoGWuagSjc4wDQYJKoZIhvcN
AQEL\nBQADggEBAAIbTU4USxqfa5Z5K08Jntleg08gygUxHzvK5jRbuVz/Y7CNc3Xi/hP\nqnlIEGZrCns/75SReUjhv3kd+w4TFR1YMoFcKP9RF0THsIBGOjwzGUWf+GBIrxP3\nnHtN9sx8
bVg9RhJ/fNPLhUsKctF2tkJz9sTvc8QEiX8KOHKIaztCZ8UGwfXeL21KtJ\n1EOJbvpa4U76SaCafPN9iOHgleFZenn87qMfsqIFiJINS5o9r0KYLfgoOrWEVc37\nn6blbKlf2AJiRu5LcGzrX
h9I3tSRw17IgTqY3dzV0AOiHY9ycXqRB8NEl2Cw?cM/k\nn8tEzie6uESRa3jfBqmm7kkrbahHpH8o=\n-----END CERTIFICATE-----\n"
  },
  "orderingServiceNodes": [
    {
      "address": "grpcs://trainervm.appdevorcl.com:5017",
      "adminAddress": "https://trainervm.appdevorcl.com:5018"
    }
  ],
  "signature":
"8afd2f040acd48a4852a7e4b569b8da5f4392cf9fae50da93bfb2cf37e0afe7eb55ab3522d7e413b966a4620a8cc0c37d710354d3422c1a2e6ef525ba46d6e90416417c87485598066
ceba79d2681253767fdd776e717b8309ff00aa714efbaec614a6937743dfead1d4eea58eb4bcae6eb19c183fd435002b6b231bdd7dc7dd"
}
```

JSON file of the orderer settings

2. Import the orderer settings to each of the participants (**ors** and **cvs**), as shown in the next few screenshots.

3. Click the **Orderer Settings** import option under the **Network** tab of the **ors** dashboard:

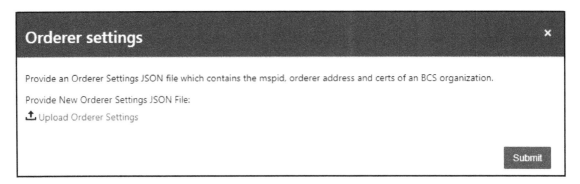

Orderer settings   ✕

Provide an Orderer Settings JSON file which contains the mspid, orderer address and certs of an BCS organization.

Provide New Orderer Settings JSON File:

⬆ Upload Orderer Settings

Submit

Orderer settings JSON file

4. Upload the orderer file exported from the **oeu** instance:

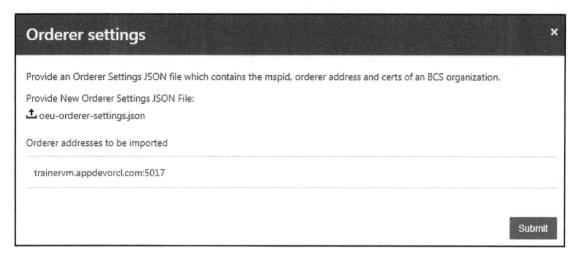

5. Once the **Orderer settings** import is complete, you can choose the **Orderer Settings View** option to verify the orderer details. Please note that the following **Orderer Addresses** instance is the same as the orderer endpoint in the **Orderer settings** JSON file exported from founder:

Configuring the OBP transaction infrastructure

After setting the base OBP network infrastructure, as seen in the previous section, it is now time to set up an OBP transaction infrastructure. Primarily, this is defining the shared ledger in system configurations and associating parties (OBP instances) who can read/write to the ledger.

For our use case, this would involve setting up a channel with OEU (the founder) and adding the ORS, CVs, and OBP instances to the same channel. Refer to the *Network topology* and *Channels* sections of `Chapter 4`, *Engage in Business Case on Blockchain Platform*, for more details.

As the name suggests, channels are logical or configuration constructs in OBP, which allow two or more network stakeholders to share data. This sharing of data is done via the shared ledger. Hence, each channel in OBP essentially also represents the underlying shared ledger associated with it.

Channel setup

Let's proceed with the necessary channel creation for the use case:

1. Go to the **Channels** tab of the **oeu** dashboard and click on **Create a New Channel**.
2. Update the following fields:
   - **Channel Name**: Provide a name for the channel.
     Keep a note of it because you will need it when making chaincode calls.
   - Select the checkboxes for the **ors** and **cvs** instances.

- Select one or more peers of **oeu** to join the channel, as shown in the following screenshot:

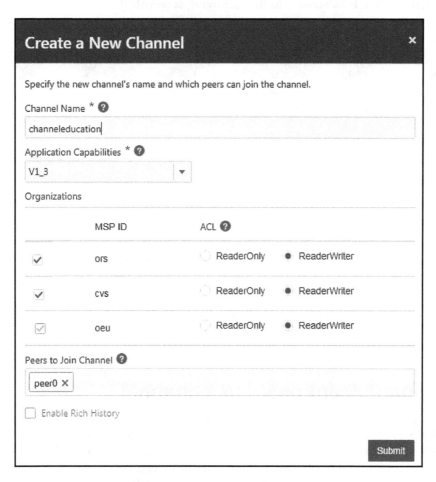

Creating a channel

Once the channel creation is successful, you can see a corresponding notification on the **oeu** dashboard, and the newly created channel will be shown in the existing **Channels** list. The **oeu Channels** tab will look similar to the following screenshot:

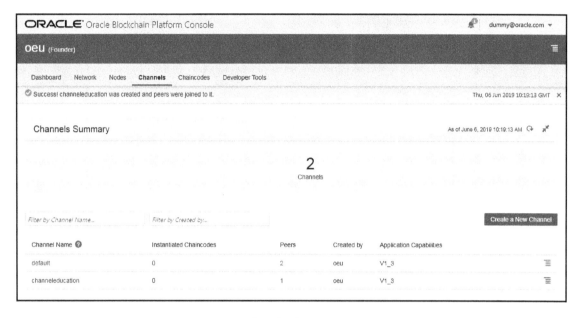

Create channel summary

Joining participant peers to a channel

After creating a channel with OEU's OBP instance, add the peer nodes of the participants, ORS and CVS, to the same channel. By doing so, we ensure that any transaction submitted by the application clients of the respective OBP instances for that channel will be taken by the peer nodes and added to the channel for validation, chaincode execution, and RWSet creation. This RWSet will then be submitted to the orderer for the sequencing of ledger blocks.

You can add a participant's peer to a channel by either of the following options:

- Using the context menu of the peer node under the **Nodes** tab of the participant OBP dashboard, as shown in the following screenshot:

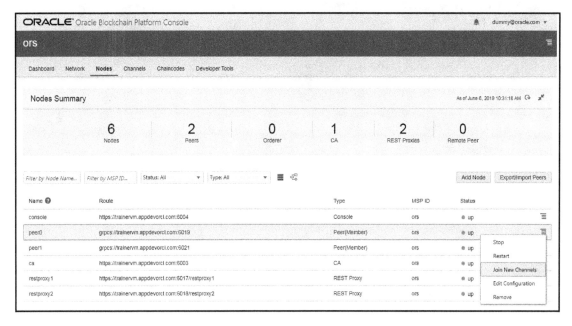

Node summary

- Using the context menu of the channel under the **Channels** tab of the participant OBP dashboard, as shown in the following screenshot:

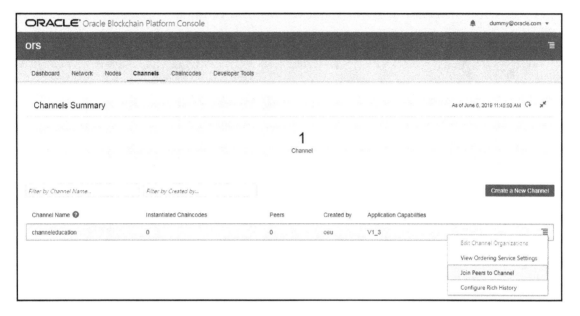

Channel summary

Moving ahead with option 2, you will be asked to select the **Peers to Join Channel** option. You can select one or more peers of the instance to join:

Joining the channel

Once the participant peers have joined the channel, the topology view of the OBP instance nodes should look as shown in the screenshots in the following sections.

Founder node summary

The following screenshot shows the node summary for the founder organization:

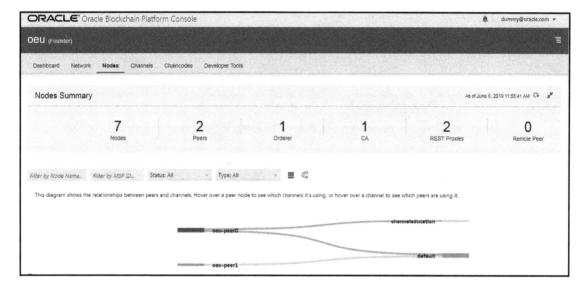

Founder node summary

Participant (ors) node summary

The following screenshot shows the node summary for the **ors** organization:

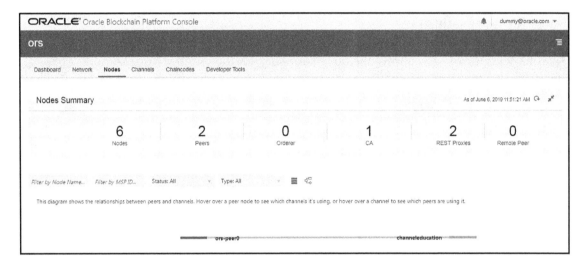

Participant node summary

Participant (cvs) node summary

The following screenshot shows the node summary for another participant (**cvs**) organization:

Participant node summary

Additionally, verify that the network topology view for OEU, ORS, and CVs are showing the visualizations shown in the following screenshots.

Founder network summary

The following screenshot shows the founder organization's (**oeu**) network summary:

Founder network summary

Participant (ors) network summary

The following screenshot shows one of the participant organization's network summary:

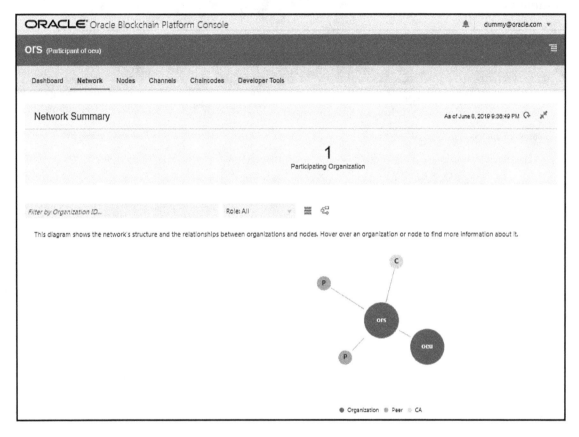

Participant (ors) network summary

Participant (cvs) network summary

The following screenshot shows the other participant organization's (**cvs**) network summary:

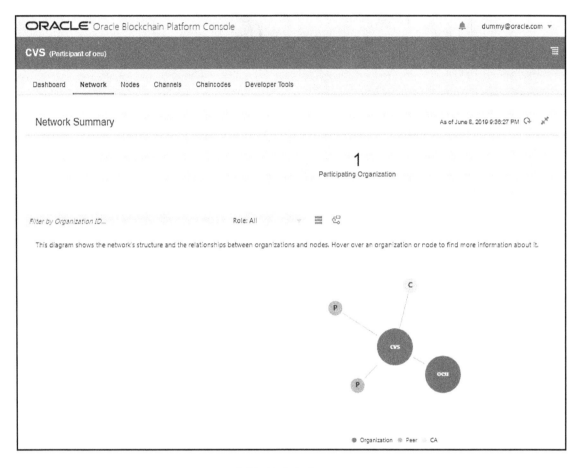

Participant (cvs) network summary

Adding smartness to the OBP network

The subsequent chapter extensively covers adding business smartness to the OBP network through chaincode development and exposing chaincode functionality to client applications. The following section provides a sneak preview of it.

Developing chaincode to add smartness to the OBP network

After completing the steps to configure the OBP network, the next set of implementation involves adding smartness to it. Typically, this means adding our use case business logic as smart contracts or chaincode. It deals with the installation and instantiation of chaincode on all the nodes of the network instances.

The next chapter of this book covers the implementation of chaincode and related network artifacts for our use case. Chapter 6, *Developing Solutions on Oracle Blockchain Platform*, covers the development, deployment, and instantiation of chaincode as needed for the use case. For more details about the design of network artifacts, refer to the *Network artifacts* section of Chapter 4, *Engage in Business Case on Blockchain Platform*.

Exposing chaincode via REST proxy configuration

These configurations typically include definitions to expose chaincode functionality to a client application (such as a dApp). For the sake of sequential continuity, refer to the chaincode deployment section of Chapter 6, *Developing Solutions on Oracle Blockchain Platform*, for details on REST proxy configuration.

REST Interface for OBP

All the administration and configuration steps for setting up and managing your OBP network (as mentioned in previous sections) can also be performed using OBP's Administration REST services. These services are useful for scenarios where the following is required:

* Reducing the manual mode of these activities

- Implementing an automated way (such as the DevOps pipeline) for setting up and managing the OBP network
- Representing OBP administration information in a customized way

These administration REST interfaces include services related to organizations, nodes, channels, and chaincode. Additionally, OBP also provides a bundle of OBP Statistics REST services.

The following is the list of OBP Administration REST services:

- Organizations REST endpoints: Under organizations REST endpoints, the following are the list of services:
  - Get organization certificates
  - Get organization admin credentials
  - Get the ordering service settings in a founder organization
  - Join a new organization to a founder organization
  - Set an ordering service to a participant organization
- Nodes REST endpoint: Under nodes REST endpoint, following are the list of services:
  - Get node list
  - Get a list of peers on a channel
  - Get a list of peers for a specific chaincode
  - Add a peer node
  - Start/stop a peer node
  - Remove a peer node
  - Get/set a peer node's attributes
  - Join a peer to a channel
  - Export/import peers
  - Start/stop an orderer
  - Get/set an orderer's attributes
  - Start/stop a CA node
  - Get/set a CA's attributes
  - Start/stop REST proxy
  - Get/set REST proxy's configuration

- Channel REST endpoint: Under channels REST endpoint, the following are the list of services:
  - Create a channel
  - Get a channel list
  - Get a channel list for chaincode
  - Get a channel list for a peer
  - Update a channel configuration
  - Get a channel information
  - Get a ledger block by block ID
  - Get blocks by ID range
  - Get blocks by time range
- Chaincode REST endpoint: Under chaincode REST endpoint, the following are the list of services:
  - Get a list of installed chaincodes
  - Get a list of chaincodes on a specific peer
  - Get a list of chaincodes on a channel
  - Install chaincode
  - Instantiate chaincode
  - Get chaincode info
- Statistics REST endpoint: Under statistics REST endpoint, the following are the list of services:
  - List of the currently existing channels and the peers joined on each channel
  - Current number and list of channels joined by the specified peer
  - Current number and list of installed chaincodes on the specified peer
  - Current number of instantiated chaincodes on the specified channel
  - List of configured chaincodes for a specified proxy or for all proxies
  - Node health status
  - Node usage related metrics (CPU, memory, disk usage)
  - Total number of asynchronous invocations
  - Number of billable transactions
  - Number of blocks
  - Number of commits

- Number of endorsements
- Total number of synchronous invocations
- Number of user transactions for peer or channel or the entire network

For more details about these services, please refer to the OBP documentation.

Summary

This chapter primarily covered the first set of steps toward experimenting with an OBP solution. We have covered translating the network topology on OBP, configuring the OBP network infrastructure, configuring the OBP transaction infrastructure, adding business smartness to the OBP network, REST proxy configuration, and administrating the REST Interface.

The next chapter explores chaincode development, such as language section, development tools, and the development environment setup. It also covers the full life cycle of chaincode from development to updates, which includes installing, initiating, testing, and versioning. It demonstrates a full chaincode with a codebase built with Go and Node.js. It also illustrates endorsement policies, private data collection, chaincode testing via shim and REST endpoints, and integrating client apps with a business network using an SDK, REST, and events.

6
Developing Solutions on Oracle Blockchain Platform

The previous chapter allowed you to experiment with doing rather than reading about doing, as it effectively demonstrated developing the samples. The preceding chapter offered in-depth facts on the **Oracle Blockchain Platform** (**OBP**) and taught the practicalities of translating network topology on OBP, creating network stakeholders, and configuring OBP instances. This concluding chapter delves into chaincode and covers details of chaincode development, including the language section, development tools, and development environment setup. This chapter also focuses on mapping asset models, operations, and developing chaincode functions and interfaces. It details the full life cycle of chaincode, from development to updates, including installation, initiation, testing, and versioning. It also demonstrates the full chaincode with a code base build on Go and Node.js. Endorsement policy, private data collections, and their functioning in concert with chaincode are also illustrated. This chapter also demonstrates chaincode testing via shim and REST endpoints and integrating client apps with business networks using SDK, REST, and events. Finally, it concludes with insights into chaincode, transactions, and channels by experimenting with the monitoring of business via chaincode logs and channel logs. The chapter covers topics such as setting up chaincode development, chaincode development, chaincode deployment, testing chaincode, and integrating client applications with blockchain.

Setting up chaincode development

In this section, you will learn how to develop chaincode for the university use case that we used in previous chapters.

Choosing the language for development (GO, Node.js, or Java)

Programming skills are very much required to write chaincode. As blockchain has a distributed ledger, only the Go language was supported in the initial versions of **Hyperledger Fabric** (**HLF**). However, with the evolution of HLF, it now supports multiple languages and plans to add more in the future. As of Fabric version 1.3, it supports writing chaincode in Go, Node.js, and Java. To explore each of these, you can download samples from under the **Developer tools** tab in the OBP instance console.

Tools for OBP solution development

This section equips you with the development tools and development environment details.

Development environment

OBP leverages HLF as its foundation, hence use the HLF documentation for help with writing valid chaincode. All the chaincode files should be packaged in a ZIP file and installed on OBP. If the chaincode is developed in the Go language and it has only one file, which is .go, then the packaging is optional. A standalone file can be installed on OBP.

Development tools

There are no specific recommended tools from either HLF or OBP. A developer can use any tools, such as a text editor or an IDE such as NetBeans, VS Code, and so on. The choice of tool depends on the interest of the developer and the language selected for the chaincode development. It is always good to use an IDE for the development to avoid syntax errors, to format the code to be easy to read, and to make development easy.

Chaincode development, for the sample use case in this book, is performed using **VS Code** (short for **Visual Studio Code**). VS Code is a source code editor from Microsoft, available for Windows, Linux, and macOS. It includes support for development, debugging, versioning, syntax highlighting, intelligent code completion, and code refactoring.

The following are a few screenshots of the chaincode file in VS Code for reference:

- Here is the source code window:

VS Code source code window

- Direct installations of plugins required:

VS Code Plugins direct installation

- There are multiple plugins available to install on VS Code for the selected language:

VS Code: plugins

Mapping the asset model

Chaincode results in the creation of assets (key-value pairs) on the ledger, as HLF represents assets as key-value pairs. Assets state changes are recorded as transactions on the channel's ledger. There are few ways to represent assets—in binary or JSON form. For the university use case in this book, two assets are defined:

- One for student information
- Another for the certificate generated

This chapter includes the creation of basic assets and chaincode to enable quick learning of the development process. The inclusion of more assets and a comprehensive set of operations might lead to the investment of time in the modeling of the use case itself. Later, when you've experimented more with the use case, you can add more complexity to it.

Using the Go language, the following are the definitions of the two assets:

1. An asset to define a certificate receiver:

Parameter	Description
assetType	The type of asset, for example, a receiver
receiver_id	The ID of a receiver/student
receiver_name	The name of the receiver/student
upload_org	The organization/department of the certificate uploaded

2. An asset to define a certificate:

Parameter	Description
assetType	The type of asset, for example, a certificate.
Cert_id	The ID of the certificate.
Cert_no	The number of the certificate.
Cert_name	The name of the certificate.
Cert_receiver	The receiver of the certificate. This will be fetched from the ledger by the given Cert_receiver_id parameter.
Cert_receiver_id	The ID of the receiver/student to whom this certificate is assigned.
Cert_issuer	The issuer of the certificate.
Cert_industry	The industry/department of the certificate.
Cert_create_time	The time the certificate was created at.
Cert_update_time	The time the certificate was changed if any changes are made.
Cert_remark	Remarks or comments on the certificate, if any.
Cert_url_image	The certificate image URL.
Cert_learning_processing	Certificate learning proceeding.
Cert_status	The status of the certificate.

Chaincode is a software program (a group of smart contracts) or business logic that defines an asset and allows modifications to an asset (aka state changes). Any transaction (as allowed by chaincode) will result in a new set of an asset's key-value pair or the modification of an asset's key-value pair, or the deletion of an asset's key-value pair.

Mapping operations

Chaincode (smart contracts) generates transactions that are distributed to every peer node in a network. Upon consensus, they are immutably recorded in the local copy of the ledger. Users use a client application or a dApp to invoke such transactions (aka operations). Chapter 3, *Delving into Hyperledger Fabric*, covers transactions in detail and also showcases examples of transaction flows. Notice that there are two types of transactions—deploy transactions and invoke transactions. A deploy transaction creates a new chaincode and results in the installation of chaincode on the blockchain business network, whereas an invoke transaction performs an operation on the installed and initiated chaincode.

This table concentrates on the implementation of the invoke operations/transactions:

Operation	Description
initReceiver	Creates an entry of the certificate receiver (student)
queryReceiverById	Fetches the receiver details by the given receiver ID
insertCertificateInfo	Creates an entry for the certificate
queryCertificateBytId	Fetches the certificate details by the given certificate ID
getHistoryForRecord	Gets a history of the receiver (student) information or certificate changes
queryAllCertificates	Fetches all certificates
approveCertificate	Changes the status of a certificate
del	Marks delete on a receiver or certificate

Take a look at Chapter 3, *Delving into Hyperledger Fabric*, to learn about more interesting aspects, such as concurrency checks, types of transactions (such as *ledger-query* and *ledger-update* transactions), transaction flow, and various other components involved in transactions.

Demystifying the craft of chaincode development

With HLF, chaincode must implement the chaincode interface in any of these languages: Go, Node.js, or Java. A chaincode developer can select any of these programming languages to develop in. Fabric's shim package (github.com/hyperledger/fabric/core/chaincode/shim) is paramount in chaincode development.

It provides support for all earlier languages. This package has two interfaces, which play a key role in the chaincode. The syntax of these interfaces and their methods may change, depending on the language, but their purpose is the same.

Essentially, when a transaction is received, these chaincode interfaces are called. Firstly, when a chaincode receives a transaction request, the `Init` method is invoked. This allows for the initialization of the application state. Subsequently, the `Invoke` methods are called when an invoke transaction is received to process any transaction proposals. Other interfaces that are used to modify the ledger, allowing invocations between chaincode, include the chaincode shim API called `ChaincodeStubInterface`.

Chaincode interfaces

Chaincode interface is mandatory to implement chaincode that has two methods:

- `Init()`: This method will be invoked only once in the life of the chaincode, when the chaincode is instantiated or upgraded. This method helps to set up the initial state of the ledger, such as initializing any serial numbers. It expects the `ChaincodeStubInterface` object as input and returns the `peer.Response` object.

  Syntax: `Init(stub ChaincodeStubInterface)`

- `Invoke()`: This method will help to invoke the user transaction. You may have several operations in your code, but when a client sends a request to chaincode, it only comes to the `Invoke()` method and, from here, this method will dispatch to the corresponding transaction. This method also takes the input of the `ChaincodeStubInterface` object and returns the `peer.Response` object.

  Syntax: `Invoke(stub ChaincodeStubInterface)`

ChaincodeStubInterface

Interface to stub provides functions to access history and the state of the ledger via calls to peers. The `Invoke()` method is called for each transaction and it passes the function and the parameters as a `stub` input requested by the client. This interface facilitates many functions to interact with the ledger and makes chaincode development easy.

Chaincode functions

ChaincodeStub is implemented by the fabric-shim library. It is supplied to ChaincodeInterface and encapsulates the APIs between the chaincode implementation and the Fabric peer.

Although stub has many functions, this section lists a few of them that are frequently used:

- getFunctionAndParameters() (string, []string): This method helps to get the function and the parameters from the stub. This method returns two values: the name of the function as a string and the parameters as a string array.
- getState(key string) ([]byte, error): This method fetches data from the state ledger by the given key. It doesn't read data from the ledger that has not been committed. It returns data as a byte array and error information if there is any.
- putState(key string, value []byte) (error): This method will put the given value in a transaction's write set as a proposal. This doesn't affect the ledger until the transaction is valid and successfully committed. This decision will be taken by Orderer. All the transaction data in the ledger is stored as a key-value pair only. This method takes two parameters: key—a unique string value for data, and value—a byte array of data to be stored in the ledger. This method returns the error parameter if there are any errors while executing. The same method can be used for both *insert* and *update*.
- delState(key string) error: This method deletes the value of the given key from the ledger. As the data in the blockchain ledger cannot be deleted permanently, this method marks the data deleted and the block remains in the ledger. The input for this method is a key and it returns an error if there is one.
- getHistoryForKey(key string) (HistoryQueryIteratorInterface, error): This is a read-only method to fetch the history of committed transactions of the given key in the ledger along with the transaction ID and timestamp. This method takes the key as input and returns an iterator of the history records and errors if there were any.
- getQueryResult(query string) (StateQueryIteratorInterface, error): This method executes a rich query against a state database. It is only supported for state databases that support rich queries, such as Oracle, ATP, or ADW. The input for this method is a query string in the native syntax of the underlying state database. This method returns an iterator of the result and errors if there were any.

- setEvent(name string, payload []byte) error: This sets an event as a proposal on the response to be included in a transaction. Regardless of the validity of the transaction, the event will be available within the committed transaction block.

Along with the earlier important and highly used methods in the chaincode, the stub also has the following methods:

```
getArgs() [][]byte

getStringArgs() []string

getArgsSlice() ([]byte, error)

getTxID() string

invokeChaincode(chaincodeName string, args [][]byte, channel string)
pb.Response

getStateByRange(startKey, endKey string) (StateQueryIteratorInterface,
error)

getStateByPartialCompositeKey(objectType string, keys []string)
(StateQueryIteratorInterface, error)

createCompositeKey(objectType string, attributes []string) (string, error)

splitCompositeKey(compositeKey string) (string, []string, error)

getCreator() ([]byte, error)

getTransient() (map[string][]byte, error)

getBinding() ([]byte, error)

getSignedProposal() (*pb.SignedProposal, error)

getTxTimestamp() (*timestamp.Timestamp, error)
```

Developing chaincode

This section covers the implementation in Golang. The following chaincode is developed in the Go language for the operations/transactions described in the preceding section, mapping operations using the assets mentioned in the preceding section's mapping asset model.

Chaincode in Go

Let's look at chaincode development in the Go language for the use case discussed:

1. `import`: This section imports the required libraries:

```
import (
  "bytes"
  "encoding/json"
  "fmt"
  "strconv"
  "time"
  "github.com/hyperledger/fabric/core/chaincode/shim"
  "github.com/hyperledger/fabric/protos/peer"
)
```

2. `type`: This will define the required asset structures:

```
// Chaincode implementation
type EducationChaincode struct {

}

// receiver/student struct
type Receiver struct {
  ObjectType string `json:"docType"` //docType is used to
distinguish the various types of objects in state database
  Receiver_id string `json:"receiver_id"`
  Receiver_name string `json:"receiver_name"`
  Upload_org string `json:"upload_org"`
}

// certificate data struct
type Certificate struct {
  ObjectType string `json:"docType"` //docType is used to
distinguish the various types of objects in state database
  Cert_id string `json:"cert_id"`
  Cert_no string `json:"cert_no"`
  Cert_name string `json:"cert_name"`
```

```
Cert_receiver string `json:"cert_receiver"` // student name
Cert_receiver_id string `json:"cert_receiver_id"` // student id
Cert_issuer string `json:"cert_issuer"` // org name
Cert_industry string `json:"cert_industry"`
Cert_create_time string `json:"cert_create_time"`
Cert_update_time string `json:"cert_update_time"`
Cert_remark string `json:"cert_remark"`
Cert_url_image string `json:"cert_url_image"`
Cert_status string `json:"cert_status"`
}
```

3. `main`: This is the `main` method to start execution:

```
// main - Start execution
func main() {
  err := shim.Start(new(EducationChaincode))
  if err != nil {
    fmt.Printf("Error starting Xebest Trace chaincode: %s", err)
  }
}
```

4. `Init`: This method is for initializing of chaincode while instantiating the chaincode:

```
// Init initializes chaincode
func (t *EducationChaincode) Init(stub shim.ChaincodeStubInterface)
peer.Response {
  return shim.Success(nil)
}
```

5. `Invoke`: This method is for bypassing or executing the user transaction:

```
// Invoke - Invoking user transactions
func (t *EducationChaincode) Invoke(stub
shim.ChaincodeStubInterface) peer.Response {
  function, args := stub.GetFunctionAndParameters()
  fmt.Println("invoke is running " + function)

  // Handle different functions
  if function == "insertReceiver" { //create a new Receiver or
student
    return t.insertReceiver(stub, args)
  } else if function == "queryReceiverById" { // query a receiver
by id, stupid name - -!
    return t.queryReceiverById(stub,args)
  } else if function == "insertCertificate" { //insert a cert
    return t.insertCertificate(stub, args)
  } else if function == "queryCertificateById" { // query a
```

```
certificate
    return t.queryCertificateById(stub, args)
  } else if function == "getRecordHistory"{ //query hisitory of one
key for the record
    return t.getRecordHistory(stub,args)
  } else if function == "queryAllCertificates"{ // query all of all
students
    return t.queryAllCertificates(stub,args)
  } else if function == "approveCertificate" { // change status
    return t.approveCertificate(stub,args)
  }else if function == "deleteRecord" { // delete student or
certificate
    return t.deleteRecord(stub, args)
  }

  fmt.Println("invoke did not find func: " + function) //error
  return shim.Error("Received unknown function invocation")
}
```

6. `insertReceiver`: This method is for creating/inserting a student or receiver of the certificate into the chaincode state:

```
// initReceiver - insert a new Receiver into chaincode state
func (t *EducationChaincode) insertReceiver(stub
shim.ChaincodeStubInterface, args []string) peer.Response {
  var err error

  if len(args) != 3 {
    return shim.Error("Incorrect number of arguments. Expecting 3")
  }

  fmt.Println("start insert receiver")
  receiver_id := args[0]
  receiver_name := args[1]
  upload_org := args[2]

  // Check if the receiver already exists with the id
  receiverAsBytes, err := stub.GetState(receiver_id)
  if err != nil {
    return shim.Error("Failed to get receiver: " + err.Error())
  } else if receiverAsBytes != nil {
    fmt.Println("This receiver already exists: " + receiver_id)
    return shim.Error("This receiver already exists: " +
receiver_id)
  }

  // Create receiver object and marshal to JSON
  objectType := "receiver"
```

```
    receiver := &Receiver{objectType, receiver_id,
receiver_name,upload_org}
      receiverJSONasBytes, err := json.Marshal(receiver)
      if err != nil {
        return shim.Error(err.Error())
      }
      fmt.Println("receiver: ")
      fmt.Println(receiver)
      // Save the receiver to ledger state
      err = stub.PutState(receiver_id, receiverJSONasBytes)
      if err != nil {
        return shim.Error(err.Error())
      }

      // receiver saved and indexed. Return success
      fmt.Println("End init receiver")
      return shim.Success(nil)

    }
```

7. `queryReceiverById`: This method fetches the receiver record by the given ID:

```
    // queryReceiverById - read data for the given receiver from the
    chaincode state
    func (t *EducationChaincode) queryReceiverById(stub
    shim.ChaincodeStubInterface, args []string) peer.Response {
      var recev_id, jsonResp string
      var err error

      if len(args) != 1 {
        return shim.Error("Incorrect number of arguments. Expecting
    receiver_id to query")
      }

      recev_id = args[0]
      //Read the Receiver from the chaincode state
      valAsbytes, err := stub.GetState(recev_id)
      if err != nil {
        jsonResp = "{\"Error\":\"Failed to get state for " + recev_id +
    "\"}"
        return shim.Error(jsonResp)
      } else if valAsbytes == nil {
        jsonResp = "{\"Error\":\"receiver does not exist: " + recev_id
    + "\"}"
        return shim.Error(jsonResp)
      }
      return shim.Success(valAsbytes)
    }
```

8. `insertCertificate`: This method is for inserting new certificate information into the ledger state:

```
// insertCertificate - insert a new certificate information into
the ledger state
func (t *EducationChaincode) insertCertificate(stub
shim.ChaincodeStubInterface, args []string) peer.Response {
  if len(args) != 11 {
    return shim.Error("Incorrect number of arguments. expecting 11
args")
  }

  cert_id := args[0]
  cert_no := args[1]
  cert_name := args[2]
  cert_receiver_id := args[3]
  cert_issuer := args[4]
  cert_industry := args[5]
  cert_create_time := args[6]
  cert_update_time := args[7]
  cert_remark := args[8]
  cert_url_image := args[9]
  cert_status := args[10]


  // check if receiver exists
  ReceAsBytes, err := stub.GetState(cert_receiver_id)
  if err != nil {
    return shim.Error("Failed to get Receiver:" + cert_receiver_id
+ "," + err.Error())
  } else if ReceAsBytes == nil {
    fmt.Println("Receiver does not exist with id: " +
cert_receiver_id )
    return shim.Error("Receiver does not exist with id: " +
cert_receiver_id )
  }

  //Fetch receiver name from the state
  receiver := &Receiver{}
  err = json.Unmarshal([]byte(ReceAsBytes), &receiver)
  if err != nil {
    return shim.Error(err.Error())
  }
  cert_receiver :=receiver.Receiver_name;
  fmt.Println("cert_receiver: "+cert_receiver)

  objectType := "certificate"
  certificate :=
```

```
&Certificate{objectType,cert_id,cert_no,cert_name,cert_receiver,cer
t_receiver_id,cert_issuer,cert_industry,cert_create_time,cert_updat
e_time,cert_remark,cert_url_image,cert_status}
  certificateJSONasBytes, err := json.Marshal(certificate)
  if err != nil {
    return shim.Error(err.Error())
  }

  // insert the certificate into the ledger
  err = stub.PutState(cert_id, certificateJSONasBytes)
  if err != nil {
    return shim.Error(err.Error())
  }

  // certificate saved - Return success
  return shim.Success(nil)
}
```

9. `queryCertificateById`: This method fetches the certificate details from the ledger state by the given certificate ID:

```
// queryCertificateById - read a certificate by given id from the
ledger state
func (t *EducationChaincode) queryCertificateById(stub
shim.ChaincodeStubInterface, args []string) peer.Response {
  var cert_id, jsonResp string
  var err error

  if len(args) != 1 {
    return shim.Error("Incorrect number of arguments. Expecting id
of the certificate to query")
  }

  cert_id = args[0]
  //Read the certificate from chaincode state
  valAsbytes, err := stub.GetState(cert_id)
  if err != nil {
    jsonResp = "{\"Error\":\"Failed to get state for " + cert_id +
"\"}"
    return shim.Error(jsonResp)
  } else if valAsbytes == nil {
    jsonResp = "{\"Error\":\"certificate does not exist: " +
cert_id + "\"}"
    return shim.Error(jsonResp)
  }

  return shim.Success(valAsbytes)
}
```

10. `approveCertificate`: This method is used for approving a certificate by an authority:

```
// approveCertificate - approve the certificate by authority
func (t *EducationChaincode) approveCertificate(stub
shim.ChaincodeStubInterface, args []string) peer.Response {

  var err error
  // check args
  if len(args) != 3 {
    return shim.Error("Incorrect number of arguments. Expecting 3")
  }
  if len(args[0]) <= 0 {
    return shim.Error("1st argument must be a non-empty string")
  }
  if len(args[1]) <= 0 {
    return shim.Error("2nd argument must be a non-empty string")
  }
  if len(args[2]) <= 0 {
    return shim.Error("3rd argument must be a non-empty string")
  }

  cert_id := args[0]
  status := args[1]
  update_time := args[2]

  //Read certificate details from the ledger
  valAsbytes, err := stub.GetState(cert_id)
    if err != nil {
      return shim.Error(err.Error())
    } else if valAsbytes == nil {
      return shim.Error("certificate not exist")
    }
  certificate := &Certificate{}
  err = json.Unmarshal([]byte(valAsbytes), &certificate)
  if err != nil {
    return shim.Error(err.Error())
  }
  certificate.Cert_status = status
  certificate.Cert_update_time = update_time

  valAsbytes, err = json.Marshal(certificate)
  if err != nil {
    return shim.Error(err.Error())
  }
  //Update the certificate in the ledger
  err = stub.PutState(cert_id, valAsbytes)
  if err != nil {
```

```
        return shim.Error(err.Error())
    }
    return shim.Success(nil)
}
```

11. `queryAllCertificates`: This method is used to query all certificates from the ledger state:

```
// queryAllCertificates - Query all certificates from the ledger
state
func (t *EducationChaincode) queryAllCertificates(stub
shim.ChaincodeStubInterface, args []string) peer.Response {

    queryString := "{\"selector\":{\"docType\":\"certificate\"}}"

    queryResults, err := getQueryResultForQueryString(stub,
queryString)
    if err != nil {
        return shim.Error(err.Error())
    }
    return shim.Success(queryResults)
}
```

12. `getRecordHistory`: This method fetches the historical state transitions for a given key of a record:

```
// getRecordHistory - Fetches the historical state transitions for
a given key of a record
func (t *EducationChaincode) getRecordHistory(stub
shim.ChaincodeStubInterface, args []string) peer.Response {

    if len(args) < 1 {
        return shim.Error("Incorrect number of arguments. Expecting an
id of Receiver or Certificate")
    }

    recordKey := args[0]

    fmt.Printf("Fetching history for record: %s\n", recordKey)

    resultsIterator, err := stub.GetHistoryForKey(recordKey)
    if err != nil {
        return shim.Error(err.Error())
    }
    defer resultsIterator.Close()

    // buffer is a JSON array containing historic values for the
key/value pair
```

```
  var buffer bytes.Buffer
  buffer.WriteString("[")

  bArrayMemberAlreadyWritten := false
  for resultsIterator.HasNext() {
    response, err := resultsIterator.Next()
    if err != nil {
      return shim.Error(err.Error())
    }
    // Add a comma before array members, suppress it for the first
array member
    if bArrayMemberAlreadyWritten == true {
      buffer.WriteString(",")
    }
    buffer.WriteString("{\"TxId\":")
    buffer.WriteString("\"")
    buffer.WriteString(response.TxId)
    buffer.WriteString("\"")

    buffer.WriteString(", \"Value\":")
    // if it was a delete operation on given key, then we need to
set the
    //corresponding value null. Else, we will write the
response.Value
    //as-is (as the Value itself a JSON goods)
    if response.IsDelete {
      buffer.WriteString("null")
    } else {
      buffer.WriteString(string(response.Value))
    }

    buffer.WriteString(", \"Timestamp\":")
    buffer.WriteString("\"")
    buffer.WriteString(time.Unix(response.Timestamp.Seconds,
int64(response.Timestamp.Nanos)).String())
    buffer.WriteString("\"")

    buffer.WriteString(", \"IsDelete\":")
    buffer.WriteString("\"")
    buffer.WriteString(strconv.FormatBool(response.IsDelete))
    buffer.WriteString("\"")

    buffer.WriteString("}")
    bArrayMemberAlreadyWritten = true
  }
  buffer.WriteString("]")

  fmt.Printf("Result of getHistoryForRecord :\n%s\n",
```

```go
buffer.String())

   return shim.Success(buffer.Bytes())
}
```

13. `getQueryResultForQueryString`: This method executes the given `rich` query on the ledger state if required:

```go
// getQueryResultForQueryString executes the passed in query
string.
// Result set is built and returned as a byte array containing the
JSON results.

func getQueryResultForQueryString(stub shim.ChaincodeStubInterface,
queryString string) ([]byte, error) {

   fmt.Printf("getQueryResultForQueryString queryString:\n%s\n",
queryString)

   resultsIterator, err := stub.GetQueryResult(queryString)
   if err != nil {
     return nil, err
   }
   defer resultsIterator.Close()

   // buffer is a JSON array containing QueryRecords
   var buffer bytes.Buffer
   buffer.WriteString("[")

   bArrayMemberAlreadyWritten := false
   for resultsIterator.HasNext() {
     queryResponse, err := resultsIterator.Next()
     if err != nil {
       return nil, err
     }
     // Add a comma before array members, suppress it for the first
array member
     if bArrayMemberAlreadyWritten == true {
       buffer.WriteString(",")
     }
     buffer.WriteString(string(queryResponse.Value))
     bArrayMemberAlreadyWritten = true
   }
   buffer.WriteString("]")

   fmt.Printf("getQueryResultForQueryString queryResult:\n%s\n",
buffer.String())
```

```
        return buffer.Bytes(), nil
    }
```

14. `deleteRecord`: This method will mark the record deleted by the given key:

```
// deleteRecord - Mark the record deleted by given key

func (t *EducationChaincode) deleteRecord(stub
shim.ChaincodeStubInterface, args []string) peer.Response {
    if len(args) != 1{
        return shim.Error("Incorrect number of arguments. Expecting 1")
    }

    id := args[0]
    err := stub.DelState(id)
    if err != nil {
        return shim.Error(err.Error())
    }
    return shim.Success(nil)
}
```

The preceding chaincode can also be downloaded from the GitHub repository referenced in this book. The filename is `education.go`.

Chaincode in Node.js

Let's look at the procedure for developing chaincode in Node.js:

- Create a Node.js file using the `fabric-shim` package
- Create a `package.json` file with the details of the Node.js file and dependencies, if any
- Package all the files in a ZIP file including `package.json`, the main Node.js file, and other JavaScript or config files or dependencies, if any
- Deploy the package under the **Chaincode** tab in OBP (refer to the *Chaincode deployment* section)

 Note: You are only required to create a `package.json` file; there's no need to run `npm` commands to install `node_modules`, as the OBP does this for you internally.

Sample Node.js file named `education.js`.

Create a Node.js file using the `fabric-shim` package:

```
const shim = require('fabric-shim');
const Chaincode = class {
    async Init(stub) {
        return shim.success();
    }
    async Invoke(stub) {
        let ret = stub.getFunctionAndParameters();
        let method = this[ret.fcn];
        console.log("Inside invoke. Calling method: " + ret.fcn);
        if (!method) {
            shim.error(Buffer.from('Received unknown function ' + ret.fcn +
' invocation'));
        }
        try {
            let payload = await method(stub, ret.params);
            return shim.success(payload);
        } catch (err) {
            console.log(err);
            return shim.error(err);
        }
    }

    //Method to save or update a user review to a product

    async insertReceiver(stub, args) {
        console.log("inside insertReceiver: " + JSON.stringify(args));
        if (args.length != 3) {
            throw 'Incorrect number of arguments. Expecting ID,Name and
Org.';
        }
        var receiver = {};
                            receiver.ObjectType = "receiver";
        receiver.Receiver_id = args[0];
        receiver.Receiver_name = args[1];
        receiver.Upload_org = args[2];
        await stub.putState(receiver.Receiver_id,
Buffer.from(JSON.stringify(receiver)));
    }//End of method
}

shim.start(new Chaincode());
```

Sample JSON file named `package.json`.

Create a `package.json` file with the details of the Node.js file and dependencies, if any:

```json
{
    "name": "education",
    "version": "1.0.0",
    "description": "Chaincode implemented in node.js",
    "engines": {
        "node": ">=8.9.0",
        "npm": ">=5.5.0"
    },
    "scripts": {
        "start" : "node education.js"
    },
    "engine-strict": true,
    "license": "Apache-2.0",
    "dependencies": {
        "fabric-shim": "~1.3.0"
    }
}
```

This sample Node.js code with the `package.json` file can be downloaded from the GitHub repository referenced in this book.

Adding events to chaincode

Chaincode can also post events to notify a subscribing application to process further client actions. For example, after purchase orders, invoices, and delivery records have been matched by chaincode, it can post an event so that a subscribing application can process related payments and update an internal ERP system.

OBP supports the following types of events, which can be subscribed via a REST proxy:

- `transaction`: Events for a transaction ID
- `txOnChannel`: Events for every new transaction on a channel
- `txOnNetwork`: Events for every new transaction in the entire network
- `blockOnChannel`: Events for every block on a particular channel
- `blockOnNetwork`: Events for the creation of a new block in the entire network
- `chaincodeEvent`: Custom events emitted by chaincode logic

Publishing events

Here, we'll see how to trigger events from chaincode. Using the `SetEvent()` method of `ChaincodeStubInterface`, events can be triggered by chaincode. Add the following code in the `approveCertificate()` method to emit the event after the certificate status is changed:

```
var testEventValue []byte

testEventValue=[]byte("Certificate "+cert_id+" status is changed to "+status)

stub.SetEvent("testEvent",testEventValue)
```

Subscribing to events

Events can be subscribed to via a REST proxy or HLF SDKs. The following is the procedure to subscribe via a REST proxy:

- REST endpoint: `<host name>:<port>/<REST proxy>/bcsgw/rest/v1/event/subscribe`
- REST method: `POST`
- Headers:
    - **Content-Type**: `application/json`
    - **Authorization**: `<Basic authorization>`
    - **Accept-Charset**: `UTF-8`:

- The JSON input to be passed to the REST API:

```
{
  "requests":[
  {
    "eventType":"chaincodeEvent",
    "callbackURL": "--- call back webhook url---",
    "callbackTlsCerts":{
      "caCert":" -- mandatory field which is the callback server's
CA certificate in PEM format. It will be verified by REST proxy",
      "clientCert": "--Optional field which refers to the REST
proxy certificate should use during callback --",
      "keyPassword": "--clientCert's encrypted private key in
base64 encoded"
    },
    "expires": "1m",
    "channel": "channeleducation",
    "chaincode": "cceducation",
    "eventName": "testEvent"
  }
  ]
}
```

- It responds with `subid`.

Unsubscribe from events

Events can also be unsubscribed. To do this, follow the same procedure as for subscription but replacing the endpoint and the input as follows:

- REST endpoint: `<host name>:<port>/<REST proxy>/bcsgw/rest/v1/event/unsubscribe`
- JSON input:

```
{

    "request":{

      "subid": "---subscription id received---"
  }

}
```

Chaincode deployment

Chaincode deployment is a multistep process. It includes chaincode deployment (quick or advanced methods), chaincode instantiation, enabling chaincode in a REST proxy, and upgrading chaincode. Prerequisites to chaincode deployment on OBP include having administrative access to the OBP instance to deploy the chaincode. Chaincode can be installed and instantiated from any instance by either a founder or a participant of a channel. Once it is instantiated, other instances of the channel just need to install the chaincode. The instantiation will be applied automatically on those instances. In this section, we will deploy the chaincode from the founder instance.

Deploying chaincode

OBP offers two different deployment options. A quick deployment option for one-step chaincode deployment and advanced deployment options. The quickstart deployment option is recommended for chaincode testing, while the advanced deployment option allows you to specify various advanced deployment settings such as choosing the peers on which the chaincode will be installed, the endorsement policy to use, and so on. This section shows both deployment options.

The following is the procedure for deploying the chaincode:

1. Navigate to the **Chaincodes** tab:

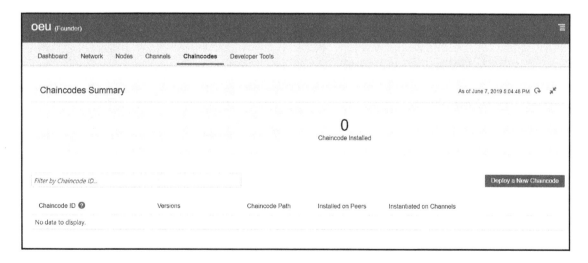

Chaincode deployment

2. Click on the **Deploy a New Chaincode** button. The following screen will be opened with two deployment options:

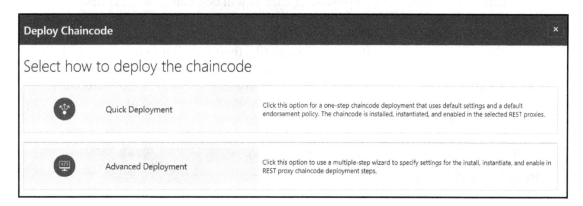

Chaincode deployment options

3. **Quick Deployment**: The one-step chaincode deployment option uses default settings and is enabled in the selected REST proxies. However, we'll use the **Advanced Deployment** option to deploy our chaincode in this section. The following is the screen for you to refer to for **Quick Deployment**:

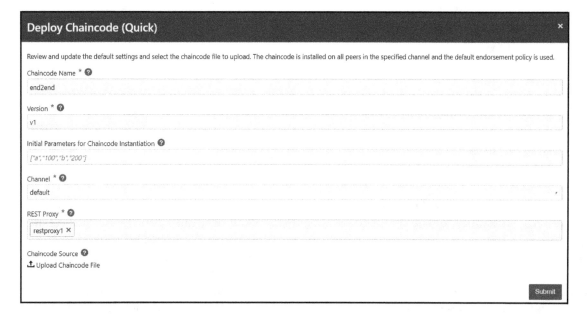

Quick chaincode deployment

4. **Advanced Deployment** provides a multi-step wizard to install, instantiate, and enable the REST proxy for chaincode. Select this option from the **Deploy Chaincode** menu. The step-by-step wizard will be opened and the first step follows, where you provide details of the chaincode such as the chaincode name, version, target peers on which the chaincode should be deployed, and the actual chaincode package. (If it is a single `.go` file, then there's no need for a package. The single file can be selected, but if it has multiple files or the code is written in Node.js or Java, then package all the files in a ZIP file.) Fill in the fields shown in the following screenshot and click on **Next**. Remember, none of these values can be altered after installing the chaincode:

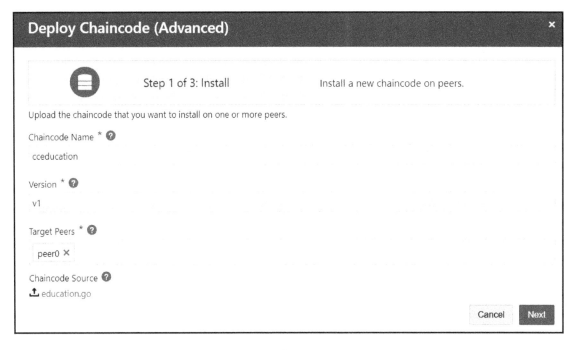

Details page

5. When the **Install** process is successful, the wizard will show step 2, which is **Instantiate**. The chaincode will be instantiated only once per channel per version. In this step, you specify which channel the chaincode should be applied to; the peers to participate; the array of the initial parameters if any, are to be passed to the `Init()` method in the chaincode; the endorsement policy, if any (see the next section for details on the endorsement policy); and the private data collection (see the next section for the details). Fill the form as follows and click **Next**; it may take a while to go to the next step:

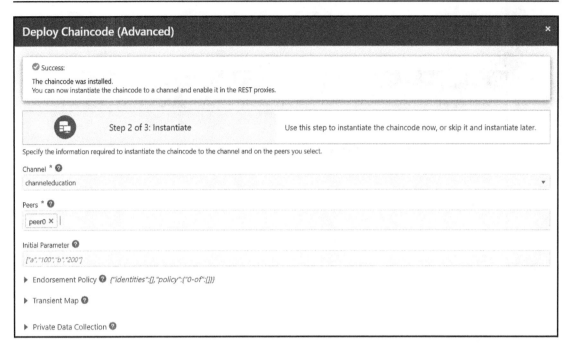

Advance chaincode deployment

6. After the chaincode is instantiated successfully, the wizard will show step 3, which is to enable the chaincode in a REST proxy. OBP provides multiple REST proxies. You can choose more than one REST proxy to enable the chaincode. Fill in the fields as follows and click **Next**:

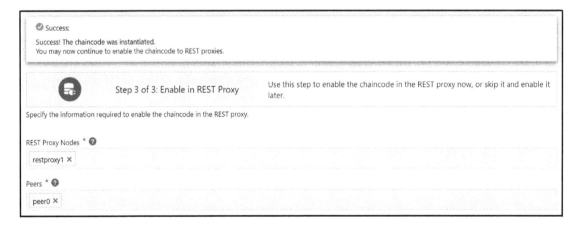

REST proxy

7. After completing all of the steps in the wizard, finally, you will see this success screen. Click on **Close**:

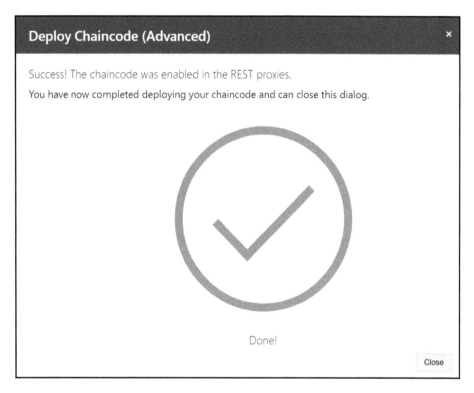

Deployment completion message

8. So far, you have deployed the chaincode in the founder instance. You need to deploy the chaincode in all the participant instances. Repeat the deployment process as we just saw; however, you just need to deploy the chaincode—instantiation will be applied automatically as it is done from the founder of the channel. So, in the **Advanced Deployment** wizard, after step 1 installation is done, in the step 2 screen, click on the **Close** button.

9. Go to the **Channels** tab. You will find that the chaincode is instantiated. Look at the following references.

The following is the channel before chaincode installation:

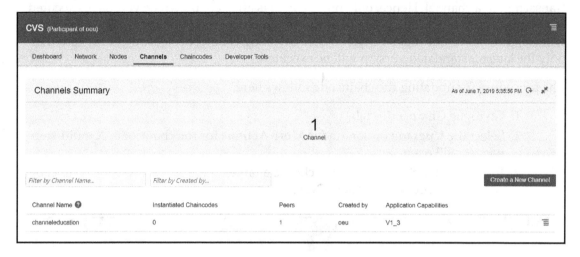

Channel before chaincode installation

The following screenshot is the channel after chaincode installation:

Channel Name ❓	Instantiated Chaincodes	Peers	Created by	Application Capabilities	
channeleducation	1	1	oeu	V1_3	☰

Channel after chaincode installation

Multiple chaincodes can be installed on a channel. Also, a chaincode can be enabled on multiple REST proxies.

Updating chaincode

HLF supports chaincode versioning and upgrading. You can update chaincode when a smart contract needs to be altered, the business logic is changed, or any changes are required in the chaincode. Chaincode can be upgraded to a new version, as long as you maintain the same name of the chaincode, else it will be considered different chaincode.

An update is a transaction on the blockchain network and it results in the binding of the new version of the chaincode to the channel. What happens to the old version of the chaincode? All of the other channels that are binding to the previous (old) version of the chaincode can continue to execute the older version. You submit the chaincode *upgrade* transaction to a channel. Hence, only one channel is affected, on which you have executed the upgrade transaction. All other channels, on which upgrade transaction is not executed, will continue to run the older version. When invoking chaincode, it's always the case that only the latest instantiated version will be executed.

The procedure for updating the chaincode follows here:

1. Go to the **Chaincodes** tab.
2. Select the **Upgrade** option under **More Actions** for the chaincode. A multi-step wizard will open.
3. In **Step 1 of 2: Select a version**, choose a target peers and browse the chaincode source package. Then click on **Next**:

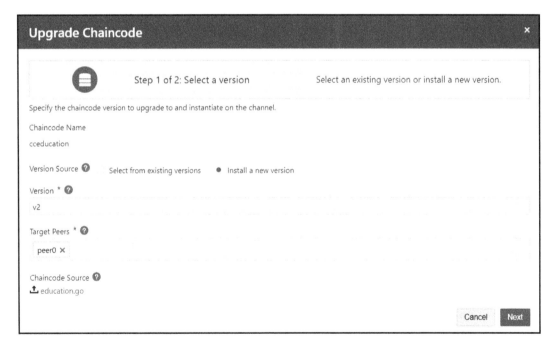

Upgrade chaincode—select version

4. In **Step 2 of 2: Upgrade**, provide the channel name, the peers, the initial parameters, if any, and an endorsement policy, if any. Click on **Next**:

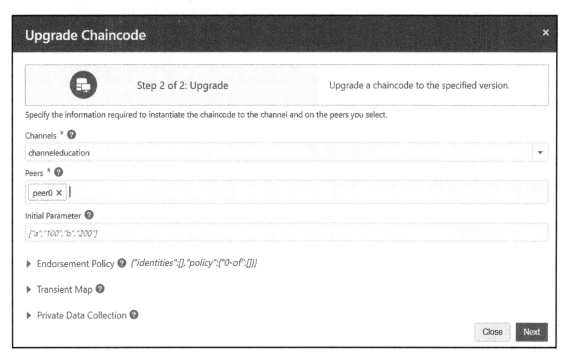

Upgrade chaincode—instantiate information

5. After the chaincode is upgraded successfully, you will see the following screen. Click on **Close** and repeat the same procedure for other participants:

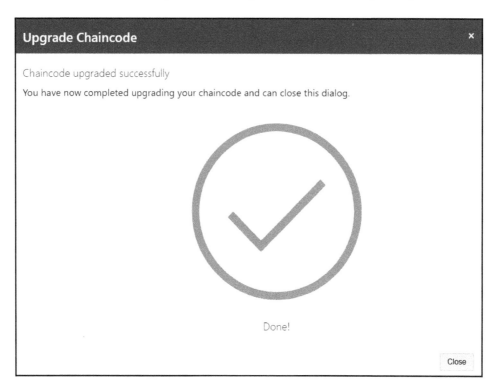

Chaincode upgrade

Endorsement policy

An endorsement policy specifies the organizations with peers that must properly approve or endorse a chaincode transaction before it's added to a block and submitted to the ledger. You can add an endorsement policy in OBP when you instantiate chaincode, which is step 2 in the chaincode deployment process. Endorsement guarantees the legitimacy of a transaction. If no endorsement policy is specified, then the default endorsement policy is used, which gets an endorsement from any peer on the network.

An organization's endorsing peer must have read-write permissions on the channel. When a transaction is processed, each endorsing peer returns a read-write set, then the client bundles these endorsing peers with their signatures and sends everything to the ordering service, which orders and commits the transactions into blocks and then to the ledger.

In the following screenshot, you can see the endorsement policy configuration while instantiating the chaincode. You can simply specify in the **Signed by** field how many have to participate in the endorsement, or by selecting **Advanced**, you can specify this through an expression too. In our use case, we are using the default endorsement policy:

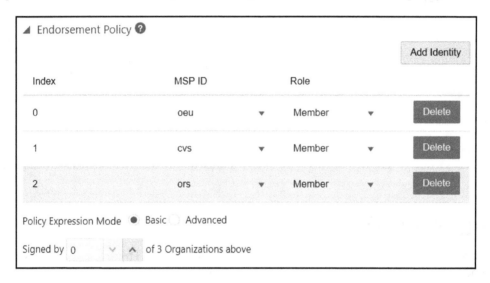

Endorsement policy

Private data collection

OBP version 19.1.3 and later has a feature for specifying subsets of organizations that endorse, commit, or query private data on a channel—private data collections. Private data collections are useful if you want a group of organizations on the channel to share data and to prevent the other organizations on the channel from seeing the data. One or more private data collections can be associated when the chaincode is instantiated, shown as follows. Also, you should specify a transient map to pass the private data from the client to the peers for endorsement.

The following screenshot shows the **Private Data Collection** while instantiation of the chaincode:

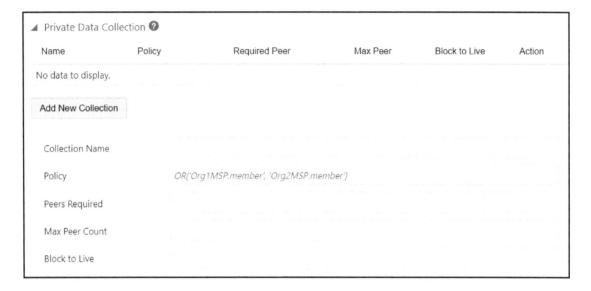

Testing chaincode

A chaincode can be tested locally, without installing it on OBP. There are two ways to test chaincode: using mock shim and using REST endpoints.

Testing chaincode using the shim

Let's see how to test the earlier chaincode developed locally in the Go language. Before that, here are some key points to note:

- Install the Go language locally on your machine.
- This test filename should take this form: `<Go file name>_test.go`.

    For example: if the chaincode name is `education.go`, then this test filename should be `education_test.go`.

- Keep both files in the same folder.
- Set `GOPATH` to the folder.
- Install the dependent packages used in the chaincode if they can't be found.

  For example: `go get github.com/hyperledger/fabric/protos/peer`
  `go get github.com/hyperledger/fabric/core/chaincode/shim.C`

- Code snippet file `education_test.go` at the GIT repository (`https://github.com/PacktPublishing/Oracle-Blockchain-Quick-Start-Guide`), is a test case with an explanation for only one method: `initReceiver()`. Similarly, you can write test cases to all other methods.
- Each test case should be prefixed with `Test<function name>`.
  For example: `TestInitReceiver`.
- After the test cases are ready, test them using the following command:

  `go test -run <<function name>>`

  For example: `go test -run Education`.

Here, `Education` is the test case name.

To test a function, create a stub using `NewMockStub()`. The stub has a `MockInvoke()` function, which invokes an actual function of chaincode.

For example, `stub.MockInvoke("001", [][]byte{[]byte("insertReceiver "), []byte(key),[]byte("Anand Yerrapati"), []byte("Blockchain")})`.

Here, `001` is a transaction ID to be returned upon the success of this test and `insertReceiver` is a function to be invoked in the `education.go` file. The remaining are the parameters to be passed to the `insertReceiver` function.

Refer file 'education_test.go' at the GIT repository "https://github.com/PacktPublishing/Oracle-Blockchain-Quick-Start-Guide-".

Test filename to test the chaincode (education.go), is test file "education_test.go". This file is referred in this section for testing chaincode using the shim.

This test case is consolidated for flow, from inserting a receiver, querying the receiver, inserting a certificate, verifying the certificate, approving the certificate, and querying the certificate again, to verifying the changes. The following are the results of the earlier test case after executing the `go test -run Education` command:

```
D:\Anand\OBP\chaincode\testing\go>go test -run Education
 Inside TestEducation
 invoke is running insertReceiver
 start insert receiver
 receiver:
 &{receiver std1231 Anand Y Blockchain}
 End init receiver
 Result insertReceiver:
 {200 [] {} [] 0}
 invoke is running queryReceiverById
 Result queryReceiverById:
 &{receiver std1231 Anand Y Blockchain}
 invoke is running insertCertificate
 cert_receiver: Anand Y
 {200 [] {} [] 0}
 Result insertCertificate:
 {200 [] {} [] 0}
 invoke is running queryCertificateById
 Result queryCertificateById:
 &{certificate cert123 12345 ORU Blockchain Certificate Anand Y std1231 ORU
IT 06/04/2019 06/04/2019 Blockchain course completed Active}
 invoke is running approveCertificate
 {200 [] {} [] 0}
 Result approveCertificate:
 {200 [] {} [] 0}
 invoke is running queryCertificateById
 Result queryCertificateById:
 &{certificate cert123 12345 ORU Blockchain Certificate Anand Y std1231 ORU
IT 06/04/2019 06/04/2019 10:41:50 Blockchain course completed Approved}
 PASS
 ok _/D_/Anand/OBP/chaincode/testing/go 3.921s
```

 The mock stub doesn't support every function. You can't implement the `GetQueryResult` and `GetHistoryForKey` methods.

Testing chaincode from REST endpoints

OBP provides a REST proxy to connect chaincode via REST endpoints. Whichever chaincode you want to be executed via REST services should be configured on the respective REST proxy. This configuration can be seen in the *Chaincode deployment* section in this chapter. In this section, we see how to invoke the REST endpoints, how to connect to the required functions, and how to pass the parameters.

There are two REST endpoints available:

- **Query**: To execute any function to query data from the ledger:

  Syntax: `<host name>:<port>/<restproxy>/bcsgw/rest/v1/transaction/query`

- **Invocation**: To execute any function to save data to the ledger or query data from the ledger. The query could also be done from this endpoint, however, the execution would be slow to fetch and return the data. So, it is recommended to use the query endpoint in cases where you are fetching data from the ledger:

  Syntax: `<host name>:<port>/<restproxy>/bcsgw/rest/v1/transaction/invocation`

For both these endpoints, the request input is the same, which is a JSON request and the following is the typical structure of a JSON request:

```
{
"channel":<channel name>,
"chaincode":<chaincode name>,
"method": <method name>,
"args":[<arguments separated by comma>]
}
```

Multiple chaincodes can be configured in a single REST proxy. So, the **channel** and **chaincode** parameters in the input JSON help to dispatch the request to the corresponding chaincode. Both the endpoints are **POST** calls. Two headers, **Authorization** and **Content-Type**, should be passed in every call.

We are using the OBP SDK, which has a default username and password: `customertenant@oracle.com/` and `Welcome1`.

The header should look as follows:

- **Authorization** : `Basic Y3VzdG9tZXN0ZW5hbnRAb3JhY2xlLmNvbTpoZWxsb211lMSA=`
- **Content-Type**: `application/json`
- **Target endpoint**: `https://<host name>:<port>/<restproxy>/bcsgw/rest/v1/transaction/<invocation or query>`

These are references to test the earlier chaincode from Postman (you can use any REST client here for testing). The following are target endpoint invocation input -

- Target endpoint – invocation to insert receiver:
    - Target endpoint: `/invocation`
    - Target method: `insertReceiver`
    - Input JSON:
      `{"channel":"channeleducation","chaincode":"cceducation","method":"insertReceiver","args":["std123", "Anand Yerrapati", "Blockchain"]}`

- Target endpoint—query to query by receiver ID:
    - Target endpoint: `/query`
    - Target method: `queryReceiverById`
    - Input JSON:
      `{"channel":"channeleducation","chaincode":"cceducation","method":"queryReceiverById","args":["std123"]}`

- Target endpoint – invocation to insert certificate:
    - Target endpoint: `/invocation`
    - Target method: `insertCertificate`
    - Input JSON:
      ```
      {"channel":"channeleducation","chaincode":"cceducati
      on","method":"insertCertificate","args":["cert1234",
      "1234","ORU Blockchain
      Certificate","std123","ORU","IT","6/5/2019","","Bloc
      kchain Course Completed","","","Issued"]}
      ```

- Target endpoint – invocation to query certificate by ID:
    - Target endpoint: `/query`
    - Target method: `queryCertificateById`

- Input JSON:
  ```
  {"channel":"channeleducation","chaincode":"cceducati
  on","method":"queryCertificateById","args":["cert123
  4"]}
  ```

- Target endpoint – invocation to approve certificate:
  - Target Endpoint: /invocation
  - Target method: approveCertificate
  - Input JSON:
    ```
    {"channel":"channeleducation","chaincode":"cceducati
    on","method":"approveCertificate","args":["cert1234"
    ,"Approved","6/5/2019 05:04:45 PM"]}
    ```

- Target endpoint – invocation to query certificate by ID:
    - Target endpoint: `/query`
    - Target method: `queryCertificateById`
    - Input JSON:
      ```
      {"channel":"channeleducation","chaincode":"cceducati
      on","method":"queryCertificateById","args":["cert123
      4"]}
      ```

- Target endpoint – invocation to query all certificates:
    - Target endpoint: `/query`
    - Target method: `queryAllCertificates`

- Input JSON:
  ```
  {"channel":"channeleducation","chaincode":"cceducati
  on","method":"queryAllCertificates","args":[]}
  ```

- Target endpoint – invocation to query endpoint to get record history:
  - Target endpoint: /query
  - Target method: getRecordHistory
  - Input JSON:
    ```
    {"channel":"channeleducation","chaincode":"cceducati
    on","method":"getRecordHistory","args":["cert1234"]}
    ```

The following is the response of `getRecordHistory`:

```
POST ∨          https://stud███████████████/restproxy1/bcsgw/rest/v1/transaction/query          Params    Send ∨    Save ∨

Body    Cookies    Headers (7)    Test Results                                          Status: 200 OK    Time: 3639 ms

Pretty    Raw    Preview    JSON ∨    ⇥                                              🗐  Q    Save Response

1 ▾ {
2       "returnCode": "Success",
3 ▾     "result": {
4           "payload": "[{\"TxId\":\"c09a707713a31d954d1fced5f4cfd34824182796ecc1f772d88249700cd2be2b\", \"Value\":{\"docType\":\"certificate\",\"cert_id\"
            :\"cert1234\",\"cert_no\":\"1234\",\"cert_name\":\"ORU Blockchain Certificate\",\"cert_receiver\":\"Anand Yerrapati\",\"cert_receiver_id\"
            :\"std123\",\"cert_issuer\":\"ORU\",\"cert_industry\":\"IT\",\"cert_create_time\":\"6/5/2019\",\"cert_update_time\":\"\",\"cert_remark\"
            :\"Blockchain Course Completed\",\"cert_url_image\":\"\",\"cert_status\":\"Issued\"}, \"Timestamp\":\"2019-06-11 17:20:20.477 +0000 UTC\",
            \"IsDelete\":\"false\"},{\"TxId\":\"36f0724e9b208f8ffaf85993817654e0d2e06d6c3f5df8d1ffb5831d5d208afb\", \"Value\":{\"docType\"
            :\"certificate\",\"cert_id\":\"cert1234\",\"cert_no\":\"1234\",\"cert_name\":\"ORU Blockchain Certificate\",\"cert_receiver\":\"Anand
            Yerrapati\",\"cert_receiver_id\":\"std123\",\"cert_issuer\":\"ORU\",\"cert_industry\":\"IT\",\"cert_create_time\":\"6/5/2019\"
            ,\"cert_update_time\":\"6/5/2019 05:04:45 PM\",\"cert_remark\":\"Blockchain Course Completed\",\"cert_url_image\":\"\",\"cert_status\"
            :\"Approved\"}, \"Timestamp\":\"2019-06-11 17:23:10.435 +0000 UTC\", \"IsDelete\":\"false\"}]",
5       "encode": "UTF-8"
6     },
7     "txid": "d16a1a5fec77e122b624767e6d7d46639e379a60ec0fe244dab12a86a5fdc116"
8 }
```

Response message

Chaincode logs

Logs are available for the system generated print statements given in chaincode. In OBP, these logs can be downloaded or viewed inline. Also, we can choose logs for the selected peer or the logs for a selected chaincode version. You can access the log files for a chaincode execution on the peer on which the chaincode is deployed. The following is the procedure to open the log files:

1. Go to the **Chaincodes** tab and locate the chaincode that you want to view the log of
2. Expand the chaincode
3. Click on the chaincode version that you want—the version information will be displayed
4. On the **Installed on Peers** tab, locate the peer
5. Click on the **Log** link and the **View Chaincode Log** dialog will be opened

6. You can also open log files by selecting the **Logs** tab of a specified peer under the **Nodes** tab, as shown in the following screenshot:

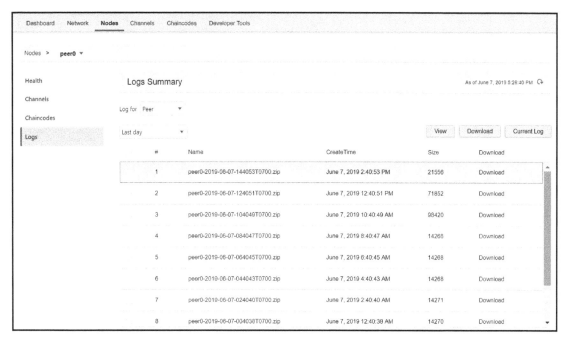

Chaincode logs

Channel ledger

The **ledger** is the ultimate storage for all of the transaction blocks of the blockchain network. Each channel has its own ledger which is common to all of the organizations in the channel. Organizations can have read, write, or both permissions on the ledger to handle transactions. The ledger can be queried or updated only through chaincode. OBP has an option in its console to view the blocks on the ledger of a channel. Each block on the ledger stores the transaction ID, the chaincode name, the status, the function name, the initiator of the transaction, the endorser, and the list of arguments. You can also see the total number of blocks and the count of the total user transactions.

By following this procedure, you can see the data on the ledger of a channel:

1. Go to the **Channels** tab
2. Locate the channel you want and click on the channel name
3. Under the **Ledger** tab, you can see all the block transactions of the channel
4. Select any transaction to see its details, as shown in the following screenshot:

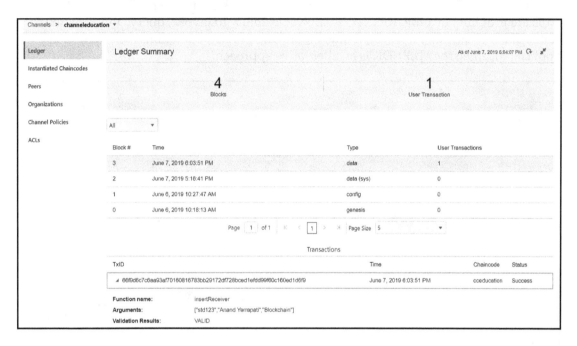

Integrating client applications with blockchain

So far, we have explored OBP and experimented with the development, deployment, and testing of chaincode on OBP. This section is a recap of the *Integration architecture* section of Chapter 3, *Delving into Hyperledger Fabric*. The following integration architecture diagram highlights three integration options with OBP: REST, SDK, and events.

When building and integrating a client with OBP using REST APIs—refer to the *Testing chaincode from REST endpoints* section—it helps to understand the use of REST endpoints to invoke chaincode transactions. REST endpoints can be integrated with the client applications and can execute them by passing the respective headers, such as authorization, Content-Type, and the input JSON, including the mandatory channel name and chaincode name fields and the required arguments. The response is also a REST JSON, which should be handled in the client application. For connecting blockchain using client SDK, REST APIs are provided by OBP. REST APIs allows flexibility to invoke, query, and view the status of a transaction. However, if much more fine-grained operations are required in applications, then the HLF SDK is an alternative approach:

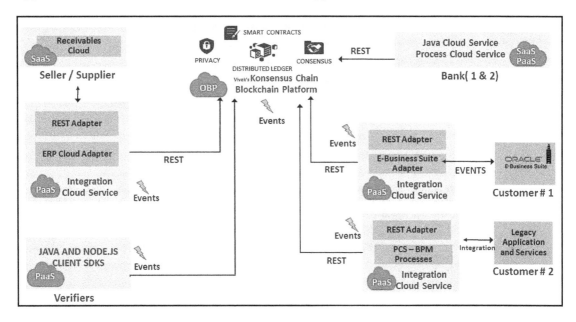

Integration architecture

Refer to the *Integration architecture* section of `Chapter 3`, *Delving into Hyperledger Fabric*, for a sample-based integration strategy for applications with blockchain.

Running an end-to-end flow

This section is a quick recap of the learning in this chapter:

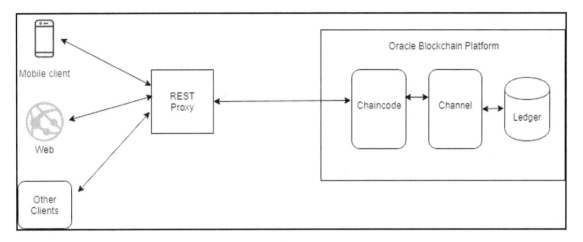

End-to-end flow

The following is a list of the steps executed so far while exploring the university use case and engaging with OBP to experiment with the development process on OBP:

- Identified who is a founder of the blockchain network (in our case, it is OEU)
- Found the participant organizations of the network (in our case, it is CVS and ORS)
- Created a founder and two participant instances in OBP
- Exported the Orderer certificate of the founder
- Imported the Orderer certificate to the network tab of both participant organizations
- Exported the network certificate of each participant organization
- Added both the organizations' certificates to the founder network
- Created a channel, `channeleducation`, in the founder for all three organizations: the founder and the two participants
- Joined peers to the channel in the founder as well as in the participants
- Exported the peers of each participant and imported them to the founder (this may require you to see the consolidated topological view of all the peers of a network; however, this step is required for the organizations participating in endorsement)

- Installed and instantiated chaincode (chaincode name: `cceducation`) in the founder
- Installed the chaincode in other participants
- Enabled/configured REST proxies to the chaincode in all of the organizations
- Used the respective organization's REST endpoints to connect to client applications

Summary

This chapter covered details about chaincode development such as the language section, development tools, and development environment setup. It detailed the full life cycle of chaincode, from development to updates, which included installation, initiation, testing, and versioning. It demonstrated the full chaincode with a code base built on Go and Node.js. It illustrated endorsement policies and private data collections and their functioning in concert with chaincode. It covered chaincode testing via shim and REST endpoints and integrating client apps with a business network using an SDK, REST, and events. Finally, it concluded with insights into chaincode, transactions, and channels by experimenting with the monitoring of a business via chaincode logs and channel logs.

This ledger of knowledge was created with the belief that, together, we will positively contribute to the evolution of blockchain technologies and continually inspire others to share their experience and further influence others to do so. Hence, the torch is with you, to continue influence by sharing, as sharing is caring, and together we contribute to creating a smarter world.

Other Books You May Enjoy

If you enjoyed this book, you may be interested in these other books by Packt:

Blockchain across Oracle
Robert van Mölken

ISBN: 978-1-78847-429-0

- A full introduction to the Blockchain
- How the Blockchain affects Oracle developers and customers
- Core concepts including blocks, hashes, and chains, assets, transactions, and consensus
- How to work with Oracle Cloud to implement a Blockchain Network
- Design, develop, and run smart contracts on the Oracle Blockchain Cloud Service
- Blockchain security and privacy for Oracle developers and clients
- Public and private Blockchain decisions for Oracle architects and developers
- Industry analysis across finance, governance, and healthcare sectors
- Industry trends and the future of the Blockchain technology

Blockchain Quick Reference

Brenn Hill, Samanyu Chopra, Paul Valencourt

ISBN: 978-1-78899-578-8

- Understand how blockchain architecture components work
- Acquaint yourself with cryptography and the mechanics behind blockchain
- Apply consensus protocol to determine the business sustainability
- Understand what ICOs and crypto-mining are and how they work
- Create cryptocurrency wallets and coins for transaction mechanisms
- Understand the use of Ethereum for smart contract and DApp development

Leave a review - let other readers know what you think

Please share your thoughts on this book with others by leaving a review on the site that you bought it from. If you purchased the book from Amazon, please leave us an honest review on this book's Amazon page. This is vital so that other potential readers can see and use your unbiased opinion to make purchasing decisions, we can understand what our customers think about our products, and our authors can see your feedback on the title that they have worked with Packt to create. It will only take a few minutes of your time, but is valuable to other potential customers, our authors, and Packt. Thank you!

Index

business-to-business (B2B) 62
business-to-consumer (B2C) 62
Byzantine fault tolerant (BFT) 50, 139

C

center of gravity (CG) 69
centralized ledger
  about 12, 13
  versus distributed ledger 11, 15
centralized network 26
certificate authority (CA) 135, 151, 215, 250
certificate revocation list (CRL) 163
certificate viewers/verifiers (CVs) 206, 243
chaincode deployment 296, 297, 298, 300, 301
chaincode development
  about 277, 281
  asset model, mapping 275, 276
  in Go 281, 282, 284, 287, 288, 291
  in Node.js 291, 293
  languages, selecting for 272
  operations, mapping 277
  setting up 272
chaincode functions 279, 280
chaincode interface 278
chaincode logs 315
chaincode, stages
  about 156
  endorsement 157
  initiated 157
  installed 156
  invocation 157
chaincode
  about 40, 183, 184
  channel ledger 316
  endorsement policy 304, 305
  events, adding 293
  events, publishing 294
  events, subscribing 294, 295
  events, unsubscribing 295
  private data collection (PDC) 305
  testing 306
  testing, from REST endpoints 309, 310, 313, 315
  testing, with shim 306, 308
  updating 301, 304

ChaincodeStubInterface 278
channel (privacy provider) 173, 174
channel ledger 316
channel
  setting up 256, 258
client applications
  integrating, with blockchain 317, 318
committing peers 158
consensus layer
  about 38
  key points 38
consensus
  about 14, 185, 186
  transaction flow 191
consortium
  benefits 65
control, systems
  centralized system 11
  decentralized system 11
CouchDB 183
crash fault tolerance (CFT) 32, 144
criticality factor (CF) 93

D

dApps 41
data layer 33, 35
decentralized applications (dApps) 58
decentralized autonomous organization (DAO) 62, 96, 102
decentralized network 26
deployment architecture 211
design strategy
  about 89, 90
  arbitrators 97
  blockchain, types 94
  business network goals 97
  business network, structure 95
  dispute resolution 97
  engage 98
  experience 98
  experiment 98
  explore 91
  governance 97
  influence 98
  use cases, identifying 91, 92

www.ingramcontent.com/pod-product-compliance
Lightning Source LLC
Chambersburg PA
CBHW080618060326
40690CB00021B/4736